P9-CFW-977

THE SEX WAR AND OTHERS

BY THE SAME AUTHOR

FICTION
The Blaze of Noon
The Greater Infortune
The Connecting Door
The Woodshed
The Shearers

MEMOIRS
Portrait of the Artist as a Professional Man

CRIMINOLOGY
A Little Pattern of French Crime
French Crime in the Romantic Age
Bluebeard and After: Three Decades of Murder in France

RAYNER HEPPENSTALL

The Sex War and Others

A SURVEY OF RECENT MURDER · PRINCIPALLY IN FRANCE

Theodore Lownik Library
Illinois Benedictine College
WITHDRAWN

PETER OWEN · LONDON

HV
6535.
FG
H44

ISBN 0 7206 0322 6

All Rights Reserved
No part of this publication may be
reproduced in any form or by any means
without the prior permission of the publishers

PETER OWEN LIMITED
12 Kendrick Mews Kendrick Place London SW7

First British Commonwealth edition 1973
© 1973 Rayner Heppenstall

Printed in Great Britain by
Bristol Typesetting Co Ltd
Barton Manor St Philips Bristol 2

To
JEAN TSUSHIMA

CONTENTS

Preface 9

1 Four Years of British Murder 13

2 *L'Amour* 25

3 Three Ritual Murders 41

4 The Homicide Act 56

5 A Garage-Hand, Five Women and a Child 66

6 *Faits Divers* 79

7 Empires Falling, Trials Coming Up 95

8 The Trial of Joseph K. 109

9 Home Thoughts 122

10 High Summer 133

11 The Little Debate 144

12 Kidnapping and its Consequences 163

13 Autumn Trials 176

Bibliography 189

| ILLUSTRATIONS

1   Haigh remanded in custody at Horsham

2   Pauline Dubuisson

3   Robert Avril

4   Jacques Algarron and Denise Labbé

5   Guy Desnoyer

6   Lucien Léger

7   Jean-Laurent Olivier

8   Pierre Tavernier

| PREFACE

To ME, it seems only the other day that Heath and then Haigh were on trial. Even in this volume's immediate predecessor, *Bluebeard and After*, I was dealing wholly with matters which had occurred in my lifetime. Everyone must have a first murderer, and mine was Landru. I remember, at the age of ten, seeing his photograph in the *Daily Mail* and, from newsprint or the conversation of my elders (the former, I think), gathering, with no great inaccuracy, the gist of it all. That Landru, though world-famous, was a Frenchman, may have given my later criminological studies a slant. That was fifty years ago. To me, anything since Hitler's war is recent. To my younger readers, however, only the latter half of this book will seem to deal, as my sub-title says the whole of it does, with recent murder. Indeed, to me also, some of the earlier cases have begun to acquire a period, a classic, flavour.

Although to us ancients it soon became apparent after the war that the quality of our national and of international life had deteriorated and would never mend, the downward trend accelerated sharply some few years ago. While inhumanity or something all-too-human has always characterised even the most respectable murderers, the new breed seem uniformly subhuman. To suggest that a period's or a country's quality of life is reflected as much in its murderers as elsewhere may strike the reader as odd, but I find that it is so. The deeper reasons I leave to deeper thinkers. In such books as this at least, I am a criminal historian and no more. Although young bulls may kill or drive out old bulls and though farmyard fowls will peck a sick sister to death, man's criminality is unique, like his organising reason, his wit and his aesthetics. I merely chronicle some variations in his peculiar murderousness within his own species.

Among the general forms this takes, none seems to me so conspicuous as murder for sexual reasons of various kinds. The

9

example of the praying mantis might lead us to expect that in
this warfare the men would come off worst, but in fact it is not
so, except perhaps in matriarchal societies. Men who support
Women's Liberation are, we may think, asking to be eaten. The
generation gap yawns also in murder, but until recently a rational
explanation for most of its manifestations was to be found in the
fact that the old were commonly richer than the young. This
might suggest to a Marxist that class war should frequently be
observed in the field of murder, but I do not find that it is so
except at certain moments, even in the history of revolutions.
This seems true also of race hostility, except when there is
organised gang warfare, as at different times in Chicago and
Marseilles, Ireland and Cyprus. In general, both private and
ideological murderers kill within their own group. In Washington,
for instance, which has a very high murder-rate and where race
hostility undoubtedly thrives, it has been recently calculated that
an overwhelming majority both of the murderers and of their
victims are black.

To this sort of statistical point some attention is paid towards
the end of my fifth chapter, within a British context. For in this
book I say most about French cases, but nevertheless nip somewhat backward and forward across the Channel. It would be
temperamentally difficult and perverse to write about murder in
one's time without paying some attention to the corpses which,
when one is at home, thud around one every other day. I even
notice matters elsewhere, but shall hope that I may best beguile
such American readers as I have with some account of what
happens on our side of the Atlantic. As to why they have more
crime than we or even the French do even now, it is they who
will have to tell me. As in the reign of Louis-Philippe or in
London at the turn of the century, I suspect that it may have
something to do with the prevalence of antinomian sociology,
dizzy-brained progressivism and sucking-up to the young, from
which we also suffer. It is frequently said, too, that the American
police are unusually corrupt.

If this is true, it is a great misfortune. A corrupt police may be
efficient, certainly, up to a point, but it seems desirable that a
modern society should trust its police and even be fond of policemen, an advantage we long enjoyed over the French. I am no
penal reformer, but I see the force of Bentham's argument that
the greatest (he did not of course use the term) deterrent against

crime would be the criminal's certainty of being caught and that, if this desirable state of things prevailed, sentences need not in general be heavy. It would require a totally efficient police, and, equipped with all the devices of criminalistics, such a police would still need public co-operation, which it would never get without good will. In criminal matters, police efficiency is almost the same thing as truth, and justice should invariably follow. These are really the only *desiderata*. We shall never quite have them. It may be doubted whether we shall ever again have as much of them as we once had. A proliferation of psychiatrists won't help, that is certain, and indeed the effect of so many home comforts in prison can only be to drive the prisoners mad by confusing them.

But these are controversial matters, and it is not required of me that I shall join in controversies, but at most that I shall take cognisance of any which constitute historical facts within my field and period. Among these, the debate on capital punishment has marked the period strongly, perhaps most of all in the United Kingdom, where, after twenty years of ups and downs, a Labour government's bill for abolition was endorsed by the leader of the Opposition, against the evident will of the people, who still grumble intermittently. This must turn out to have been an important fact in criminal history. At the point at which I abandon the French scene, a similar bill, presented by M. Claudius-Petit, seemed to stand a good chance of success until the dreadful events at Clairvaux prison, which are the last I record. It will hardly surprise the reader that these led to agonised reappraisal on a great scale.

However, I have spent four years preoccupied with murder and now begin to feel I deserve a rest. I have come to few general conclusions, as notable as any being that I don't like murderers. There is not one of them whose company I have enjoyed, unless it were Lacenaire's and perhaps Landru's. Mme Steinheil and Mme Caillaux were fun, but, as both were acquitted, I am not entitled to call them murderesses. For those who kill in sudden rage or hopelessness, it is, unless they are governed, as they so often are, by vanity, possible to feel sympathy. A high proportion of these commit suicide or try to but are prevented. And there it may be we have a partial answer to the question of capital punishment, on which I have obstinately refused to 'stand up and be counted' (dear me, what an expression). Now that suicide is no longer a crime, perhaps it should be made a rule in prisons that no convicted murderer should be prevented from committing suicide, whether by hunger strike or more violent means. They might even be given encouragement and assistance, like Socrates. A half-way form of capital punishment would be to leave a man in his cell with nothing to drink except a hemlock draught. Whether he drank it or not, he would be dead within five days.

Among criminals without suicidal impulse, I must admit a comparative and reluctant admiration for those who never confess and who therefore, alas, presumably feel no remorse. It is convenient when murderers confess. It is inconvenient when, as with Landru, we never learn just what happened. But the man preserved a certain dignity. He was not messy. There is always a certain messiness about confession, whether to the police, to a whore (this also used to be common) or to a priest. And here I may say that I cannot see why, in a non-Catholic country, the secret of the confessional should be upheld in the case of murder suspects. Or, come to that, the professional secrecy of doctors and lawyers. Where a verdict is in doubt, for instance, I suggest that counsel and their solicitors might usefully be called in evidence, with a great deal else which this might involve. The secret of the priestly confessional I take to be one reason why the murder-rate is generally higher among Catholics than among Protestants or agnostics.

Lacenaire confessed, but then he was in love with the guillotine, fearful of confinement and determined to see his treacherous accomplices off before him. The lack of a Lacenaire or even a Landru and the fact that little literature has gathered around these later matters have made this book less agreeable to write than its predecessors. The labour of writing it was greatly lightened by the recipient of the dedication, who has had my notes of hand before. I contracted a small but very distinct debt to Frank Jellinek in connection with the Jaccoud case. What I owe Nigel Morland will be clear. The debt to printed sources is, I hope, sufficiently acknowledged in an inconclusive bibliography.

1 | FOUR YEARS OF BRITISH MURDER

For England and Wales, the annual murder-rate in the 'thirties averaged 131. In the 'forties, it was 167, an increase of more than a quarter. There was some regression in the early 'fifties, though never quite to the pre-war level. Then the figures began to climb again, but of that more hereafter. To most Britons over forty, a murder on the doorstep every two and a half days is normal. This gives us roughly one to every fifty road deaths and every fifty suicides. The French are more than twice as murderous, as suicidal and as careless on the road as we are, and I understand that even worse might be said of the Americans. Even so, no more than a fraction of our statistics can be clothed with flesh, comparatively modest as these still are.

Of the eight hundred murders committed here during the war years, we may glance quickly at those which still engage the attention of criminologists. They are associated with the names of eight individual murderers and a village. Twelve of the fourteen victims were women, nine of them killed by men but three by another woman, a Mrs Ransome, who blasted off at them with a shotgun in an Oxfordshire orchard and was politely arrested in High Holborn, with a *Daily Express* photographer sitting in a taxi alongside. With the exceptions of Manton and Dobkin, the seven individual male murderers were all young. The four victims of the R.A.F. cadet Cummins were women somewhat older than himself. The taxi-driver killed by the American deserter Hulten was older than his killer. Aircraftman Heys, Gunner Buckfield and the French-Canadian Sangret killed within their age-group, as indeed (it is usual) did the two, Dobkin and Manton, who murdered their wives. The victim at Lower Quinton, Warwickshire, was an old man of seventy-four, associated in the past with witchcraft and pinned to the ground with a hayfork. Who did it is unknown. The whole village may be assumed to have been at least accessories after the fact and a majority of them younger than the victim.

13

Among the wartime murders which had not yet come to light were one of Haigh's and one of Christie's. It was a pair of Polish deserters, Malinowski and Grondkowski, who provided British murder addicts with their first good read under the Attlee government. They were responsible for the fact that a man called Reuben Martirosoff, known as Russian Robert, a crook a good deal older than themselves, was found shot dead, on November 1st, 1945, in his Opel car, on the townward side of Notting Hill Gate, in Chepstow Place, whose taller roofs are, I fancy, among those I can see from the windows of the room in which I write. It was for a while suspected that the same pair had caused the body of 'Duke' Everett, police sergeant turned taxi-driver, to be found on Lambeth Bridge (but his cab near here, in Notting Hill Gate) a fortnight before. But they had been hanged before the first full year of peace dawned. They *seem* to belong to the war years, and it is for the years immediately thereafter, for my own benefit in the first place, that I should like to sort out the order in which occurred those criminal episodes with which our shrunken newspapers presented us.

Four of the 'forties remained. By the end of the decade, between six and seven hundred further 'murders known to the police' would have been committed in England and Wales, as a result of which some fifteen of my countrymen and two women (one of them Irish) would have established their names in British criminal history and themselves effectively have vanished, though not all were hanged. As ever, most of the crimes occurred in or near London, but four were in Lancashire and one in Glamorgan. One of the Lancastrians, Walter Rowland, a casual labourer, had been sentenced to death for the murder of his daughter before the war, but reprieved. Two highly suspect disappearances of political rivals had been among the reasons for portly Thomas Ley's return from Australia, where he had once held ministerial rank, to the United Kingdom. Dr R. G. Clements of Southport had so far fallen under suspicion with regard to the death of his third wife that an exhumation was ordered, but could not take place because the lady had been cremated (it would come to seem likely that he had murdered all three of his previous wives, out of whose deaths he had certainly done well). Heath and Haigh had both served Borstal sentences. Haigh had in fact committed at least one murder, which had not yet come to light. Otherwise, none of our *dramatis personae* can reasonably be suspected of any crime of violence against persons before March

22nd, 1946, when a woman lodged a complaint against Heath for some form of vicious assault, but for lack of evidence no prosecution followed. A fortnight later, he was fined at Wimbledon for wearing uniform and decorations to which he was not entitled.

The curtain here rises on the saloon bar of the Lord Nelson in King's Road, Chelsea. The date is, unfortunately, uncertain, but must, I should have thought, be in late May or early June. The scene is described, in a letter to myself, by Nigel Morland, now editor of *The Criminologist*, then crime reporter and the author of detective stories. At present, he lives in Bognor Regis, but he then lived two doors away from the Lord Nelson.

Standing at one end of the bar, on his own, was Haigh, drinking beer. Farther along, talking to his first victim, Margery Gardner, was Heath – Heath was on beer and Margery, as always, with 'a small gin'. In the middle, chatting to friends, was 'Fabian of the Yard'. With me, saying nothing but thinking his own thoughts, was Duncan Webb of *The People*. Margery used always to wear shoes which were too big for her, and all of us knew her (affectionately, because she was quite charming) as 'Minnie Mouse'. Heath was friendly and, indeed, still owes me a borrowed pound. Haigh I knew quite well. . . .

For the moment, let us do no more than glance at Haigh, with his small, sparkling eyes and small, dark moustache. The man one would have liked to see walk in was Ley, a man already in his sixties, enormously fat, who, after all, lived not far away and whose insane jealousy was not quite yet focused on Wimbledon.

Perhaps the most famous Scotland Yard detective of our time, it was Superintendent Robert Fabian who, the previous year, had failed to break the conspiracy of silence at Lower Quinton. We shall not see him in action until the following year, when, released from Borstal, Jenkins and Geraghty go a little too far. Duncan Webb's moment of glory was yet to come, though he would write on Heath. He was a small man, with a lot of fair hair, and spectacles, a good journalist but imaginative to the point of invention. In the only photograph I have seen (except, alas, of her dead back covered with weals), Margery Gardner looks handsome, with fine hands, such as, being an artist, she might well have, her features smooth, her nose rather prominent but straight, her eyebrows carefully plucked, her hair, of a medium colour, scraped back, the mouth and chin firm. She was a

Yorkshirewoman from Sheffield, by some accounts small but according to Duncan Webb's quite tall (five feet seven or eight). She had studied drama as well as art, was writing a novel, lived separated from a wine-salesman husband, Peter. She did not confine her custom to the Lord Nelson. Webb says that, for instance, she also drank at the Nag's Head in Kinnerton Street, and that she had first met Heath there under one of his many assumed names, as Colonel Bill Armstrong.

In early June, Mrs Brook, Ley's mistress or, rather, ex-mistress, who had her own one-roomed flat in Cromwell Road, stayed for ten days at her daughter's in Wimbledon, the latter having gone into hospital for an operation. On the 11th, the owner of the house introduced Mrs Brook to one of her tenants, a nice young man, Jack Mudie, a barman, who unfortunately would soon be leaving to take a new job in Reigate. It would have been better for young Mudie if this introduction had never taken place. For, baselessly, Ley took it into his head that Mrs Brook, a woman in her late sixties, with whom his own sexual relations had long ceased, had misbehaved while staying in her daughter's flat. At first he supposed it to have been with her son-in-law and then with another lodger in the house, but was finally to decide that it had been with Mudie and would spend devious months attempting to establish that it was so, his suspicions only hardening as any foundation for them eluded him.

It seems to have been in the small hours of June 13th that, at Ley's insistence, Mrs Brook returned from Wimbledon to her tiny flat in Cromwell Road. In the course of that week, Heath took a room at the Pembridge Court Hotel, much changed since those days and concealed from these windows by an enormous tree, at present in full leaf. There, on Sunday the 16th, he persuaded a nineteen-year-old girl to spend the night with him. At his trial, she was to declare that on this occasion he had behaved quite decently to her. Just what this means we can only surmise, for the matter was not pursued. On the evening of the 20th, Heath was with Margery Gardner at a club in South Kensington. Thence a taxi took them to the Pembridge Court, where they occupied the same room with hideous effect.

That the body of a young woman no less sickeningly mutilated was found a fortnight later on a cliff path near Eastbourne might, it was commonly felt, have been prevented if the police had previously released Heath's photograph to the newspapers. The

argument for not doing so was that in court much would depend
on the taxi-driver's evidence of identification and that defending
counsel would make hay of this evidence if it were shown that
the cabby could first have seen Heath's photograph in a newspaper. Those who write on the case seem in general to accept the
soundness of this argument, however unfortunate its consequences.
Although no lawyer, I beg leave to doubt it. The taxi-driver in
fact had first identified Heath from a photograph shown him by
the police. His evidence and theirs corroborated each other
unbreakably on this point, and at need an affidavit to that effect
could have been sworn and witnessed before ever copies of the
photograph were made for distribution to newspaper offices.

Heath was sentenced on September 26th. While he awaited
execution, the body of a prostitute found on a bomb site in Manchester was traced to the saturnine Rowland. Heath was executed
on October 16th. On November 28th, having lured him to the
house in Beaufort Gardens, Ley and Smith hanged Mudie and
transported his body to a disused chalk pit in Surrey, where it
was found two days later and gave rise to an investigation which
was still going on as the year ended.

UNIQUE IN having twice occupied the condemned cell at Strange-
ways prison, Rowland was hanged there on February 27th, 1947.
On May 24th, Ley and Smith were sentenced to death, but that
was not to be the end of the matter. On April 29th, in Charlotte
Street, which runs parallel with Tottenham Court Road and
which, before the war, had been much haunted by Dylan Thomas,
a gallant motor-cyclist was shot dead in broad daylight by three
youths running away from an attempt to rob a jeweller. The case
is remembered rather by his name, Alec de Antiquis, than theirs.
They were Jenkins, Geraghty and Rolt, this last too young to
be hanged. The police work on this case was good, urgent,
complicated and, as we have noted, conducted by Fabian.

On May 5th, Ley was declared insane and sent to Broadmoor,
where a month later he died of a heart attack. As it did not seem
fair to spare him and hang Smith, the latter's sentence was also
commuted to one of life imprisonment. On the 27th, at Southport
on the Lancashire coast, the fourth Mrs Clements, married just
before the war at St George's, Hanover Square, scene of many
society weddings, succumbed to medical treatment by her husband,

who, when suspicion fell upon him, committed suicide, as did another doctor who had signed the death certificate. On June 20th, John Allen, a baby-murderer who had been there for ten years escaped from Broadmoor. For almost two years, the news was to be intermittently diversified by reports of the whereabouts of 'the mad parson'. Jenkins and Geraghty were hanged on September 19th. Next morning, Timothy Evans, a van driver from South Wales, surprisingly married a young woman of some looks, refinement and intelligence, who was not even pregnant. For the time being, the happy pair lived with Evans's mother in St Mark's Road, north-west of here, in the neighbourhood of St Charles's hospital.

In the small hours of October 18th, James Camb, a steward, pushed the body of a young actress through the porthole of her cabin on a ship bound from Cape Town to Southampton. On the 27th, outside a Welsh public house at closing time, Haydn Evan Evans, a young miner, knocked an old woman down and kicked her to death for making fun of his new suit. In mid-December, Joe Smith, a gipsy, left a public house in Slough with an old man, whom he killed and robbed and whose body he hid for a while in a gipsy encampment before dumping it in the river nearby. That month, the famous pathologist, Sir Bernard Spilsbury, gassed himself in his laboratory, apparently while in the throes of a heart attack. The prison population had grown, and that year saw the end of the idea that each prisoner should have a cell to himself.

Dr Archibald Henderson and his third wife, *née* Rosalie Burlin, had recently sold their house in Ladbroke Square, along the road from here, and moved to Dawes Road, Fulham, a piece of Mrs Henderson's property at which she had formerly run a 'doll's hospital' (new dolls had been almost unobtainable during the war). The Hendersons' names were not much to be read about in 1948 and, even the following year, would be mentioned only mutedly by way of 'showing system' in a case which did not directly concern them even as victims. Yet Dr Henderson's marital career had clearly been an interesting one. Since in any printed volume I have seen nothing said about his first marriage except (Knowles, *Court of Drama*) that he 'inherited a very substantial sum from his first wife' and since Nigel Morland apparently sees no

immediate prospect of compiling his reminiscences, I further pilfer
the letter already quoted.

> He lived in Jersey (my family's home) and was not getting along
> with his wealthy wife. One night, coming back from a party,
> he told his wife to help him into the garage by standing by
> the back wall and waving him in. She did so, and his foot
> 'accidentally' jammed on the accelerator as he reversed instead
> of the brake. Everyone was most sympathetic.

Knowles tells us that the second wife was the widow of a German
airman killed in the Great War, and, in their life of Bernard
Spilsbury, Browne and Tullett say that, in 1937, at the inquest
on her death in a Gloucester Road hotel, the future Sir Bernard
gave medical evidence which resulted in a verdict of natural
causes. Henderson might, we may think, have emulated his
professional colleague Clements had he and his third wife not,
over the sale of their house in Ladbroke Square, met and made
a friend of Haigh, who lived beyond his means at the Onslow
Court Hotel in Kensington but had use of a shed in Crawley,
Sussex. I again quote the Morland letter.

> I wondered why Haigh was so friendly when I was introduced
> to him. I did not remember that some little time before a man
> had rung me up about one of my crime novels, asking for more
> details about a bath of acid into which my detective (Mrs Pym)
> was almost dunked by a villain. I told him the two best acids
> used, which I had not named. He gave me his name as (I
> thought) 'Hay'. . . .

Then on holiday at the Metropole in Brighton, the Hendersons
were, on January 12th, 1948, lured in succession to Crawley, shot
in the back of the head and subsequently dunked. Despite suspicions aroused in the mind of a brother of Mrs Henderson's, the
crime did not then come to light, any more than had Haigh's
first experiments in the genre. Haigh was an expert forger of
documents and experienced little difficulty in disposing to his
own advantage of the house in Fulham and other Henderson
assets.

Haydn Evan Evans was hanged on February 3rd. On the 13th,
Donald Thomas, an Army deserter, shot and killed a policeman,
P.C. Edgar, who was taking his name and address. Mrs Timothy

Evans was pregnant, and at Easter she and her husband left his mother's to live not far away on the second and top floor of the last house, No. 10, in a dead end which has become famous, Rillington Place. On April 14th, the House of Commons voted in favour of a no-hanging amendment to the Criminal Justice Act. Until the House of Lords rejected it the following month, the death penalty was therefore suspended long enough to spare the lives of Thomas and of Camb, but not those of Griffiths, a young ex-guardsman who, on May 15th, raped a girl-child of four and beat her brains out against a hospital wall in Blackburn, or of Russell, a tramp who, in Maidenhead at the end of the month, battered and robbed a woman of ninety-six, then tied her up and stuffed her into a trunk, where, understandably, she suffocated, or of the unhappy Lesbian Margaret Allen, who, at Rawtenstall, Lancashire, in August, cracked her neighbour Mrs Chadwick's skull with a hammer. Timothy Evans's child, a daughter, was born in October.

HAIGH'S FINAL and best-known dunking, that of Mrs Durand-Deacon, a fellow-resident at the Onslow Court, is dated February 18th, 1949. This time, the little man was arrested, and at the height of the summer Lewes would again deprive London of the spectacle of the year's most interesting trial, with its suggestions of vampirism. In May, 'the mad parson' was recaptured and restored temporarily to Broadmoor. In August, a friend of the wife's was put up by the Timothy Evanses in their cramped premises at 10 Rillington Place. During her stay, Evans in a rage rushed at his wife, threatening to throw her out of the window, as, we may suppose, he might well have done had their guest not tripped him up. When the girl left, Evans left with her, but one night with him (because of his 'violence') was enough for her, and she sent him back to his wife. He went about for some days threatening to run the girl down with his lorry.

On October 4th, in Golders Green, Donald Hume, another former Borstal boy but too complex to be designated by a simple phrase, killed a crooked business acquaintance, Stanley Setty, with an S.S. dagger and began distributing him by aeroplane off the Essex coast, evading arrest until the 27th. Meanwhile, on the 6th, out at Edgware, the married daughter of a prosperous Jewish couple, the Goodmans, had borne a child to her husband, the clever young advertising executive, Daniel Raven, who, four days later, battered his parents-in-law to death with the base of a television aerial. Mrs Timothy Evans was pregnant again, and there was talk of an abortion. Builders appeared at 10 Rillington Place to carry out repairs mainly to a wash-house at the back. Mrs Tim was last credibly seen alive on November 5th, and it is probable that she was strangled on the 8th. Two days later, Evans was sacked from his job as a driver, and it may have been that day when his baby also was strangled. In the early morning of the 15th, he arrived at Merthyr Vale, where he sold his wife's ring. On the 21st, he went to London, on the 23rd called at Rillington Place and returned to Methyr, where on the 30th he made the first of his numerous and contradictory statements to the police. On December 1st, the top floor at No. 10 was searched, revealing a stolen brief-case and cuttings about the disappearance of Stanley Setty. On the 2nd, the bodies of his wife and daughter being found, Evans was brought back to London, where on the 3rd he was charged with both murders, brought before a magistrate and remanded in custody.

That Evans was innocent of either murder has since become an article of faith with the whole of our liberal and progressive middle class, principally for reasons connected with their opposition to capital punishment. This belief was to arise from the discovery, more than three years later, of the bodies of other murder victims in the same house, two of them already there in the Evans's time, and the conviction for murder of their ground-floor neighbour, Christie, whom Evans's second statement first incriminated and who was to give evidence at Evans's trial. Whenever, in conversation, I have challenged the belief, I have found not only that the believer had never studied the evidence but also that he or she did not even know of precisely what murders either Evans or Christie was finally indicted and convicted (of the child alone in Evans's case, of his own wife in Christie's). The circumstances of Mrs Evans's death are in fact obscure, but to this murder there seems no sufficient reason to doubt that Evans was at least an accessory after the fact, while Ludovic Kennedy's well-imagined timings and logistics do not, to my mind, dispose of the likelihood that both men were present at the murder of the child, the question being which of them tightened a tie about the little neck. It does not make very much difference to a rational estimate of their respective guilt. If I understand the legal position, an abettor (an accessory, as we might say, though the expression is not used, to the fact) has, ever since 1861, been treated as a principal punishable in the same degree. If Evans was there, it was certainly not as a passive and helpless spectator. Though small, he was a tough and violent man, more than a match for Christie. There is little to suggest that, previously, Christie had gained an exceptional moral influence on his activities, whether by hypnosis or other means, blackmail for instance.

In the winter of 1949-50, Evans, Hume and Raven, all three awaiting trial on murder charges, made up a jolly trio at Brixton, with fifteen others who 'play dominoes and games of all kinds all day'. As Hume was to be found guilty only as an accessory after the fact to the murder of Stanley Setty, readers of the *Sunday Pictorial* were in due course able to enjoy his account of that murder. His account of what transpired between him and Evans we have only at second hand, but it is good second hand and corroborated. His fellow-prisoners believed Evans guilty in the first degree, and Hume's repeated advice was largely responsible for Evans's later denials. While still a prisoner, Hume refused to testify at the Scott Henderson inquiry which, in 1953, sought to exonerate Evans posthumously. However, nothing more delights the 'liberal' heart than a good miscarriage of justice, especially if its supposed victim and a possibly embarrassing chief witness have both been silenced. I say this with the historic Lyons mail bandwagon also in mind, Lesurques its Evans and Dubosq its Christie.

From a more practical point of view, the unfortunate thing about the Evans case is that, during their investigation, the police did not find the two bodies in the garden and bring a case against Christie at the same time. It might have led to discovery of the whole truth about the deaths of Mrs Evans and her baby. Had the case been proved, it would certainly have spared the lives of Mrs Christie and three victims of the necrophily her husband finally elaborated. It would have spared the life of a Swiss taxi-driver if the full case against Hume had been proved. For capital punishment certainly deters those who have once committed murder from doing it again. A prostitute's life would have been spared if Rowland had been hanged for the murder of his daughter. As Sir Harold Scott was to point out to the impending royal commission on capital punishment, another case in our four years demonstrated its deterrent effect not perhaps in terms of annual statistics but in a specific criminal situation. This was the case of Alec de Antiquis. A brother of the Jenkins hanged for that had been found guilty of a remarkably similar shooting in wartime, but was not sentenced to death and, indeed, in 1947, was almost half-way through his prison sentence.

> All the persons concerned in this and in the subsequent Antiquis case were associated and lived in the Bermondsey district. After the result of the case against Hedley and Thomas James Jenkins they . . . became actively engaged in crime. Some of them were arrested and sentenced to varying terms of imprison-ment, but still they continued living their life of crime.
> Then came . . . the death sentence on Charles Henry Jenkins and Christopher Geraghty. Almost immediately the gang dis-banded. They have not been seen in their usual haunts since, and as far as is known are not engaged in criminal pursuits.

I quote this from Fabian, who on his own behalf adds that, for weeks after the hanging of Jenkins and Geraghty, he and his men began to find guns abandoned in parks under bushes, in dustbins, dropped through the floors of bombed houses, fished up by Thames River patrolmen in nets from the low-tide mud.

That a lenient court verdict may set up what (by, I feel sure, inaccurate analogy with nuclear physics) we now tend to call a 'chain-reaction' in crime, sometimes lasting over many years, was first suggested to me by the long succession of political murders in Paris between the world wars, which all seemed to stem, more or less directly but in several later verdicts explicitly, from the acquittal, in 1919, of the murderer of the socialist leader Jean Jaurès three days before the outbreak of the Great War. Much of the benefit wrought by the hanging of Geraghty and Jenkins was, I dare say, undone by that 1948 suspension of the death penalty which saved Thomas, making it likelier both that another young man would presently shoot a policeman and that a hanging would then be demanded at all costs. At the beginning of 1953, there was a hanging, but not of the young man who had shot the policeman, he being only sixteen, as he proclaimed at the time of the shooting. He also had a brother in prison, as he likewise proclaimed. It seems not improbable that Craig had thought much about the Rolt who was too young to hang with Geraghty and Jenkins. The wretched Bentley was hanged instead.

AFTER BRIEFLY listing a number of prominent murders in wartime, I noted that twelve of the fourteen victims were women and that one was a very old man, while most of the murderers were young. In the cases we have since considered, if we count in known previous victims, we find that fifteen women and three children died at the hands of ten men, a child and an elderly woman at the hands of our only two murderesses, that the average age of the men killed was not exaggeratedly high (though higher than that of their killers) and that two multiple murderers killed men and women equally. In so far as our cases represent a fair sample, the last four 'forties cannot therefore be described as a statistically significant phase of intensified sex warfare or abnormal generation hostility. No woman hit back. An older man killed a younger one for reasons supplied by unfounded sexual jealousy. A young man slaughtered his parents-in-law four days after their daughter had borne him a child. A sadist was first brought to the point of murder by his encounter with a masochist, if we may indeed deduce that Margaret Gardner had consented to the tying-up and the first beating.

This last we might suppose a promising situation, but, if we think about it, we may see that his partner's pleasure would frustrate a sadist's desire to inflict pain. When she had reached her limit, his enjoyment would not yet have begun. Beyond all that she could endure, he must persist in what she could not. Unfortunately for Heath, Margaret Gardner died of suffocation, not of the final horrors, the infliction of which must have been a solitary performance and therefore no doubt unsatisfying, whence the further experiment at Eastbourne. All this and much else in those four years is odd and, if you can bear to dwell on it, interesting. I find no significant general pattern in it.

By the evening of February 20th, 1949, Mrs Durand-Deacon's body, in the shed at Crawley, must have been well on its way to forming the 'sludge' her killer was so elegantly to describe. He, with another resident at the Onslow Court Hotel, had that day reported her disappearance to a woman sergeant at Chelsea police station. Intuitively, she had felt that there was something 'wrong' about Haigh and, what was more to the point, had ventured to say so in her report. Ignorant of this fact, him we may imagine with a satisfied smile in the dining-room of his Kensington hotel. Meanwhile, after a drink in the bar at Orly airport, in a restaurant on the Orleans road were dining a rich man, Marcel Hilaire, three years older than Haigh, his young mistress, Christiane Page, and the manager of his flourmill near Blois, a former policeman, Roland Petit.

After dinner, they continued along the N20 and called on a friend, a garage-owner, Bouguereau, who brought out a bottle of wine and, when they had drunk this, got into the car with them. At a quiet spot, Hilaire switched off the headlights, said that there must be something wrong with the wiring and stopped the car. He and Christiane got out. While she squatted to relieve herself on the grass verge, he shot her twice in the back of the head. His friends then got out and helped him place her body in the back seat, while they crowded into the front and drove on to Hilaire's house at Mer. As there were callers and a car standing outside, they went on to Meung, where Hilaire's father lived. There they got out spades and started to dig but found the ground too hard. They returned to Mer and dropped Christiane's body down the well. A fortnight later, when the smell had become offensive, Bouguereau brought a load of sand and, with Petit's help, tipped and shovelled it down on top of the body. Hilaire gave up the flat he had rented for Christiane at Sceaux and returned to the path of virtue with his wife and children. The girl had become a nuisance.

25

Somewhat more than fifty miles south-east of Blois lies the small town of Loudun, historically associated with a notable outbreak of witchcraft hysteria. There, in the summer of 1949, started what I suppose may be the longest-drawn-out and most wretched legal process for murder on record anywhere. On July 21st, a woman in her fifties, a Mme Besnard, *née* Marie-Joséphine-Philippine Davaillaud, twice a widow, was arrested and charged with thirteen acts of culpable homicide. The remains of thirteen bodies, including that of her mother and those of both her husbands, were exhumed. They had been buried on dates between a year and a half and a quarter of a century before. Like so much in rural and provincial France, the case had started with vindictive gossip. It was to be kept going by incompetent local experts, who seemed never to have heard of that omnipresence of arsenic in the soil of graveyards which had so often led to forensic confusion during the past hundred years. I shall not enlarge on the case of Marie Besnard. It was to be a good deal heard of abroad, and we may read in English the unfortunate woman's own account, admirably translated and presented.

Another case which was to make both legal and police history started that summer. On August 3rd, just after noon, the Aga Khan and his Begum were seated in a hired Cadillac on the way to Nice airport, whence they were to fly to Deauville. The Begum had two hundred million francs' worth of jewellery and a quarter of a million francs in notes with her. A Corsican gang from Marseilles held the car up on the Cannes road, an accomplice with a bicycle having brought it to a halt by mending his chain in the middle of the highway. They took possession of the jewellery and notes, punctured the Cadillac's tyres and made a smooth getaway. There was to be a little bloodshed later, but in essence we may regard this case as non-lethal and thus outside our competence.

The year bore a normal crop of gang shootings. The two most notable took place in Paris. They were, by accident, of a parliamentary deputy and his secretary and, with carefully plotted intent, of another of his henchmen by deadly little Émile Buisson, who thus precariously maintained his position as Public Enemy No. 1, though the henchman was himself no loss to the public. He was a Corsican. The deputy had been mistaken for a Corsican by other Corsicans.

The mortal remains of Christiane Page still lay beneath a ton of sand down a well at Mer, while at ground level her former lover, previously her employer, the franc-millionaire Marcel Hilaire (for the past two years, he had also imported and resold American farm machinery), continued to tread the path of domestic virtue. On December 13th, he was arrested, the former policeman, Roland Petit, having cracked under questioning. The police investigation had taken almost ten months. The judicial inquiry was to last almost three years. For his own defence, Hilaire retained the formidable Maître René Floriot, for that of his friend Bouguereau, the garage-owner and sand-provider, the even more distinguished Maître Maurice Garçon, a member of the Académie Française.

In 1950, two of Pierrepoint's customers were Timothy Evans and Daniel Raven. Neither execution caused much heart-searching at the time. Much was caused in France by that of Michel Watrin, a young man from Verdun who, within a week in 1946, had shot two taxi-drivers in the back of the head within jurisdictions as far apart as those of Metz and Mâcon. He had thus faced two trials, been convicted and sentenced twice. On the outskirts of Paris, without sound of shots or bloodshed, Émile Buisson was arrested for the last time. His associate in an escape three years before, lame and bespectacled René Girier ('René la Canne'), escaped again, uniquely (but lamed himself further), by sawing through the floor of a police van on its way to the prison at Fresnes. That was on November 20th. On December 3rd, an elderly caïd of the Corsican vice empire, Ange or Angelo Saliceti, was shot dead as his wife drove him into Paris. The culminating point of one feud which had gone on for twelve years, this règlement de compte marked an important stage in the general course of post-war French gang warfare.

There was less bloodshed in the London milieu. Even before the war, it had been dominated by the five Messina brothers, of Sicilian origin, who, by way of Malta, had acquired British passports but were in due course found to be of Egyptian nationality. Their Soho and Mayfair women had nevertheless been recruited largely in France, brought over after being provided with British ghost husbands. Among them was the splendid Martha Watts, née Marthe Hucbourg, of La Neuville-au-Pont on the Marne. On September 3rd, 1950, in the person of Duncan Webb, The People

had opened its campaign against the Messina brothers, greatly
to the embarrassment of Chuter Ede, who, in the manner of
Labour Home Secretaries, preferred to know nothing about the
underworld. By the end of the year, questions in the House of
Commons had forced his hand, however. Four of the brothers had
already left Britain and were spending most of their time in
Paris or at Pau in the Pyrenees. The one who remained, Alfredo,
was arrested in February 1951. He was defended by John Scott
Henderson, K.C., later to be so prominently associated with the
agitation about Timothy Evans. The defence consisted largely of
allegations against the police so manifestly invented that they
disgusted even Chuter Ede.

That year's principal British murders were to be those of three
little girls and two older women, committed by a person unknown,
by the mentally defective Straffen, by two of the Lancashire Irish,
Burns and Devlin, and by a literary youth in Nottingham, Leonard
Mills. There was a certain sexual content, as there almost
invariably is, in the child-murders and, though it seems to
have been of revulsion due to her age, in Mills's strangulation of Mabel Tattershaw. In France that year were performed
four murderous acts three of which, like Hilaire's two years
before, involved 'the eternal triangle'. As the fourth also
involved shooting of a wife, a sequence of trials for *crimes
passionnels* was clearly promised. In the terms I prefer, all five
cases were certainly episodes in the sex war. In none of them did
a man kill a man or a woman a woman. The fatal casualties were
equal. In four out of the five cases, a 6.35 mm. automatic pistol
was employed. They were all middle-class crimes, with either
money or education somewhere in evidence.

FÉLIX BAILLY, aged twenty-five, a good-looking and evidently
good-natured third-year medical student from St Omer had a
small flat in the Rue de la Croix-Nivert on the Left Bank in
Paris, very much in the district of the teaching hospitals. He was
engaged to be married to an excellent and beautiful, fair-haired
young woman, Monique Lombard. On the morning of March 17,
1951, he was shot three times, at close quarters, with a new 6.35
automatic, in his flat, by Pauline Dubuisson, aged twenty-four,
who had been his mistress during the first year of his medical
studies at Lille. He had been apprehensive of something of the

kind for the past three days, Pauline's landlady having warned
his father at St Omer that her lodger had left Lille for Paris with
the weapon in her handbag. He had taken precautions, staying
the night of the 15th with an uncle, having a friend stay with him
the following night. This friend had just departed, and another,
expected to take his place, was at that moment held up in a
traffic jam, a public transport strike that day filling the streets
with more than the usual number of private cars. Each of the
three shots would have proved fatal, and the third appeared to
be a *coup de grâce* behind the ear. Pauline Dubuisson had, it
appeared, intended the fourth shot for herself, but the pistol
jammed, so she wrenched off the pipe of a gas-cooker, turned on
the gas and lay down. Bailly's expected friend arrived an hour
later, smelled gas on the landing and called the fire brigade, who
broke in. Pauline was unconscious but in no immediate danger.
Reading what had happened next morning in his newspaper, her
father, living in Malo-les-Bains, which is the residential quarter
of Dunkirk, gassed himself in the bathroom, having first swallowed
gardenal and written a note to say that the shame was more than
he could outlive.

A building contractor, M. Dubuisson might have found it
difficult, during the Occupation, in Dunkirk, not to collaborate
with the Germans. He had done it willingly. He was a Lutheran
protestant with authoritarian views. Pauline's head had been
shaved at the Liberation. She had flirted with Germans from the
tender age of thirteen and at seventeen had been the mistress of
the colonel in charge of the military hospital. At one time, Félix
Bailly had wanted to marry her, but she had refused and had been
openly promiscuous. When he transferred his studies from Lille
to Paris, a period of eighteen months had elapsed without the
two meeting. They had met again in Paris twelve days before the
shooting, Pauline then returning to Lille, visiting Malo-les-Bains
on March 10th, her birthday, promptly obtaining a firearms
certificate and buying the 6.35 automatic with the money her
father had given her. From hospital she was taken to the Petite
Roquette prison, where she was to spend eighteen months under
examination and awaiting trial.

HENRI DEMON, aged twenty-six, was a manufacturer of agricultural machinery near Lille. By his wife Alice he had two young

children, boys. He possessed two 6.35 mm. automatic pistols. His house adjoined the factory, and in a yard between the two he kept a private workshop. There, in June 1951, he set up a contrivance of his own invention for firing one or other of the two weapons. Late at night on the 12th, he got up, telling his wife that he had heard a prowler in the yard. He took a pistol and went down. Alice heard six shots. Her husband returned and told her that the intruder had fired twice at him, that he had returned the fire, but that in the dark he had missed and that the prowler had got away. Next day, Demon reported this incident to the police. A month later, at one o'clock in the morning of July 10th, he again went downstairs, pulled the kitchen curtains apart, moved a flowerpot off the window-ledge, called out to his wife that somebody wanted to see her and went out into the yard, one pistol in a holster on his belt. When, from outside, he could see his wife in the kitchen, he fired at her and saw her fall. He then went into his workshop, pulled the string which activated his pistol-firing contrivance and, at the third attempt, wounded himself in the left arm. He removed his second pistol from the contrivance, hid it temporarily and returned to the kitchen. Alice Demon was conscious, but could not get up. The two little boys were trying to help her. A bullet, lodging in the pericardial region, had damaged her spine, depriving her of the use of her legs for the rest of her life.

She knew what had happened. At first, she confirmed her husband's story of an intruder, but a priest, visiting her in hospital, persuaded her that it was her Christian duty to tell the truth, which indeed was more readily consonant with police findings and with ballistics *expertise* into ten spent cartridges ejected by two similar weapons.

On August 11th, 1951, Pierre Chevallier, aged forty-one, mayor and elected parliamentary representative of Orleans, was given ministerial rank (Under-Secretary of State for Technical Education) in the new government of René Pleven. His record was excellent. He came of a family of doctors. As a medical officer during the ten months France was at war in 1939-40, he had been decorated for tending the wounded under fire. During the German occupation, he had both worked tirelessly as a doctor and led the local Resistance. Mayor of so important a town at thirty-five, he had done marvels in the way of reconstruction (as anyone who travelled through Orleans in those post-war days could see). He had two sons, aged eleven and six, by his wife Yvonne, a nurse whom he had married on his departure for the Front in 1939. On August 12th, 1951, he went down to Orleans from Paris for what was to be a brief visit, largely to pick up clothes. His wife shot him five times with a 7.65 mm. automatic bought some days before.

It was known that, for five years past, Pierre Chevallier had had a mistress, the plump, pretty, younger, red-haired wife of an Orleans businessman, Léon Perreau, who was *complaisant*. It was also understood in Orleans that the Chevalliers had never quite accepted Pierre's marriage with Yvonne Rousseau, a daughter of the circumambient folk, and that, when he became a figure in public life, she had at once shown herself to be a social liability.

A FORTNIGHT later, on August 26th, in a hotel bedroom off the Champs Élysées, Michel Gelfand, forty-nine, a hosier of Latvian origin, having made a will and intending initially to kill only himself in front of her, first, with the inevitable 6.35 mm. automatic, shot his mistress, Edith Tarbouriech, a tart in her later thirties, and then missed his own heart, so that a fortnight later he left hospital and went to the Santé prison. During the whole course of the judicial inquiry, he was to insist that his motive for both suicide and murder had been to save the honour, threatened by the blackmailing Tarbouriech, of a Mme X., in good society, with whom his relations had been platonic and whose name he was never going to divulge, though in due course the examining magistrate would discover it. About Michel Gelfand it may be said here that he had been a great frequenter of night-clubs and that a friend of his was the novelist Joseph Kessel, co-founder of the weekly magazine *Détective,* himself of Baltic origin.

ONCE AN arrest has been made, criminal proceedings in the United Kingdom are conducted with what by continental standards is great speed, while after conviction there is no such protracted appeal procedure as seems to us characteristic of the American system. In the United States, it seems to us, there are always convicted criminals awaiting either the passing or the execution of their sentences, while in Europe the unconvicted await trial, not idly, however, for all this while the judicial inquiry is continuing, the *dossier* being compiled, and twice or even three times a week the prisoner may be driven from prison to see the examining magistrate, until such time as the *instruction* or *information* is closed and a grand jury of the Court of Appeal non-suits it or finds, as we say, a true bill. The result is that criminal history, year by year or over a longer period, presents quite different patterns here and abroad. In general, a single case will occupy our attention here in Britain for a while and then leave the columns of our newspapers, while another takes its place. It is not so elsewhere. In other countries, names may be inter-mittently in the news for a very long time, and, in France, they will commonly be the names of those awaiting trial. By the time a case comes up for public hearing, French readers may, on the other hand, have quite forgotten what aroused their interest at the time of the discovery of the crime, the police investigation, the arrest. A year at least will commonly have elapsed.

These differences cannot but find reflection in any attempt to write consecutive criminal history. For the United Kingdom, it will be comparatively easy, and the result should seem neater. From a lack of personal experience in the matter, I can only surmise what difficulties would arise in a similar enterprise for the United States. I beg the reader to believe that it is not perversity or the tortuousness of my own mind which alone causes the French names in a book like this to disappear for a while and then suddenly to recur. Between the murder of Christiane Page and the verdict on Michel Gelfand, four years and nine months elapsed. For almost fifteen months, from late August 1951 to early November 1952, Marcel Hilaire, Pauline Dubuisson, Henri Demon, Yvonne Cheval-lier and Michel Gelfand were in prison at the same time, all five awaiting trial. Before the first of their trials came up, a great deal of a criminal nature happened in France which we may ignore, but in the late summer and early autumn of 1952 occurred two events of distinct Anglo-Saxon interest.

On the morning of August 5th, the bodies of Sir Jack Drum-mond, a senior British civil servant, and his second wife were found shot dead beside a desolate stretch of road in hilly northern Provence, that of their eleven-year-old daughter battered to death in a field nearby. Driving through France in a green Hillman shooting-brake, they had camped out the previous night at this unpromising spot. The adjacent land was farmed by a family called Dominici. A fair amount about this case has appeared in English, and in France it has never quite been allowed to rest. Here, it is perhaps sufficient to remind the reader that the old patriarch, Gaston Dominici, was, two years later, to be sentenced to death for the murders, that he was nevertheless released in 1960 and has since died, that in 1968 Maître Floriot again pointed the finger of suspicion at one of the sons, Gustave Dominici, and that, more recently still, the Detective Chief Inspector from Marseilles who was originally in charge of the case and whose findings were largely brushed aside has published his own account. It was his suggestion in the first place that a political motive lay behind the crime, and in England, where of course more attention had been paid to the antecedents of the victim, this view is widely held, the murder of Sir Jack Drummond being taken to have been the consequence of an old story of the wartime Resistance. The case indeed bristles with unsolved difficulties, although, to my mind, some of these appear only if you become greatly concerned to find an adequate motive.

To be adequate, a motive must no doubt be rational, and we may perhaps expect reason in educated persons, but hardly among peasantries or proletariats. To the former, especially, mere foreignness may be at least an exciting circumstance, heightening at once greed and sexual curiosity, with the sense also that the stranger is unprotected. To Greenwall's catalogue of Britons murdered in France had been added, two years before, the name of Jacqueline Richardson, and at that very moment a young man called Liger was in prison at Versailles, charged with her murder, for which he was to be very indulgently treated. Contrariwise, it is not long ago since a timid English youth shot three young French campers, not, apparently, as a result of xenophobia but because their very presence and situation (as it must have seemed to him, there was one girl spare) stimulated in him expectations which, though otherwise friendly, they declined to fulfil. From the site of the Drummond murders, watches and a camera had disappeared, though we don't know who took them. What we do know is that the Dominicis possessed such firearms as are commonly found about a farm and that one of these was used, an American .22 rifle as it happened. In the annals of Anglo-French murder, I have not, I may say, yet met a case in which it appeared that xenophobia itself was the motive, while even run-of-the-mill political murder, uncommon in the United Kingdom, has in France as a rule taken place between compatriots, not infrequently foreigners living in Paris.

Not for a long time had either the Parisian or the Marseilles *milieu*, in both cases largely composed of Corsicans, been content solely to exploit the basic commodity of women. To drugs and the rest had been added, since the war, American cigarettes. The great warehouse was Tangier. Genoa was as interested as Marseilles, and so there had come into existence a generically Mediterranean *milieu*, the Italian names of whose members might equally be of Corsican or mainland provenance. Indeed, they might have come from Sicily by way of New York, for 'Lucky' Luciano was apparently much involved. There were also plain Americans, chief of them a former naval officer, Elliot Forrest, who masterminded the act of piracy by which, on October 5th, 1952, the cigarette-laden *Combinatie*, with a Dutch skipper, was boarded and forced to change direction by a torpedo-boat, formerly British. The wariness of French customs vessels caused her to be unloaded in Corsica itself. This accident was to lead to a sequence of *règlements de comptes* or settling of scores (the only expression French has yet found for gang feuds and gang warfare) on a barely precedented scale, its course following a 'chain-reaction' logic which I fear I cannot follow even with Montarron's help. Forrest himself was eventually brought to trial in France, with what reflection in American newspapers I do not know.

OF OUR five warriors in the sex war, the first to come up for trial was Yvonne Chevallier, *née* Rousseau. She was tried at Rheims, and the result was acquittal, largely, it was felt, because of the bad impression made by the dead politician's mistress and her compliant husband. That was on November 7th, 1951. Yvonne Rousseau had trained as a midwife and had first met young Dr Pierre Chevallier on hospital service in Orleans. There, the case would have aroused local passions, and that was why it had been tried at Rheims. After her acquittal, widowed Mme Chevallier nevertheless returned to her mother's cottage in the countryside near Orleans, but within a matter of months was to take the two sons of her marriage to French Guiana, appointed sister in charge of the maternity wing of the hospital for the natives at St Laurent du Maroni, where sick convicts had once died if they were lucky.

There were promotions among the magistracy of Rheims, so

that we shall presently see prosecuting Pauline Dubuisson and presiding over her trial in Paris the MM. Lindon and Jadin who had played corresponding parts in the trial of Yvonne Chevallier at Rheims. Next, however, came up, in Paris, the trial of the rich miller, Marcel Hilaire, who had murdered his mistress unaided and then, with some help, tipped her body into his own well near Blois. The presiding judge at his trial, in February 1953, M. Chapar, had only recently risen from the ranks of *juges d'instruction* or examining magistrates, in which capacity he had prepared the case against the soulful mistress-murderer, Michel Gelfand, not to be heard till November, so that for the moment his functions were rather complicated. Hilaire's defending counsel was, it may be remembered, the redoubtable Maître Floriot, whom presently we should see, acting for the family of Félix Bailly, deceased, in the case against Pauline Dubuisson, with Jadin presiding and Lindon, the official prosecutor, somewhat taking a back seat. For Hilaire, on February 13th, Floriot just managed to avert a capital sentence.

In ENGLAND, it was Coronation year. A fortnight before the trial of Marcel Hilaire, Bentley had been hanged for an ambiguous phrase. Christie, who had made away with his wife in December and Kathleen Maloney in January, disgustingly finished off Hectorine McLennan on or about March 3rd. A week later, Philip Henry, a coloured soldier, entered a house in York, raped and beat a woman in her late seventies, then took her upstairs and dropped her out of the window. As Sir John Hunt's expedition toiled up the lower slopes of Everest, the bodies were discovered at Rillington Place, and on April 13th, in Blackpool, a Mrs Merrifield administered rat poison and rum to a Mrs Ricketts in her eightieth year. As the anthems pealed in Westminster Abbey, in the Thames at Richmond was discovered the body of the second of two girls stabbed to death and raped subsequently* by a young labourer,

---

* Nothing is apparently easier for a pathologist to determine than the order of proceedings in such a case, where this order seems to be common. Whiteway's previous hobby had been knife-throwing, but, like all repetitive posthumous rapists, he must either have been both a necrophilist and a coprophilist or have wondered whether the same displeasing accident would happen the second time. For crime reporting regularly errs on the side of gentility, which, I suggest, does harm, in that some potential murderers might be deterred by a proper realisation of how

Alfred Whiteway. On July 2nd occurred a peculiarly vicious juvenile gang-stabbing at a bus-stop on the edge of Clapham Common. On the 15th, Christie was hanged, on the 30th Henry, on September 18th Mrs Merrifield. On the 23rd, a woman murdered her epileptic son and stuffed him into the base of a divan bed on which her husband slept that night. In Wales, a young farm-worker killed his uncle and aunt.

That was on October 16th. On the 22nd, a young man received a death sentence (never carried out) for the Clapham Common stabbing. That same day, at Douai, Henri Demon was brought to trial for the attempted murder of his wife, carried into court to give her evidence against him. On the 24th, he received a life sentence. On the 28th, Pauline Dubuisson was due to stand trial in Paris, but that morning was found in her cell at Little Roquette unconscious and bleeding from cut wrists. Thus, of that autumn's two great trials in Paris, it was that of Michel Gelfand which came up first, on November 12th. The aging playboy was acquit-ted and made straight for Fouquet's in the Champs Élysées, where his friends assembled to congratulate him. The name of his high-born, platonic *inamorata* had not come out in court. The post-poned case of Pauline Dubuisson came up on the 18th.

THE FRENCH magistracy is divided into two main branches, the *magistrature assise*, seated magistracy or Bench, and the *magistra-ture debout,* procuracy, Directorship of Public Prosecutions or Parquet. There is very little transference or secondment between one branch and the other. A judge remains a judge, whether he presides over some lower court in the provinces, pursues judicial inquiries and is known as a *juge d'instruction* or examining magistrate, lords it over the court of assize in Paris, flanked by two junior or superannuated judges, his assessors, hears proceed-ings before the Cour d'Appel (which considers appeals not against sentence but against committal and thus acts as a grand jury) or, at the height of seniority, deliberates with his fellow-members of the Cour de Cassation, which is the supreme court and which considers appeals against conviction and sentence and may quash

disgusting murder, especially sex murder, is to most tastes. At the moment of natural death or perhaps, rather, of final collapse, evacuation of the bladder and colon is usual. In the case of violent deaths, this is commonly accelerated by fear.

these (the common word for breaking, *'casser'* also means to quash in the legal sense, so that *cassation* is quashing) and order a new trial, but which also promulgates rulings which will have the force of statutes, just as though new parliamentary legislation had been involved.

The *magistrature debout,* equally red-robed, prosecutes, generally in the person of a man whose civil-service grade is that of *avocat-général* (but it may be the departmental *procureur-général* himself or other *substitut*). He sits in some isolation and is known as the *représentant du ministère public,* this *ministère public* not being the Ministry of Justice or any specific ministry but rather a general concept. He is in effect our prosecuting counsel. He raises points with the presiding judge, who may allow him to question the defendant or a witness directly, and he delivers his concluding speech for the prosecution, known as the *réquisitoire.* (He does not deliver an opening speech for the prosecution of the kind with which our criminal trials begin. Its place is taken by a prepared *acte d'accusation* or protracted indictment, which is read by the clerk to the court and which may be very long.) Counsel for the defence always speaks last.

Members of the black-robed Order of Advocates do not, officially, prosecute. They are generally employed as defending counsel (and, incidentally, you approach them directly, not through a solicitor). In France, however, civil and criminal actions may lie together, as they may not with us, and, before the *réquisitoire,* there may be a *partie civile* for whom an advocate speaks (or advocates speak) on behalf of civil complainants who will in general be the next-of-kin of victims. The essential purpose of this arrangement is to put in claims for damages or compensation, which will be discussed after the criminal verdict and sentence have been pronounced. In practice, however, what an advocate of the *partie civile* says, imploring sympathy for the bereaved, will, in a murder trial, commonly amount to a speech for the prosecution. It may be more vehement and damaging than the official *réquisitoire* which follows. It often is, no doubt in part because barristers who normally defend feel frustrated and like to remind us now and then that they also have teeth.

For twenty-five years, Maître René Floriot has been regarded as France's leading criminal advocate, and generally he is to be found acting for the defence. He is a man of modest origins, and a style of simple factuality and hard logic, at first peculiarly his own, has largely driven out that fine rhetoric and sobbing appeal of the great *ténors du barreau* of whom Moro-Giafferi was the last. Though he wears and always has worn spectacles, Me Floriot, who has never married, is or was a good shot and once did a lot of amateur boxing. This side of his character has more than once come notably to the fore when he was not defending but doing the *partie civile*. He was to overdo it badly in a case at Rheims fifteen years later. In many opinions, he overdid it at the trial of Pauline Dubuisson.

In an English murder trial, the accused need never be heard. If his counsel calls him in evidence, he leaves the dock and goes into the witness-box. Having then told his story at the prompting of his own counsel, he becomes liable to cross-examination. In France, he remains in the dock, but from the outset is questioned, not only on the offences charged against him but on the whole course of his life, by the presiding judge, who also questions witnesses. Our routine of examination-in-chief, cross-examination and re-examination of witnesses does not exist in France, though what amounts to the same thing seems latterly to have become increasingly frequent. In principle, all questions, whether those of *avocat* or *avocat-général*, are put through the presiding judge, the president of the court. In practice, he often gives counsel their heads. Here, for example, is Me Floriot in effect cross-examining Pauline Dubuisson even before the president, M. Jadin, has closed his initial *interrogatoire*. M. Lindon, the *avocat-général*, has already had a go at her, and at last the mask of pride has fallen, the defendant is in tears. Floriot wants precise details of the last interview and shooting.

FLORIOT. In fact, you didn't let him speak.

DUBUISSON. He seemed distant.

FLORIOT. I thought you'd called to discuss something with him.

DUBUISSON. He didn't speak.

FLORIOT. He didn't have time. He struck you as distant, and that was enough for you : you fired. You move fast.

DUBUISSON. I don't know how it happened.

FLORIOT. And you don't miss. You open fire, and he falls. How?

DUBUISSON. I couldn't say.

FLORIOT. At the first shot, the second? . . . The first shot, that was the one in the forehead?

DUBUISSON. How should I know?

FLORIOT. When you fire at point-blank range, you see where you've hit.

DUBUISSON. If I knew, I'd tell you.

FLORIOT. I doubt it.

DUBUISSON. After all the admissions I've made to day!

FLORIOT. That doesn't relieve you of the need to be frank about the rest. And this third shot?

DUBUISSON. I don't know.

FLORIOT. A fine display of indifference! You put a revolver to the ear of a man you love, you act like a real killer, and you remember nothing at all about it. . . . Pauline Dubuisson, you're a liar in this as in everything else.

DUBUISSON. No.

FLORIOT. And now let's talk about your attempt at suicide. The pistol was found jammed. All right, I grant that, though we don't know how it got jammed. So you turned on a gas tap. You waited quite a while, didn't you?

DUBUISSON. No.

FLORIOT. Didn't you wait till you heard the firemen in the staircase before you turned the tap on and lay down by the stove?

DUBUISSON. No.

FLORIOT. You're accustomed to that sort of thing: it was only the third or fourth time you'd failed in a suicide attempt. You're more efficient when it comes to a murder.

FOR THE DEFENCE, ME BAUDET. There's no need to muck it all up with this hunting talk.

An English judge would have allowed very little of that. Most Parisian judges would have stepped in, if not earlier, at the point when it was suggested that the gas tap had not been turned on until firemen were in the staircase. The fact had not yet come out in evidence, but from the files in front of him M. Jadin well knew that it was in part the smell of gas which had caused Bailly's late-arriving friend to call the fire brigade. His impartiality was clearly in doubt. He and his prosecuting side-kick, M. Lindon, seemed a provincial pair putting on a determined double act in Paris, a bit awed by Floriot. As a *Figaro* reporter pointed out, they were the same who, at Rheims, had displayed indulgence in full measure towards Yvonne Chevallier.

In the end, the jury brought in a verdict of *assassinat*, that is to say, of wilful and premeditated murder, but with extenuating circumstances, which meant a life sentence. M. Lindon had asked for a capital sentence. It would have made no difference. The death sentence might still be passed on a woman, but, in peacetime, none had been carried out since 1887. It sometimes seems, however, as though French juries do not trust even so long-established a precedent. The case against Pauline Dubuisson had been pressed with exceptional vigour, even viciously. And the motive had indeed been hideous. It had been to prevent a happiness in which the murderess could not share and which she had once rejected. Though incidental to the sex war, it was a crime of pride and left another woman conspicuously damaged.

That was, we may note, the last Parisian *grand procès* at which photography was permitted in court. We may see the sufficiently handsome murderess in the dock and the far more attractive *fiancée* at the witnesses' bar. Thereafter, for Paris, we have to be content with artists' impressions, though at Digue, for example, we have photographs of the Dominici trial a year later. A week after the verdict, the big, sentimental Slav heart which Michel Gelfand had missed with his 6.35 was stopped by a clot of blood. Pauline Dubuisson was taken to Haguenau, near Strasbourg, where to begin with they put her on rough leatherwork.

3 | THREE RITUAL MURDERS

MERRETT-CHESNEY flew over from Germany for a last fling, but otherwise the most notable British murders at the end of 1953 and in 1954 were the work of foreigners, Onufreczyk, Hepper and Mrs Christofi, while an Irish regular in the British armed forces, Sgt Emmett-Dunne, was brought to trial in Germany for a sergeants' mess *crime passionnel* thought at first to have been suicide. In the United States were heard the names of Lorraine Clark, Chapin and Stacey, all three sex-driven. Into Article 64 of the Code Pénal was introduced the notion of diminished responsibility. Marie Besnard was brought to trial again, this time in Bordeaux.

On February 25th, a banker's son, Jacques Fesch, whose father had refused him the money he wanted to buy a new boat, entered the Silberstein *bureau de change* and numismatics shop near the Paris Stock Exchange, knocked out the assistant with a hammer and made off with over three hundred thousand old francs, pursued by the elderly Alexander Silberstein shouting *'au voleur'*. In the Rue St Marc, he was knocked off his balance by a printer but pulled out a revolver and continued. Taking refuge in a house in the Boulevard des Italiens but pursued by police, he shot and killed the first who approached him and ran to the nearest *métro* station, where he was felled and captured by a bank clerk who slammed a gate in his face. There was no shortage of witnesses to this adventure, but Jacques Fesch was to spend three years in prison awaiting trial.

On May 1st, at a dance in Rennes, a typist who worked in Paris, home for the weekend, had made the acquaintance of Jacques Algarron, a cadet from the Army school at Coëtquidan. The following weekend, they had become lovers. Neither was a novice. Denise Labbé had an illegitimate child, a daughter aged two, Catherine, by a house-doctor at Lorient, with whom she had lived until his departure for Indo-China and whom she had refused to marry on his return. The child was farmed out with entirely respectable foster-parents, a retired nurse and her husband, in the western outer suburbs of Paris, where her mother visited her quite regularly on Sunday afternoons. Algarron had two illegitimate children, whose mothers seem to have borne him no ill will, though he had refused to marry either.

He was himself the illegitimate son of an elderly Army officer, and a much older half-brother of his had at the Liberation been sentenced to death as a collaborator but reprieved. He was twenty-four. Denise Labbé was four years older. Her father had been a postman, who committed suicide in August 1940, throwing himself in the canal one Sunday morning when his daughter was fourteen. Her mother was still alive and lived in Rennes, where Denise still had friends. An intelligent and an industrious girl she had received little formal education, and the only connections she had were those she had made by promiscuous frequentation of university circles in Rennes. Despite his illegitimacy, Algarron's background was bourgeois, and for a while he had attended a very good school indeed, Louis-le-Grand. Frequenting the bars and cellars of St Germain des Prés, he had picked up the jargon, read some of the fashionable books and would philosophise in a pretentiously half-baked manner which no doubt impressed his girls. It impressed Denise, that is certain. She was not at all bad-looking, round-faced, with a nice figure. Both were fair in colouring, he the more so. He had green eyes and was faunlike, with a nasty slit of a mouth.

He clawed and bit her, and she liked it. They even bought a penknife. On her summer holidays, with her mother and little Cathy, she proudly paraded her scars on the beach. He kissed the blood he drew and particularly enjoyed making love to her during her periods. He made her sleep with other men, though she did not want to. He thought that the human couple, to become a super-couple, ought to be united by something more than the pleasure of the senses, even with such sado-masochistic refinements. On August 7th, the day on which he passed out as an officer, as they rode in a taxi, he suggested killing the driver. But that would be a meaningless sacrifice. Her surest way of showing that she belonged wholly to him would be to kill her child. The suggestion was made and somewhat insisted on. By then, he had been posted to garrison duty with the gunners at Châlons-sur-Marne, and they met infrequently in Paris. She became pregnant, and he ordered her to have an abortion, which she did on the cheap and badly, so that later curettage was needed.

On September 22nd, she held Catherine over the balcony of her mother's second-floor premises in Rennes, but had not the heart to force the clinging fingers loose. A week later, she dropped the child into the canal from an iron bridge, but the child's clothes kept her afloat and she was rescued. On Saturday, October 16th, Cathy was found blue with cold in a stream near the children's home. In early November, Denise Labbé took her daughter to stay in Vendôme with her sister and brother-in-law, a shady lawyer called Dusser. On the 8th, she held Cathy head down in a vessel kept for washing clothes in the yard. At the funeral, suspicions were voiced by the foster-mother, but not until December 6th was Denise Labbé arrested.

Presently, Jacques Algarron joined her at Blois, charged under Article 60 of the Code Pénal, which deals with what we call accessories before the fact, 'those who, by gifts, promises, threats, abuse of authority or power, machinations or culpable artifices, shall have provoked the act or given instructions for it to be committed'. The original charge against Denise Labbé had, it may be noted, been under Article 63, for 'non-assistance to a person in danger'. Under our law, this is not a criminal offence. We may think it should be. That it is not may, at least, cause us to miss the point of such literary works, well-known and greatly admired in translation, as *The Fall* by Albert Camus. The lawyer in that book is guilty of a criminal offence under French law. It is not mere self-contempt which has led him to take refuge in Amsterdam.

In the days before the contraceptive pill, it was one of the disabilities of women that only the chaste, the careful, the undesired and the abnormal could be sure of avoiding unwanted pregnancy, the abrupt termination of which, whether by miscarriage, abortion or parturition, might induce a state of emotional disturbance verging, if not on madness, at least on diminished responsibility. This has sometimes been recognised in English law, in cases of infanticide by the mother. No doubt, among other factors, Denise Labbé's personality had been somewhat disturbed by her bungled abortion and its after-effects. In early April, 1955, a London woman of the same age, Ruth Ellis, had a miscarriage. It left her very quarrelsome, and the racing-driver with whom she had been living chose that moment to go and stay with friends, who were doubtless better fun, in Hampstead. On Good Friday, she followed him and made a nuisance of herself at their house. The police twice removed her, but either they did not search her or it was during the next thirty-six hours that she procured a revolver, for on Easter Sunday she reappeared in Hampstead and shot her lover dead as he emerged from a public house.

In Minneapolis, a woman seven years younger, Mary Moonen, was three months gone with a child not by her husband but by a dentist, Dr Axelrod, with whom she had an appointment on the evening of April 22nd. A quarrel indeed took place, but in the morning it was Mrs Moonen's body that lay strangled in the roadway of a fashionable street. In Paris, Simone Soursas was seven months gone, again not by her husband, who was in the Sudan, but by Pierre Clair, a clerk, aged thirty-five, who talked Gide and Sartre. Simone Soursas was forty-two and plain, if not downright ugly. Pierre Clair was no Adonis either, but had lately acquired a younger and prettier girl-friend. He was not a blood-drawing sadist, but had always beaten Simone heartily before making love to her. She bought a .22 pistol, the only kind which it was possible to buy without a licence. Armed with this, she took up her stand outside his Left-Bank hotel on the morning of May 18th and, as he emerged to go to work, put four bullets in him.

Two months later, in prison, she gave birth to a pretty girl-child, Christine. At about that time, on the morning of July 13th, they were hanging Ruth Ellis at Holloway. The case of Simone Soursas came up before M. Jadin, more clement that day. He awarded her a suspended sentence, which meant that she went free at once. But Ruth Ellis would have been treated more lightly than Pauline Dubuisson by a French court, for, on the one hand, hers was more truly a *crime passionnel*, and, on the other, her victim lacked any great sentimental appeal. That summer, however, approached its close with yet another display of incompetence by the French police when faced with the murder of an English-woman in France.

The victim was Janet Marshall, a schoolteacher from Nottingham, aged twenty-nine. Riding a man's bicycle with a high seat, she had travelled as far as the Pyrenees, visited the Gurdjieff centre in Fontainebleau, stayed at a youth hostel in Paris and was approaching Amiens on the way home. Near Breteuil, she turned off the road and, in a sunken path, removed her shorts and was squatting to relieve herself when there appeared a rough-looking man in a corduroy jacket, beret pulled down to his ears, powerfully built but with a badly mutilated left hand, aged in fact forty-three. As she stood up, he attempted to kiss her, but she repulsed him violently. He then whipped out a handkerchief, slung it round her neck and strangled her by twisting the handkerchief with his one good hand, which, since his childhood misfortune with the other, had developed unusual strength. She was already dead when he tore a branch from a tree, broke it and clubbed her repeatedly about the head. Then he stole her wrist-watch, camera, money and provisions of food, which were what had tempted him in the first place, for it was two days since he had eaten.

He had been riding a stolen bicycle. On this, he continued towards Amiens. Questioned by a gendarme outside a tobacconist's in a village on the way, he abandoned the bicycle, walked into Amiens, caught a train into Paris and again walked out to a hamlet on the north-eastern outskirts where his sister lived. There he remained undisturbed until the end of the year, while the police questioned other suspects, and statements were taken in the United Kingdom from young men known or thought likely to have been in Janet Marshall's company at one point or another in the course of her protracted tour. A new inquiry had just been ordered into the Dominici affair, and this time the French police and the French press were determined that the murderer should turn out to be English. They complained of unco-operativeness on the part of Scotland Yard. Our press, of course, in the meantime made derogatory remarks about the poor protection afforded British subjects in France.

The man was Robert Avril, casual labourer, petty thief and wandering rapist of a kind, though not on quite the same scale, archetypally represented in French criminal history by Joseph Vacher sixty years before. His record for rape and attempted rape was long, and he was only just back in circulation after serving seven of a ten years' sentence. He remained at his sister's house in Brie while, in the United States, the names of John G. Graham and Gerry Cornwell made news, and, round Glasgow, Peter Manuel pursued the earlier stages of a career of personal savagery without parallel. Robert Avril was arrested in January

1955 and confessed. He was to die in prison. As successive electro-encephalographs showed, he had developed a brain tumour between his last previous conviction and first murder.

THE TRIAL of Denise Labbé and Jacques Algarron opened at Blois on Wednesday, May 30th, 1956, in a thunderstorm, which rose to its height while the clerk to the court was reading the indict-ment, and briefly extinguished the lights, so that for a while the courtroom was illuminated only by flashes of lightning at the windows. The president of the court was M. Lecocq, bespectacled, white-moustached, gentle in manner. Of the two assessors, M. Sorlin, on his left, seemed too young for his place, and on his right sat a good-looking woman in her thirties, Mme Kopenski. Before them, on a broad dais, stood Exhibit A, the *lessiveuse* in which, eighteen months previously, Catherine Labbé, then aged two and a half, had been held head downward till she died. On to the dais from the wall to their right projected the little box in which sat M. Gay, *avocat-général,* for the prosecution. Beyond him was the dock and, in front of it, the bench and long desk for counsel for the defence, among whom were two very eminent Parisian barristers indeed, for Algarron our old friend René Floriot, for Denise Labbé a man ten years his senior and of even greater if quieter distinction, Maurice Garçon, a member of the Académie Française, known as a writer on subjects commonly thought remote from jurisprudence and case law, demonology for instance, which in fact did not seem remote that sultry afternoon.

Maître Garçon's first intervention was to ask whether his client could be moved to the end of the dock, just behind himself and thus farther away from Algarron, at which Maître Floriot was heard to ask sarcastically whether the latter was expected to hypno-tise Labbé in open court, with the solid figure of a gendarme between them and two others in the dock. After consultation with his assessors, M. Lecocq allowed counsel's request. Floriot had two juniors. With Me Garçon, a man of unusually narrow, clean-shaven face, his short grey hair parted in the middle, sat the leader of the Loir-et-Cher bar association, M. le Bâtonnier Simon, venerably white-bearded. The jury was all male, seven farmers. There was no shortage of journalists from Paris, but few distinguished visitors, at best a couple of actresses (resting at the

height of the season) and two singers from the existentialist base-
ments of St Germain des Prés, probably there less from general
interest than to lend moral support to later witnesses, of whom
several had been Algarron's girl-friends in those Left-Bank
surroundings. Yet all France was interested in the case, none
more so than such eminent writers as François Mauriac, Jean
Cocteau, Jules Romains, André Breton, Jean Schlumberger and
Marcel Jouhandeau, all of whom would have their say when it
was over, Cocteau describing it as the case of the century.

It is not uncommon for accomplices on trial together to be
found making every effort to place the main burden of guilt on
each other. Here, the cases against and for the two defendants
were at once of a different nature and diametrically opposed.
Even in an English court, it seems unlikely that Denise Labbé
would have pleaded guilty, but she admitted all the facts with
which she was charged, claiming only that she had acted under
improper influence strongly and persistently exerted, so that her
guilt if not indeed her responsibility was diminished. Jacques
Algarron admitted no more than a few idle words, not intended
to lead to any practical result. It would be Me Floriot's aim to
show that there was really no case for his client to answer, the
only evidence that could be brought against him being the allegations of his former mistress, a proven liar, and some few scraps of
letters of ambiguous import. There was no *partie civile*, the victim's
next-of-kin being in the dock. But Floriot would be as much out
for Denise Labbé's blood and hers alone as though he had been
partie civile. Me Garçon, on the other hand, since nothing alleged
against his client could be disproved, must go all out for the case
against Algarron. M. Gay could play it which way he pleased,
but, since the case against Labbé presented no difficulty, he might
be expected to concentrate on that against Algarron. Journalists,
it may be noted, had long since dubbed the two *'les amants
maudits de Vendôme'*. This introduced an error of fact into the
popular conception of the matter. The murder of little Cathy
had indeed been committed in Vendôme, but, apart from a very
little at a seaside resort, the defendants, however accursed, damned
or doomed they might be, had done all their love-making in
Rennes or Paris.

Spirited during the preliminary inquiry, especially when con-
fronted with her lover, Denise Labbé, in a shabby two-piece
tailor-made and white blouse, a handkerchief screwed up in her

hand, made a poor, depressed showing in court, breaking down
and sobbing at Algarron's vicious interjections. He, on the other
hand, though his articulation was indistinct, had an answer to
every question. His manner was defiant to the point of insolence.
It did him no good. M. Gay demanded sentences of death for
her, of life imprisonment for him. After hearing what Me Floriot,
Me Garçon and again, more briefly, Me Floriot had to say, the
jury awarded sentences of life imprisonment to Denise Labbé,
twenty years to Jacques Algarron. In practice, it would probably
turn out that his sentence was the longer.

Among the books which, as it came out in court, Algarron had
lent his mistress was *Les Nourritures Terrestres* by André Gide.
During the past five years, François Mauriac had made it plain
that he derived consolation from the thought of Gide roasting
in hell. In his *bloc-notes* in *Le Figaro Littéraire*, he seemed nevertheless to regret that his youthful hero and later foe had been
transferred to another jurisdiction.

> On the evidence of a single person, his mistress, contradicted
> by that of all the other women he knew, Algarron has been held
> responsible for a crime which he did not commit but which he
> may have inspired, without being impelled thereto by any
> discoverable motive. If such a verdict were to create a precedent,
> there would be no reason to stop there and not to charge the
> writer who may have inspired the young man.

In the same paper, Jean Schlumberger considered that from no
point of view could the mind be satisfied by such a verdict, while
to André Breton it was hopeless to expect understanding from
such down-to-earth jurors. A Catholic writer of no less orthodox
piety than Mauriac, M. Stanislas Fumet, thought the verdict quite
normal, there was nothing scandalous about it, and Jules Romains
wrote in :

> This verdict seems to me as rational as anybody could wish. I
> have tried to imagine what were the thoughts and reactions of
> the jury : mine would have been much the same. . . . It does
> seem beyond doubt that works of literature named in the
> course of the trial exercised an influence on one of the char-
> acters in this drama and, through him, on the other. But that
> raises the vast question of the freedom of literature and the
> arts.

In another paper, the weekly *Arts*, Marcel Jouhandeau is quoted by Montarron, in his book on the case, as writing :

It remains for us to wonder what will take place to-night or to-morrow, after the sight of this catastrophe, between those of the same age as Denise and Jacques, who are in love with each other, as Jacques and Denise thought they were. How can they fail to cast a look of suspicion on each other, at the thought that some uncontrolled deed or word, though dictated by tenderness, may one day bring them into opposition and make them enemies eternally irreconcilable?

But, indeed, phrasing this thought somewhat differently, M. Jouhandeau was, six years later, to include his Labbé-Algarron reflections in a volume touching at more length on two other 'ritual murders' of which, at the time of the verdict in Blois, the fatal seed had been sown, two hundred miles to the east, in one which was to prove of uncommon interest not only to Catholic writers and the hierarchy.

IN THE small village of Uruffe in Lorraine lived the Fays family, modest folk with daughters aged nineteen and seventeen and twins aged nine. The elder daughter, Régine, worked at the glassworks in Vannes-le-Châtel, nearby and not very much larger. By the late summer of 1956, it could no longer be concealed from Mme Fays that Régine was pregnant. She refused to say who was the father. No doubt it was some young man at the glassworks, though in a neighbourhood like that not even young workmen were anonymous. The Fays were good Catholics and collectively amiable. It was a Catholic village, with a calvary by the roadside not far out. The *curé*, M. Guy Desnoyers, was a man in his early thirties, of peasant stock, remarkable neither for spiritual fervour (his sick, saintly predecessor had died at the altar) nor for intellectual distinction, but always active in good works, organising amateur theatricals, choir outings and even excursions to the remote seaside. All doors were open to him. He was welcome at every table.

Not that the breath of scandal had quite failed to touch him in the past. A girl from the glassworks, for instance, had gone away to somewhere in the south of France to be cured of fatty anaemia or sprue, one symptom of which is a protuberant stomach.

At the same time, the priest had been absent from his parish. An older woman said that the girl had in fact been pregnant and had gone away either to have the baby or an abortion and that he was the father. He had threatened her with proceedings at law, and she had withdrawn the allegation. When it turned out to be true that the girl had borne a child, a diocesan emissary had appeared from Nancy, but reported back to his bishop that the culprit had evidently been not the priest himself but a cousin of his who had been staying at the presbytery. The scandal had died down. It was clearly a good-natured community. The *curé d'Uruffe* had been lucky in his parishoners.

For he was the father of Régine Fay's unborn child. She would not divulge the fact, but neither would she go away or have an abortion. He was afraid that the child might conspicuously resemble him. Régine was already eight months gone. On Sunday, December 2nd, 1956, he announced to his flock that there would be no church services for a few days, as he felt in need of rest and, after a visit to Nancy the following day, proposed to stay for two nights with his brother at Haplemont. The following evening, he drove over from Nancy to meet Régine Fays by the calvary. She got into the car, and they turned along the Baudricourt road, stopping again less than a mile and a half from the village. The girl again refused to go away and have the baby elsewhere. Why should she, since her family were prepared to make it welcome? He wanted to absolve her. She said she had forgiven him, but he could keep his absolution. The crime would no doubt have been even more 'ritual' if he had given her absolution, for we may suppose that he would then have shot her while she was kneeling. Instead, she got out of the car and said she would walk home. As soon as her back was turned, he took a 6.35 mm. automatic from the glove-compartment, and she was less than two yards in front of him when a bullet entered her head. The priest turned back and switched his lights off.

In the dark, on the frozen verge, the rites were performed. Later that evening, the telephone rang in M. Desnoyers's house at Haplemont. The call was from Uruffe. The caller, a young woman, wished to speak to the Reverend Father Desnoyers, the subscriber's brother, Guy. The caller was Régine's friend, Michelle, none other than the girl whose child by the priest was growing up elsewhere. Régine had gone out at 6.00. Now it was 10.00, and she had not returned. The Fays were out of their minds with worry. Would he come? He got out the car and drove to Uruffe, where he called on the mayor and obtained permission to ring his church bell as though for a fire. A hundred villagers turned out. Their parish priest and the mayor split them up into search parties and sent them off in various directions. Fr Desnoyers telephoned for a doctor from Vaucouleurs to come to Mme Fays, whose heart was weak. Then he took Michelle into the car and himself drove slowly along the Baudricourt road. It was 2.30 a.m. There was something untoward on the grass verge. He reversed. There, in the headlights, lay a young woman's body, its clothes stripped off, the belly ripped open, near her a baby, pierced to the heart, its face a mess of blood.

The two got out of the car. We do not know whether the girl shrieked. We do know that the priest took off his cloak and spread it over the dead mother and her dead premature child and also that, after he had done this, he put his hands under the garment and moved the child's body closer to the mother's. We know that he said, 'Let us pray!' and himself knelt and that he distinguishably recited the *De profundis*. We do not know just how quickly others were on the scene, but we know that it was not long and that they included the doctor from Vaucouleurs and M. Fays. The priest said: 'Poor Régine, I hope she had time to prepare herself for death.' He told her father that he was sure it could not be suicide. He said that he must now go and break the news to her mother, but the doctor intervened. It was *his* duty, he said. Mme Fays was his patient, and her heart might not stand it.

There seems to be some little doubt also about the point at which, and to whom, Desnoyers first intimated that he knew something about the matter but that he was bound by the seal of the confessional. This could only be taken to mean that he knew who the father of Régine Fay's baby was and that that man would turn out to be the murderer. At daybreak, he was in his presbytery, being questioned (it was he, after all who had found the bodies) by a warrant officer of the *gendarmerie*, to whom one of his men presently brought a spent cartridge found at the scene of the crime. In the absence of a ballistics *expertise*, it could at least be said that this was of 6.35 calibre and that it was for a weapon of that calibre that the priest held a licence. He admitted his responsibility. He also produced a knife and said that the handkerchief with which he had wiped it would be found in the graveyard at Haplemont.

It was noon, and the angelus was ringing, when Guy Desnoyers, *curé d'Uruffe,* in an ordinary suit and open-necked shirt, handcuffed, was ready to leave his presbytery for the last time. As the door opened to let the *gendarmerie* and their prisoner out, a villager of good sense, standing outside, begged them not to come out for a moment, as the children would just be leaving school. They waited and then took him to the town hall. The examining magistrate, who had driven out from Nancy, was a woman. The priest made a statement on oath. He had extracted the child from its mother's womb to baptise it. Then he had stabbed it from the back and slashed its face to remove anything tell-tale from its features. Even Jouhandeau, who, I should have thought, would be sensible to just such details, does not say or surmise with what water the sacrament was performed. There would be some in the car's radiator, of course. The priest might have brought water with him, ready blest, in a bottle. He might, with the heat of his fingers, have melted sufficient hoar frost off the grass. At any rate, the child's soul was safe. And Desnoyers had not, he was careful to insist, severed the umbilical cord, though, if that is either a theological or a legal point, it escapes me.

The bishop's palace in Nancy issued a statement which, in the United Kingdom, would have exposed the bishop to proceedings for contempt of court.

Public opinion has been deeply shocked to hear of the tragedy which has just occurred in a parish of this diocese. This monstrous act defies understanding. Human justice must now follow its course.

We share the grief of a family so fearfully tried, and, from the bottom of our heart, we must express a deep sense of humiliation that such a crime should have been committed by one of our people.

In the face of deeds which beggar human imagination, Christians, nevertheless, are not left without resource. It remains a comfort to us that, before God and man, we may still confidently pray for the victim and ourselves expiate this man's guilt.

The canon who conducted Régine's and the baby's funeral service pointed out that among the Apostles there had been Judas and that the shame of this act struck not only at the priesthood and the Church but at the whole human race. The Fays family set up

a tombstone over the grave. Upon it, their daughter was described
as having died murdered by the vicar of her parish.

JACQUES FESCH, it may be recalled, the son of a banker, had
killed a policeman while fleeing from his failed attempt at armed
robbery, with extreme violence, of a jeweller's shop. In the spring
of 1957, he came up for trial in Paris, with Floriot again acting
for the *partie civile* and in effect prosecuting. The young man
was sentenced to death. In June, a Dr Évenou staged a scene in
which, before his eyes and at his orders, his wife was stabbed to
death in her bed by one of the less attractive of his mistresses,
dressed in nothing but a red-lined cloak. The only account of this
case I have seen is that in Jouhandeau's *Trois Crimes Rituels*. The
murder was apparently committed, in some sense, in the Forest of
Sénart, south-east of Paris. Jouhandeau attended the trial,
presumably at Melun. Among the long-term prisoners then at Melun
was Marcel Hilaire, the millionaire miller. In the month of the
Évenou-Deschamps murder, it was announced (I take this detail
from Goodman) that Hilaire had been made chief accountant of
that important *prison centrale* and that, indeed, he had worked
out a prison accounting system which seemed likely to be adopted
for the whole of the French penal administration. Jacques Fesch
was executed on October 1st.

At Nancy, in January 1958, the former parish priest of Uruffe
was tried before a jury of nine, the number of jurors at a French
criminal trial having been raised by two in a recent promulgation,
to be embodied in the new Code de Procédure Pénale which, the
following year, would supersede the old Code d'Instruction
Criminelle, encumbered with a hundred and fifty years' amend-
ments. The priest was defended, *ex officio*, by the leader of the
Meurthe-et-Moselle bar association, from which it may be inferred
that no prominent criminal defence lawyer had been willing to
accept a brief on behalf of a defendant so universally execrated.
As he pleaded guilty, there would in effect have been no trial in a
British court, but, although the expression *'plaider coupable'* has
come into use, it means little in France, where the whole case must
be heard and the accused defended. This, I am bound to say,
strikes me as more reasonable than our own rule. It is not at all
uncommon for a man to confess to a murder he has not committed,
and it is at least conceivable that, in the United Kingdom, he

should be found guilty (and that some of his predecessors may have been hanged) entirely on the basis of such false admissions, whether these were prompted by hysteria, exhibitionism, a remarkable death-wish or (now) a taste for prison, or by a firm determination to shield someone else.

Among the murderous priests in French criminal history, we may be sure that le curé d'Uruffe will not be forgotten. The most famous of his predecessors are, I suppose, Frs Mingrat, Delacollonge, Verger, Auriol, Boudes and Bruneau, whose crimes were committed between 1821 and 1894. All but Fr Verger (whose vow greatly bothered him) had recklessly broken their vows of celibacy, though only Frs Mingrat and Delacollonge murdered the women with whom they had sinned. The only two to be executed were those who had murdered other priests, in Fr Verger's case his archbishop, in Fr Bruneau's the elderly vicar to whom he acted as curate (in English and indeed in Anglican terms, for in French the parish priest is the curé and any assistant he may have his vicaire). Though it did not affect their position before courts of law, this may have made a great difference to Catholic jurors. A priest may, it appears, be deprived a divinis only if he denies the doctrine or defies the authority of the Church. Verger had been suspended from his priestly functions before he stabbed Monseigneur Sibour in a Paris church, and, as he struck, he shouted a controversial anti-Marian slogan. When he came up for trial and sentence, he was therefore no longer a priest. The position of Fr Bruneau is perhaps more obscure, but no doubt to murder your immediate superior in the hierarchy shows some lack of obedience. Like Frs Mingrat, Delacollonge, Auriol and Boudes, Fr Desnoyers remained both orthodox and submissive. His bishop could not quite disown him. As he proclaimed in his last words from the dock, he remained a priest.

His orthodoxy had, indeed, been made quite plain by the sheer horror of his actions. He had wished to absolve the mother before he shot her, and he had ripped the child from her womb in order to baptise it before it died. Throughout his trial, he had held a crucifix in his hands. The prosecution demanded his head, of course. The jury refused it by finding extenuating circumstances. There are, it seems, certain types of case in which a reprieved murderer's fellow-prisoners are always anxious to remedy the law's omission. In British prisons, child-murderers are said to stand in particular danger. 'They'll get him,' it is said, 'as surely as a cat will get a canary.' That, one understands, is why Hindley and Brady were long kept in a kind of solitary confinement and are so glad to see Lord Longford. At Loos, where the former parish priest of Uruffe began his life sentence, the matter was no doubt further complicated by the notorious anti-clericalism of the French industrial proletariat. At any rate, he was considered to be in danger of his life at Loos and was moved to St Malo, where he was made librarian.

4 | THE HOMICIDE ACT

To BE a sadist in the proper sense, a man must either gain sexual gratification from the dreadful things he does to a woman or need cruelty as a stimulus to normal intercourse. This latter peculiarity accounts for most wife-beating, as well as for the biting and scratching of couples like Labbé and Algarron. Indulged recklessly, it could lead to the death of one's partner, but that is not its intention, and the result would be something less than murder. If the whole pleasure lies in the dreadful things themselves and these are expected to lead to orgasm and, because this is delayed, things go too far unintendedly, we have a sort of 'constructive' sadistic murder, which may be what we had in the case of Heath. The guilt is much greater if the sadist knows that only the other person's death will relieve him. He could always masturbate, or so one supposes, though some apostle of total permissiveness will no doubt presently tell us that he should be provided with victims on the National Health Service.

If that is the only true sadistic murder, yet we may think that it need not be committed strictly à deux or in a closed room, but is practised by arsonists, train-wreckers and possibly some motorists, to whom murder from whatever motive is so difficult to bring home that the attempt has been largely abandoned. The Marquis de Sade used accomplices. So did the butcher of Hanover, Haarmann, though perhaps we should not regard him as a true sadistic murderer, since it seems likely that he enjoyed 'normal' sodomy with all those boys before slaughtering them for meat. Among the French murders we have so far considered, it does not seem to me that any of them was committed by a full-blown sadist or in a truly sadistic context, though Henri Demon's attempt on his wife bears an awkward resemblance to the behaviour of the prewar Breton fox-farmer, Michel Henriot. Although to rip a woman's belly open may strike us as the very hallmark of extreme sadism and little importance as most of us may attach to infant baptism,

56

I do not think for a moment that the parish priest of Uruffe derived sexual gratification from those posthumous horrors or that he performed them for reasons other than sacramental ones. His main fear was that he would lose his job, and his working-class fellow-prisoners at Loos might have viewed him with sympathy had a shop steward explained it all to them as the only kind of work-to-rule men in his minority trade could hope to get away with.

The great succession of individual German mass-murderers was extended in 1956 by Werner Boost, in Düsseldorf, scene of the activities of the most famous of them all, Peter Kürten. To what extent we should regard Boost as a sadistic killer is as obscure as it is in the case of the between-wars 'vampire of Düsseldorf' himself. In both cases, they were 'sex crimes' certainly. Boost was a peeping Tom who spied on couples in stationary cars, then, seized with indignation, shot the man and raped the woman. His downfall was brought about by enlisting an accomplice who shared his tastes as a *voyeur* but did not care for the killing and spared a victim who must inevitably become a dangerous witness.

Peter Manuel committed rape and murder, but quite separately, though the manner of some of his murders seems to indicate underwear fetishism. He also killed men for money or sheer bravado and indulged in simple housebreaking. His activities were largely, though not exclusively, confined to the Glasgow area, and he was clever enough to persuade the Scottish police, in September 1956, that not he but their husband, father and brother-in-law had shot three women in Fennbank Avenue, so that for two months he and the innocent, bereaved man were in prison together, he, the following month, having been sent down for housebreaking, which was to keep him out of mischief for thirteen months. As a dedicated killer, Manuel was anybody's equal. That he operated outside any gang framework makes him almost unique, though it seems that he had applied to join a London gang and been sternly rejected because of the intemperance of his speech.

In London, the unsmart *milieu* of Kilburn, in which it seems that face-slashing was then as common as it had long traditionally been in Glasgow, was enlivened on June 23rd, 1956, by Maltese gangsters executing a *règlement de compte* with one Tommy ('Scarface') Smithson, himself presumably once given the treatment, who advanced upon them, in a gaming club, armed with a pair of scissors. That summer also, in both hemispheres, doughty Amazons, heroines of the sex war, in the jurisdiction of Bristol, Freda Rumbold, in South Carolina, Joyce Turner, the latter egged on by her neighbours, shot sleeping husbands. In Massachusetts, Lorraine Clark had acted with no less resolution in the same cause two years before. In October 1956, Morris Clarke, a young Huntingdonshire man, battered, robbed and drowned a bachelor farmer, his wife's former employer, perhaps wholly out of jealousy but not liking to see good money wasted. On November 27th, a young man in far North Kensington, Brian Burdett, put cyanide in his wife's tea. He, Clarke, Mrs Rumbold and the Maltese gangster Ellul were all convicted but reprieved.

THE COMPARATIVE euphoria of the early 'fifties was over, ending, as far as Europe was concerned, with the Suez fiasco and the Russian massacres in Budapest. When it took office in 1951, the first post-war Conservative administration had inherited from the Attlee government a Royal Commission on Capital Punishment, which published its findings, four years later, in the year of Churchill's resignation. In 1957, the Macmillan government brought in the Homicide Act, which divided murder into two varieties, the capital and the non-capital. In fact, the distinction already existed. It was the distinction between murder and manslaughter or, as the Americans put it, murder in the first and second degrees, *assassinat* and mere *meurtre*. The demarcation line was simply shifted.

It was shifted both explicitly and implicitly. Explicitly stated to be no longer murder but manslaughter were participation in suicide pacts; killing in the course of furtherance of an offence if the malice were merely 'constructive' and not so much afore-thought as to have made it murder anyway; and whatever would have been murder had not the person who committed it lost, for one reason or another, his self-control. Implicitly, though still to be known as murder, most forms of murder would henceforward be treated as manslaughter. Apart from those affecting policemen and prison officers, the sole exceptions were murders (not, it must be understood, mere killings) committed in the course or further-ance of theft; those affected by shooting, or causing an explosion; and those the perpetrator of which had been convicted of murder previously.

The Act was criticised on many grounds and in most quarters. None criticised it more severely than those 'abolitionists' to placate whom the Bill had been brought in. That is perhaps natural enough. For them, it abolished too little. The nervous and those who simply saw no reason for change (known as 'retentionists' just as non-motorists had, to their astonishment, come to be known as 'pedestrians') were dismayed to find that no more than a 'life' sentence (averaging ten years) thenceforward awaited those who, for the first time as far as the law knew and when not actively engaged in robbery, for any reason or none, killed anyone but a policeman or prison officer with poison, cold steel, a blunt instrument, drowning, strangulation, smothering, burning, gassing, starvation, driving a car at the victim or tampering with his brakes, infecting him with a fatal disease, pushing him off a tall building or over a cliff, torturing him beyond what his constitution would bear, shutting him in with dangerous animals, inducing madness with drugs, hypnotic suggestion or sustained ill-treatment and then putting the means of suicide into his hands or leading him to believe that a fatal trap is a way to safety, anything in fact that a writer of detective stories might plausibly imagine. Apart from prison officers and policemen, the victim might be anyone at all, a child or the Queen. To poison an elderly person in order to inherit, collect insurance or practise subsequent fraud would presumably not be murder in the course or furtherance of theft. Nor, presumably, would it if the robbery were an afterthought, as, in anticipation of the Bill becoming an Act, it had been argued to be in the case of Morris Clarke six months before.

In general, what might have been is not a profitable field for speculation, but the purpose of the Act itself was largely speculative, and it may throw light on them, as creatures before the law, if we glance back at our list of British murderers to date and see how they might have stood had the Act existed for them. The first thing to note is, perhaps, that at least some of the multiple murderers would have had to be tried differently. Heath's murder of Margery Gardner would have been non-capital, and, to hang him, it would have been necessary to convict him separately for Doreen Marshall, even supposing that his counsel unsuccessfully urged diminished responsibility within the meaning of the Homicide Act. Although at need other murders could have been proved against him, Haigh, on the other hand, would have gone to the scaffold for Mrs Durand-Deacon alone, since, although it is the acid bath we remember, he had previously dispatched her with a firearm. For Christie, it would have been much as for Heath, though, as he murdered other women both before and after his wife, the Director of Public Prosecutions would have had to choose which of his crimes should be made capital. During the war, this would have been the case also with Cummins, in other respects more like Heath.

Had I been a lawyer, I might not have been willing to use the confident conditional tense. As I am not, I ought, I dare say, to be even more chary of it, as indeed I am, but find it convenient and have not much feared contradiction so far. In the case of Whiteway, also much like Heath, there might, I suppose, have arisen the question of whether he killed the two girls on different occasions. This must certainly have arisen in the case of Timothy Evans, had he been charged with the murders of both his wife and his daughter. In the case of Walter Rowland, it must, as I read the Act, have been his earlier conviction for the death of his daughter, not the fact that he was reprieved, which decided whether his second murder was capital. Undoubtedly capital would still have been the crimes of Hulten, Malinowski and Grondkowski, Jenkins and Geraghty, Thomas, because they used firearms, and of Russell and Joe Smith if it were beyond doubt that the deaths of their victims had been foreseen to be essential to their robbery, a consideration which might have got Burns and Devlin off. As to the women who were in fact hanged, Ruth Ellis, like Mrs Ransome, must, if I have understood the Act correctly, have been charged with capital murder and very probably convicted of it, though, had she waited two years before shooting her faithless lover, I imagine that she would have been reprieved by the Home Secretary, because of a change in the climate largely brought about by her own execution. Although by no means averse to robbery, Margaret Allen might have been thought to have lost her self-control in the first place through provocation. Two of her prison companions might have been Mrs Merrifield and Mrs Christofi. Also still in prison would no doubt have been Haydn Evan Evans, Daniel Raven, Leonard Mills, Peter Griffiths and Hepper, unless these last two had been seen off by their fellow-prisoners for murdering children. Five already released should have been Manton, Dobkin, Heys, Buckfield and Sangret.

As I have said so little about any of these individually, I can hardly suppose that thus to regroup the mere list of their names will convey much to the reader who is not a murder addict. My point for the criminologist must be that, while our three chief monsters might not have fared very differently, the 1957 distinction between capital and non-capital murders would quite have failed to separate the worse from the not so bad among the well-known other murderers of the past fifteen years. Among those spared would certainly have been some of the likeliest to commit the second murder the Act allowed their successors. Personal guilt was totally disregarded. Not even social guilt was considered, but only social danger. There had been no attempt to classify types of murder by any but police standards and those of bank clerks, post office employees, train guards, persons involved on a large scale with weekly wages and those of the rich who kept much of their wealth around them in portable and negotiable form. Although to many minds worse was to come, almost everyone thought it a bad Act. The exceptions were psychiatrists frequently called as expert witnesses.

It came into force on March 21st, 1957. The murder-rate for England and Wales went up at once, though even then not quite to the average for the 'forties. For the years which followed, it was to become increasingly difficult to make statistical comparisons with earlier years because of the increasing skill shown by lawyers in 'sandpapering down' murder to manslaughter. There were two executions in 1957, those of Vickers in August at Durham and of Howard in December at Birmingham. That of Vickers, the first for two years, was of a young man who had killed an old woman while robbing her shop. Howard also was young. On the same errand, he killed a shopkeeper of his own age and sex with a revolver, one of six or seven he possessed. There was little edification to be got out of the courtroom arguments in either case, though clearly points were raised which had to be raised and though Labour back-benchers no doubt rightly questioned the verdict on Vickers, who may not have intended to kill the old woman, at any rate in the first place. It was the leniency of the new law which first aroused public indignation. This was in the case of a factory worker in his early thirties, just south of London proper, who had killed a girl of four with the intention of subsequently raping her, but had then 'suffered remorse' and had not carried out his fell purpose. In view of what is said in a footnote on page 35, we may wonder whether in such a case remorse is not a consequence of surprised disgust (the man had committed indecent

Theodore Lownik Library
Illinois Benedictine College
Lisle, Illinois 60532

assaults on little girls in the past, but had killed none). This was non-capital murder, and the fact that it was treated as such incensed the local populace, so that there was a riot. How the man fared subsequently in prison, I have not heard.

A case tried at Leeds assizes that December had already made international criminal history. This had been the first recorded murder by insulin, committed in Bradford by a male nurse at a hospital, St Luke's, in Huddersfield (my native town, as it happens), where he had frequently been put in charge of insulin injections for diabetics and psychiatric cases undergoing chemical shock therapy. The idea that insulin (because of its rapid absorption by the bloodstream, leaving no trace) might be used to commit 'the perfect murder' had occurred to this Kenneth Barlow two years before, when he had indiscreetly communicated it to a colleague. It was this fact, turned up by police inquiries, which had put him where he was, since it had given direction to an exceedingly delicate and complicated piece of toxocological research at Harrogate police laboratory. For all the detail of this, the interested reader may be referred to Thorwald (in the English paperback edition, the volume called *Proof of Poison*), who devotes a whole chapter to the case. The police work had been as distinguished, in its way, as the forensic science, for, though also careless, Barlow had been clever, arranging that his wife should go into hypoglycæmic coma while in her bath, so that the actual cause of death would be drowning. There is strong presumptive evidence that, in essentials, his method had been employed, only the previous year, on a first wife, but by the time of his arrest it was far too late for renewed autopsy to prove that she had not died of unascertained natural causes, as stated on her death certificate. And so Barlow could only be indicted for a non-capital first murder.

I suppose that a murder is 'perfect' only if it is never thought to be murder. In the very nature of things, we cannot know how frequent such murders are. Insulin had (and possibly still has) its advantages. These are nothing, I understand, to those of paraquat, whose use might perhaps be demonstrated circumstantially but which, it seems, could never be shown to have caused death. Of more than half the murders 'known to the police' the perpetrator is never discovered, but that is hardly perfection. A Kensington example of such crude half-success had been achieved that year on May 24th, when an old but still admirably active Polish gentlewoman, Countess Lubienska, was stabbed five times in Gloucester Road tube station at no unreasonable hour in the evening.

The year ended, and 1958 began, with the fearsome Peter Manuel active again, at first on Tyneside and then once more in the Glasgow area. The first of this second group of his murders was committed little more than a week after his release from prison on November 30th. Frustrated for the past eighteen months, he used both gun and knife on a taxi-driver. His last four victims were very evenly divided as to sex and age. Arrested and charged on January 14th, 1958, he was to be brought to trial at unusual length before a Scottish court on May 12th, to dismiss counsel and conduct his own defence, to be executed on July 11th, shortly before the celebrated but comparatively innocuous Notting Hill race riots. In England and Wales, there were four executions that year.

In FRANCE that year, political events seem to have driven private murder off the streets and out of the home. There were notable gang killings. The Corsican *règlement de comptes* with Robert Juan on March 28th was spendthrift of bullets, of which thirty spattered buildings in Montmartre and two killed passers-by, so that clearly it was an inexpert job, entrusted to beginners. Juan had been an Algerian, one of the generation of North African ponces who had largely taken Pigalle over from the Corsicans, one of whose most senior figures he had killed in his own night-club four years previously. In Marseilles on the 14th of July, a Corsican night-club proprietor was indeed killed in the old way by a compatriot, a man who had been involved with the theft of the Begum's jewels. The Algerians, no less the political idealists than the ponces, had for long dealt with each other mainly in Paris, where, during the past thirteen years, members of the two main Arab political groups, the F.L.N. and the M.N.A., had killed each other at an average rate of something like a thousand a year. In 1958, having somewhat composed their differences, they began to pick off policemen, of whom eight were killed that year, four on August 25th, in a raid on Préfecture motor transport headquarters.

Of murders in the private sector, however, that year's most interesting continental examples occurred elsewhere than in France. In Geneva, on May 1st, Charles Zumbach, an elderly and highly respectable man, was stabbed and shot at home, and, though at first with some incredulity, suspicion pointed sharply at the city's most prominent lawyer, former *bâtonnier* of the bar association, Pierre Jaccoud. It appeared that he had gone to the Zumbach house to recover letters from the son, André Zumbach, for whom his mistress had left him. He may have meant to kill André, only attacking the young man's father (and mother, though her he only injured) in surprised panic. The case had its international aspects, in that various United Nations officials and secretaries were questioned. Moreover, because of Maître Jaccoud's prominence in Swiss legal circles and public life, he was encouraged to choose a French advocate to defend him. This was none other than René Floriot, who two years later would appear in full regimentals before a court in plain dress.

That was at least in French-language territory. The year's other outstanding continental murders were conducted in German, the first of them at Stuttgart in mid-April. In kidnapping cases, murder frequently ensues because of the abductor's growing fear of discovery and arrest. In this case, Emil Tillmann, a forty-year-old jobbing gardener of minute stature, strangled seven-year-old Joachim Goehner in the woods before making any attempt to communicate with the boy's father. A tape-recording was made of his eventual telephone call to demand ransom. This was repeatedly broadcast and finally led to the recognition of Tillmann's voice by a former employer, a woman. In late May, he hanged himself with a bed sheet in his cell.

In respect of his victims, with whom he made contact through matrimonial advertisements, Max Gufler may be described as an Austrian Landru. He characteristically doped their coffee with barbiturates, then stripped them and dumped them in ponds or rivers. He was to be convicted of eight murders, and ten other probable victims were named, dating back as far as 1946. Three 1958 victims were murdered, respectively, on June 3rd, a date unknown in early September and October 15th. It was his indiscretion over the September victim which led to his arrest (he wrote pseudonymously to her former husband to say that he had seen her killed in a road accident). At the time of his arrest, a further intended victim waited in vain at the registry office.

By then, a small girlish-looking young man of markedly nordic colouring, Heinrich Pommerenke, had entered upon the last phase in a career of attacks on women and girls which had begun five

1 Waiting outside the court at Horsham, Sussex, where Haigh is remanded in custody
 for the second time. March 11th, 1949.

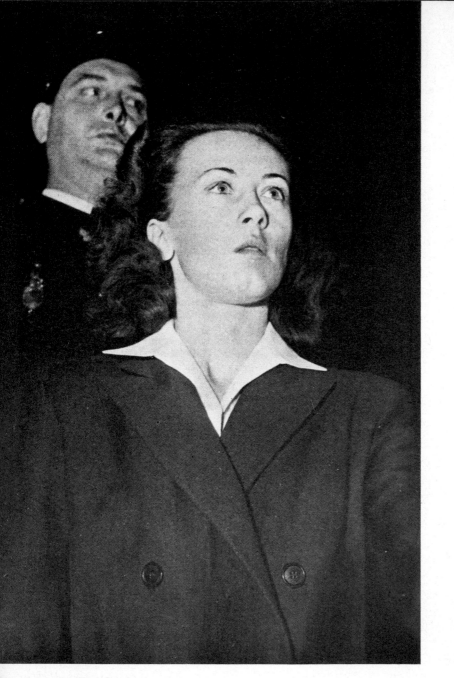

2 Pauline Dubuisson, November 18th, 1953.

years previously, in East Berlin, from which he escaped, but which was to reach its climax in Baden, so that he became known as the monster of the Black Forest. The number of his murders seems uncertain, but there were at least four, with twenty or thirty cases of rape achieved by wounding his victims, knocking them unconscious or even hurling them out of moving trains and leaping after them beside the track. The explanation was said to be that he suffered from an inferiority complex.

German murderers have often made their mark abroad. It will be six years more before we find anything like a worthy successor to Eugen Weidmann in Paris. In London, in the summer of 1959, great excitement was created by a visitor from Düsseldorf, Günther Podola, who, at first intending only blackmail, killed a C.I.D. detective-sergeant. That was on July 13th, ten days before Pommerenke's arrest. Podola resembled Weidmann in having, before his brief return home, been expelled from Canada. Penally, he would have done better to stay in Germany, for the result of his activities in London was that on November 5th he was hanged.

C

5 | A GARAGE-HAND, FIVE WOMEN AND A CHILD

AT HAGUENAU in Alsace, Pauline Dubuisson had long ago been taken off saddlery and put on hospital duty, for which she was qualified and at which she acquitted herself well, so that her release during the course of 1959 was envisaged without anxiety. Among twenty million other Frenchwomen, we may note eight from whose circumstances at the beginning of that year their immediate futures could not have been so confidently predicted. Three lived in Marseilles, one of them a regular prostitute, the other two wife and mistress of the same man. Four lived in Paris, none of these quite a regular prostitute, two of them attached to one young man, one to another, one for the moment unattached, though she had deaf-mute twins. An old lady in Normandy, crippled with arthritis, had a grown-up granddaughter for company, a daughter and other grandchildren in the next village.

The names of the four Parisians were Marie-Christine, Arlette, Muguette and Nadine. These last two were younger, Nadine barely nineteen. They were childless. Marie-Christine had seven children, two of them by the very curious young man with whom she lived. He was not much to look at otherwise, but even in those days wore his fair hair curling in the nape of his neck, though he was only a paint-sprayer at a big garage. His name was Guy Trébert. The other young man's name was Georges Rapin. His hair was vivid, too, luxuriant and a natural Titian-red, with moustache to match. He worked, though without much need to do so. He worked in some capacity with an insurance company. He also owned a bar, but was selling it piecemeal to the manager he had installed when he grew tired of running it. Guy Trébert had some kind of second-hand car. Georges Rapin had a gleaming black Dauphine Gordini.

He was very much a *fils à papa*. We seem to have no equivalent to this expression. 'Daddy's boy' wouldn't translate it at all. It means the spoilt son of a rich and influential father. The animal

66

exists here, but we have somehow failed to classify it, perhaps because (one would like to think so) it is both less common and less vicious here than in France, where also what makes fathers influential is somewhat different. M. Rapin was in mines, a mining engineer with government pull. He and his wife lived in the Boulevard St Germain, and Georges, who had been delicate, seems to have been their only child. As he was fond of night life, M. Rapin had bought him a bar of his own, refitting it, driving out the old customers with the zinc and *belote*. It was renamed Bill's Bar, and Georges became M. Bill, but found himself too far away from the more exciting and deadlier bright lights around Pigalle. Nadine was the pretty daughter of *concierges* in the Rue de Gergovie, in outer Montparnasse. She had a room behind the caretaker's lodge, and Georges Rapin had a key. He had been her first lover, when she was fifteen, and most days he drove her to and from her job as a hairdresser out at Rueil.

His evenings he spent in Montmartre, more especially at the Sans-Souci, where he had picked up one of the hostesses, Muguette Thiriel, from Rheims, known as Dominique 'la Panique'. She was a girl of too independent a turn of mind to suit any of the regular *ponces*, and she was not to be found on the streets, though she 'did' ('*faisait*') a few clients, so that, once he became her lover, 'M. Bill' fancied himself a regular *souteneur*, with 'Dominique' his woman, working for him, turning in her earnings to him, bound to him by the rules of *le milieu*. That was not the position as she saw it, nor did the serious *ponces* think him anything but a *demi-sel*, one of the many young fools who hung around their world. But let us now turn to Arlette, the unattached mother of deaf-mute twins, who had a room in the Avenue Parmentier.

On the evening of March 15th, she went along the Avenue de la République and the Boulevard St Martin to see a film. She wore a coral pink frock. In front of her in the cinema queue stood a young man in a shabby blue suit with long, fair hair, Guy Trébert. They sat next to each other and became acquainted. They met once or twice by arrangement during the next ten days, but he was rather a bore. When, on the 26th, she went to visit her twins in the country, she did not bother to let him know and, on her return, was surprised to find a succession of scribbled notes to the effect that he must see her without delay. They met again and drove in his old car west of Paris to the forest of St Germain, where, on April 5th, her body was found, strangled and subsequently mutilated with a savagery which would not have disgraced Heath.

That same day, Georges Rapin committed his first murder, that of a garage-hand who had filled up the Dauphine Gordini without showing what the young man considered due respect. It was done with a 9 mm. German revolver, borrowed from the man who was buying Bill's Bar from its owner. This crime was not brought home that month to the red-haired playboy-gangster, but Guy Trébert soon saw the murderer of 'the lady in red' identikitted in the newspapers, and the shearing of his locks did not prevent him being traced to the Rue St Augustin, where he was forced to leave Marie-Christine and the seven children, two of them his, while Arlette's deaf-mute twins became a public charge.

Muguette, *dite* Dominique, had had quite enough of 'M. Bill' and proposed to get out of Pigalle altogether. This did not please the mock-ponce's vanity. It was a *milieu* rule that, if a woman left one *souteneur* for another, this last must pay his predecessor an indemnity, the current rate ranging from half a million to two million old francs, according to the woman's earning capacity. If, as Sacotte tells us, the woman is simply leaving the game or going to live with someone who works and doesn't belong to the *milieu,* it is she who must pay. Her earning capacity being small, Georges Rapin demanded a mere half million from 'Dominique' and went round Pigalle announcing that he would get it or else. A barman at the Sans-Souci (this Montarron tells us) warned him that he was making a mistake. She made it clear that in her view the position had never been as he described it and that of course she did not mean to pay. He went round to his manager-purchaser at Bill's Bar, whose revolver he still had, and told him that he meant to liquidate a wench who was misbehaving and that he proposed to bury her in the cellar. His friend pointed out the disadvantages of such a proceeding (the sound of picks, the smell) and suggested a grave in some lonely spot out of doors. This conversation took place on May 25th, a Monday. On Friday, Muguette-Dominique made her great mistake. She agreed on a 'last ride together' in the Dauphine Gordini. They took the Fontainebleau road and no doubt passed the filling station at Villejuif, scene of Rapin's earlier triumph.

Nadine, the caretaker's daughter in the Rue de Gergovie, had not seen her lover for some time and thought that the idyll was over. At two o'clock that Saturday morning, he let himself in, made love to her, put on a clean shirt, left her with a bloody shirt, gloves and a woman's handbag to get rid of, a suitcase, a revolver and a flick-knife to clean, an alibi (he had been there earlier) to swear to at need. He returned later and drove her out to the hairdresser's at Rueil. The body of Muguette Thiriel was found that morning off the circular road in the forest of Fontainebleau. Five shots had been fired, from the front and from behind. Then petrol had been poured over the body and lighted. It had burnt well.

IN MARSEILLES, dome-headed M. Court-Payen took up a knife and slaughtered both wife and mistress on October 31st. In Normandy, Marguerite Bertrand, aged seventy-one, took to her bed. The pain of her rheumatoid arthritis was, she told the neighbours, at times more than she could bear. Her old doctor had, moreover, hinted at cancer of the liver. Besides, the grand-daughter, Jacqueline Letondeur, who had tended her for almost five years, wanted to marry and go away. Julienne Letondeur, Jacqueline's mother and the old lady's daughter, with her husband, Eugène Letondeur, and one of their sons, Louis, moved into the house at Pierreval from the neighbouring hamlet with the apparently ungrammatical name, La Vieux Rue. To ease the old lady's sufferings, Mme Letondeur mixed her a green drink, which she said was Pernod. Jacqueline held the glass to her grand-mother's lips, and the old lady said that it burned her. That was on December 15th. Louis was out. Mme Letondeur had been deaf from the age of nine. M. Letondeur was reading a detective story.

The doctor signed a death certificate. There was neighbourly rumour, but at the time nothing more. The house was put up for sale. Jacqueline married and went to live elsewhere. They were a much-interrelated family. Marguerite Bertrand, *née* Letondeur, and her sister Louise, who had never married, had borne Julienne and Eugène Letondeur, respectively, to their own father, so that the parents of Jacqueline and ten or eleven other surviving children were not only first cousins but rather closer than half-brother and half-sister commonly are. They lived very much to themselves, not much liking each other and shunned by everyone else in La Vieux Rue, except when they needed Eugène's services as a tiler and thatcher. The eldest of those at home, Albert, could read and write. A younger daughter, Janine, worked as a roadsweeper. The

State, through the municipality, had provided the simple-minded François, second youngest of the surviving sons, with a pair of spectacles and a surgical boot.

In Paris, Nadine, the little hairdresser, had been released after a month in prison and taken in by the Rapins, since Georges had said that he wanted to find her waiting for him at the house in the Boulevard St Germain when he was acquitted and discharged. For their son's defence, they had engaged Maîtres Floriot and Schwab. Neither was optimistic. The case against 'M. Bill' had been completed with speed and would come up for hearing in April. To save his head was the utmost that could be expected. The case against Guy Trébert, on the other hand, would take long to prepare. Like M. Court-Payen of Marseilles, he was psychiatrists' meat. In all, nine of them were to give him their attention.

The two young men were in the Santé together, Trébert visited by his motherly mistress, Marie-Christine, Rapin by his parents but not by Nadine, for whom no permit could be secured and to whom he wrote grandiloquently, copying the sentiments out of novels. His counsel had no easy time with him. One day, he would declare his total innocence. The next, he would boast of thirteen other murders. But a change is as good as a rest, and in mid-January Maître Floriot went to Geneva for three weeks to defend the eminent Swiss lawyer, Maître Jaccoud, whom on February 4th he got off with seven years, later reduced to three. A child-murderer of 1935, Gabriel Socley, was discharged from the special prison at Château Thierry. Sentence of death was passed on Georges Rapin, and he moved to a cell where the lights burned all night.

Within a month, Gabriel Socley was back at Château Thierry, having been caught, in the streets of Dijon, with a little girl struggling in his grasp. The Peugeot kidnapping was in the news, and on April 28th opened the month-long Ballets Roses trial, a delicious scandal involving, among other dignitaries, the former Speaker of the National Assembly, with orgies at an official residence and some of the nymphets seated on occasion in the President's box at the Opera. Since it involved minors, the trial was held *in camera*, not of course in the assize court but in the 15th Chamber at the Paris Law Courts on the Île de la Cité, the evidence not being published but only the findings against the twenty-two defendants. The original charge sheet, however, had left only fine detail to the imagination, the old Speaker's way of satisfying himself being at least as clearly delineated as in a Krafft-Ebing case-history. But we must keep these pages clean, dear reader, and sternly confine ourself to homicide or rather, for the moment, feminicide.

In Marseilles, on May 9th, 1960, the nameless regular prostitute among our eight women was taken home to his mother's house by a little, dark, pale-faced, shifty-eyed, quiet young man, André Pauletto, who wanted to reform her. When she made light of this project, he stabbed her to death as she lay in bed, then took barbiturates and lay down beside her. Afterwards, he said that he had killed her because he loved her too much. He too was psychiatrists' meat, and for this first serious criminal offence a great Marseilles advocate, Maître Émile Pollak, got him off with four years, so that in no time at all he would be out and ready to start again. In Paris, the *bois de justice* were set up in the Santé yard on the night of July 25th, and at first light Georges Rapin was abridged.

No VOLUME of criminal history is complete without a good miscarriage of justice. Because it may be easily read up in English, I have barely touched on the case of Marie Besnard, which in 1961 was to reach its conclusion, with a third trial and acquittal. Nor, in a sense, does that case really concern us, since no criminal homicide had occurred. Five months before the happy termination of Marie Besnard's ordeal, at the source of a legal process which was to last two thirds as long as hers, eight years to her twelve (but all of them spent in prison, whereas only five of hers were), a real and most shocking murder was committed. On July 7, 1961, between half past three and a quarter to four in the afternoon, in the cellar of a butcher's shop, that of the Bessards, in Bron-Parilly, five miles east of Lyons, near the airport, somebody cut the throat and opened the belly of their seven-year-old daughter, Dominique. A tenant in the house, Mme Cannard, going down to the cellar, found her and, screaming, brought Mme Bessard down. She carried her child half-way up the cellar steps to a landing. The young assistant, a lad of nineteen, Jean-Marie Deveaux, who was working in the shop, boning and rolling beef and veal and washing the dishes on which they had stood, telephoned the police at 4.15. The body was still warm and limp when they arrived at 4.30. There was a pool of blood on the floor of the cellar, but very few spots on the walls and no signs of a struggle.

All the knives of the trade were clean and in place.

A dog-handler was fetched. The police dog sniffed the blood and at first would not leave the cellar but nosed obsessively in a farther corner. When it did go outside, it followed a trail south through the park to Berliet, where there were hutments housing foreign workers, but then lost the scent. Neighbours had seen Dominique outside the house somewhat after 3.00. Several had noticed an Arab (or, as the French prefer to say, a North African) and one a brown patch on his white shirt. Mme Bessard had come down to the shop from upstairs at 3.10, and Deveaux had been with her from that point until, while she was answering the telephone at 4.00, Mme Cannard screamed in the cellar. Inspector Charrié from the Sûreté in Lyons saw no signs of blood on Deveaux's shoes or clothes and did not suspect him, while, on his return from the slaughterhouses, M. Bessard said he'd always wondered why the lad wanted to be a butcher, since the sight of blood upset him.

An autopsy was performed on July 10th. A knife had indeed entered the child's belly forcibly three or perhaps four times, but death had resulted from a violent and possibly repeated cutting of the throat to the bone. This must have occurred first, since there was almost no blood about the nevertheless terrible wounds to the viscera and beyond. There are a few cardinal rules in forensic medicine which even a layman may feel he understands. The most cardinal of all seems to be that wounds inflicted after death do not bleed, no doubt because, once the heart has stopped beating, the blood no longer circulates. In this particular case, the haemorrhage from the throat had been so rapid and, as it were, exhaustive, that there would in any case have been little blood left to show elsewhere. The importance of this finding was not at first apparent. Rather little importance would ever attach to the fact that there were no signs of sexual assault.

For seven weeks, the investigation made no headway. Inspector Charrié went on leave. Superintendent Durin returned from leave. The public was discontented with the police, and Superintendent Durin was discontented. A murder mystery can only be solved by finding the murderer. The only suspect to hand was young Deveaux. He must have felt this himself. On August 29th, on the landing half-way down to his employer's cellar, he feigned an attack on himself, being found apparently recovering consciousness and stating that he had been hit on the head from behind and that, as he fell, he had just caught sight of a pair of trouser legs, those of his assailant. A doctor examined him and disbelieved his story. Next day, a police surgeon came out from Lyons and confirmed the findings of his colleague. At Sûreté headquarters on September 1st, he confessed that he had made the story up to remove any suspicion that might attach to himself of having murdered Dominique Bessard.

He was questioned by Superintendent Durin, and the following dialogue is on record (I quote, or rather I translate from, Thévenin, *Meutriers sans Aveu*).

DETECTIVE CHIEF SUPERINTENDENT LUCIEN DURIN. I saw you this morning for the first time, and I had the impression you must be hiding something. If you told lies about this attack, you weren't telling the whole truth about the murder of Dominique either, were you? (*Deveaux hangs his head.*) Have you heard people talk about the truth serum? No? The suspect is given an injection, and if he isn't telling the truth, it shows on a machine. Shall we give you a shot?

J-M. DEVEAUX. No, sir.

DURIN. Why?

DEVEAUX. I'm scared.

DURIN. You're afraid?

DEVEAUX. Yes, I'm afraid it'll hurt.

DURIN. All right. Let's forget it. But you must tell me the truth.

DEVEAUX. It was me, then. I killed Dominique.

DURIN. It was you, was it? But just when did it happen?

DEVEAUX. Five minutes before the boss's wife came down.

DURIN. So you went down to the cellar with a knife?

DEVEAUX. More than one. And a bucket. I was going to sharpen them.

DURIN. And Dominique?

DEVEAUX. She followed me. And then, half-way down the steps, I realised I'd forgotten the keys to the cellar.

DURIN. Yes, I see. But what made you think of killing Dominique?

DEVEAUX. It just happened. All of a sudden.

DURIN. Go on.

DEVEAUX. So we went down to the cellar. When we got to the little passage, I said I'd dropped my watch. She bent down to pick it up. Then, before Dominique stood up again, I planted the knife in her tummy. And as she was yelling out loud, I put my hand over her mouth. Then I struck her on the throat.

That was in the course of the afternoon. In the evening, Deveaux was questioned again.

DEVEAUX, *shouting.* It wasn't me that killed Dominique!

DURIN. Shall we give you the serum?

DEVEAUX. No! No! It was me. . . .

As the police well know, here no less than in France, there are always people eager to confess to murders they haven't committed, the majority of such false claimants being exhibitionists, sensation-seekers and miscellaneous nut-cases, who come forward of their own accord and tell stories which stand little chance of being believed, if only because the only details they have got right are those they could have learnt from the newspapers. This being so, it is astonishing how often in our courts (not in French ones) conviction and a capital sentence have resulted from nothing more than a plea of guilty, no evidence whatsoever being heard in court, however much may be known to the police and on record at the office of the Director of Public Prosecutions. By continental standards, every conviction resulting from a plea of guilty in our courts has been a miscarriage of justice. This does not mean that the defendant may not in every case have been guilty as charged, but it does mean that justice was not seen to be done.* This, I know is a digression, but it may be some excuse for French policemen like Chief Superintendent Durin that on occasion they have to work harder than ours to make a charge stick.

From the statements of witnesses, Inspector Charrié had compiled a timetable which gave Deveaux no opportunity to kill Dominique Bessard. The means had been handy, certainly, and, if there had been no evident motive, there had been none either for anybody else. There was no past history of violence, but some

---

* At Winchester assizes, on December 14th, 1959, Brian Cawley, thirty, was found guilty of non-capital murder and sentenced to life imprisonment at a trial lasting under a minute. At Liverpool assizes, on February 3rd, 1929, Joseph Clark, twenty-three, at a trial lasting between four and five minutes, was found guilty of murder, sentenced to death and, in due course, hanged.

of mythomania. At the moment at which he spoke to the police over the telephone, how can he have known that the little girl had been murdered, unless he had murdered her? He said he had followed Mmes Bessard and Cannard down to the cellar, but they denied this. While he was in his confessing phase, he described how he had made the belly wounds (as though he were boning meat), and this corresponded with the pathologists' findings. These indicated, on the other hand, that the throat had been cut first, while he said that he had cut it last.

The Bessards were by now coming round to the view that it *must* have been young Deveaux. Mme Bessard conceded that, when she came downstairs, it might have been rather 3.20 than 3.10, a neighbour that Dominique might have been back home by 3.15. This would have given the butcher's assistant five minutes in which to carry out his fell work, clean himself up and be washing the knife. As to the expert findings, the examining magistrate got a *contre-expertise* from Paris, based solely on photographs and merely allowing (as though in response to a suggestion from Lyons) that the blood position might have been as found if the throat had been cut immediately after infliction of the abdominal wounds. The tendency is for provincial experts to bow (before they are overridden) to Paris opinion. There is much to justify this, historically. Medico-legal scandals had often resulted from the incompetence of provincial experts (were being shown at that moment to have done so in the case of Marie Besnard). In the matter of forensic science, however, Lyons was hardly provincial. From Lacassagne to Locard, Lyons had often led Paris. The present head of the department, Professor Roche, how-ever, seems to have been a weak and compliant man, deferring to Paris not so much from conviction or lack of it as because to do so would relieve him of pressure from the regional police and magistracy.

The judicial inquiry dragged on all through 1962. On August 22nd of that year took place the Bastien-Thiry attempt on the life of President de Gaulle, so vividly described in the opening pages of a recent English novel. Colonel Bastien-Thiry himself was arrested on September 17th. In November, Guy Trébert came up for trial not in Paris but at Melun, which seems odd in view of the fact that *la dame en rouge* had been killed not in Seine-et-Marne but in Seine-et-Oise. As a paint-sprayer, he had been a satisfactory workman, but in the Army he had been hopeless. A ferocious masturbator, he had also acquired masochistic tastes from the brutalities he had suffered at home and elsewhere in his youth. He seems to have been fond of Marie-Christine, the motherly mistress who had added two children by him to the five a husband had left her. The unfortunate Arlette had been the fourth woman he had taken for a drive in the forest of St Germain. One he had attacked with a spanner. Two he had tried to strangle while sexually engaged, sweating, as one of them said in evidence, as though a bucket of water had been poured over his head. The prosecution demanded that head. The jury gave him life imprisonment.

THE FOLLOWING year, Colonel Bastien-Thiry was to be executed by firing squad, a thing which has not happened in the United Kingdom for a long time, though it was done abroad to members of our armed forces during the Second World War. It is interesting to note that, among French crimes in the private sector, the penal result of those we have seen brought to trial in this chapter would have been much the same under our Homicide Act. Of the four male killers of women, only Georges Rapin would have been hanged here, on the double ground of having committed two murders on separate occasions and of having committed them with firearms. The total of those hanged in England and Wales from the passing of the Act to the end of 1962 had in fact been far greater than that of those guillotined in France.

There had been four in 1958 (plus Manuel in Scotland), six in 1959 (the best-known of them Marwood and Podola), three in 1960 (two of them, Forsyth and Harris, for the same murder), seven in 1961, three (one of them Hanratty) in 1962. From the admirably detailed Morris and Blom-Cooper 'breakdown' of the statistics for those years, we may note that, since the Act came into force, a mere 95 females had been indicted for murder, but 669 males, while there had been 399 female to 342 male victims. No more than three mistresses had killed their lovers, but 47 lovers their mistresses, 24 wives their husbands, 132 husbands their wives. As to generation hostility within the family, more than a hundred parents (52 fathers, 56 mothers) had murdered their children, while only two daughters had killed respectively a mother and a father, but 38 sons had killed parents, twice as many mothers as fathers. In general, however, both murderers and their victims were most numerous in the age-groups 15-24 and, a bit less so, 25-34. After the middle fifties, the numbers both of murderers and of victims fall off, but, as we might expect, among these older people there are more than twice as many victims as murderers.

Two tabulations one might wish Messrs Morris and Blom-Cooper had provided would have shown where the various crimes were committed and what proportion existed between locally born and, in the very largest sense, foreign protagonists. They do indeed show, in their summaries of individual cases, at what assizes these were tried. This gives us a broad (and unremarkable) jurisdictional and thus geographical distribution, but does not tell us what took place in country districts and what in towns, and which towns. As might be expected, the proportion of recent immigrants is high among both killers and their victims. During that period of somewhat less than six years, acts of culpable homicide were, for instance, committed in England and Wales by ten Poles, nine Cypriots, one Cypriot woman and one Turkish Cypriot, five Hungarians, two Maltese, two Germans and one German woman, two Dutch seamen, one Italian and one Italian woman, one Ukrainian, one Polish Ukrainian, one Latvian and one Lithuanian; by twenty-one Indians and ten Pakistanis, one Eurasian, one gipsy and two Arabs, two Moslem Somalis, two Moslem Nigerians (one male, one female) and one Ghanaian; by thirty-four male and two female coloured West Indians and by twenty-eight Irish born males and two females. An Irish ponce was dispatched by a pregnant and thus currently non-earning prostitute of unspecified provenance, and there were somewhat more than twenty native-born Britons killed by some of those listed above. In general, however, they murdered within their own group, or members of one immigrant group killed those of another, sometimes in self-defence or greatly provoked. The balance was usually favourable to women in that, among the victims, men outnumbered them by two to one. An exceptional amount of insanity and mental sub-normality was found in mitigation by the courts.

A failure to appreciate this tendency to kill within the group gave rise, more recently, to a dangerous piece of journalistic display. On October 14th, 1971, three children and (subsequently, of her burns) their mother died in a fire, deliberately started, at a house in Bradford, a city in which one in ten persons is an immigrant, a high proportion of the immigrants being Pakistanis. The children and their mother were Kenya Asians. There had been a series of such fires at the homes of immigrant families, but none previously had produced fatal results. The tragedy happened at half past two in the morning. That very day, a London morning newspaper bore on its front page, in letters more than an inch deep and a quarter of an inch thick, the headline :

RACE MURDER COMES TO BRITAIN

Letterpress underneath boldly assumed that these deaths could only have been the deliberate work of white men activated by race hatred.

There was talk of fingerprinting a thousand males in the vicinity, but presently, to those who read small paragraphs in small type, it was made clear, from police statements and the reports of court proceedings, that the arsonists were two immigrant youths of fourteen and seventeen. The younger's name was withheld, while the elder's was unmistakably Mohammedan. It seemed likely that they had been responsible for the whole sequence of fires. Appropriate proceedings were taken against them. I have not heard that the journalist and his newspaper were so much as reported either to the Press Council or to the Race Relations Board.

ON RELEASE, Pauline Dubuisson went to Morocco, with a house physician's job in a hospital at the former Mogador. The chief surgeon knew her story but did not reveal it. As her surname was not an uncommon one, all she herself did to conceal her identity was adopt a different Christian name and be known as Andrée. Her mother went out and spent a month with her. At the beginning of 1963, she had no boy-friend, but was known to be very fond of animals.

On February 4th, at Lyons, Jean-Marie Deveaux came up for trial. On the 7th, he was convicted of the murder of Dominique Bessard and sentenced to twenty years' imprisonment. Then just approaching his majority, intelligence tests gave him a mental age of eight. As I understand these things, a person's intelligence quotient or IQ, as determined by valid and properly conducted intelligence tests, will not vary from nineteen to, say fifty, in the absence of disease or traumatic brain damage. In view of Deveaux's behaviour at a later trial, it seems to me that those first intelligence tests must have been either improperly conducted and marked or confused with personality tests. The young man had indeed been lonely and introverted. He had made stories up about himself in order, as he put it, to be like everybody else. And late development there may have been. At his first trial, photographs show Deveaux chubby-faced, with bewildered eyes.

My account of this case is taken in the main from Raymond Thévenin, who, six years later, was to cover Deveaux's second trial day by day for Radio Luxembourg, and from J.-M. Théolleyre of *Le Monde*. But neither attended the first trial. What we have for that are the impressions of a Jesuit, Father Boyer, the prison chaplain at Lyons, to whom the butcher's boy was one of his flock. It was, he says, only the second criminal trial he had attended, and at both the presiding judge had been the same, as had the official prosecutor. The latter, M. Quatre, he found moderate and fair, the former, M. Combas, a hideous bully. He was shocked by the revised timetables, the awful docility of certain witnesses, the lack of logic and of fidelity to the written texts. After giving his evidence, one of the psychiatric experts sat next to Fr Boyer and complained bitterly of the misuse that was being made of his findings. Deveaux did not understand in the least what was going on. After the verdict had been pronounced, he said to his counsel, Me Soulier, 'So Maître, I shall be going home this evening?' He was not to go home for six years. Even then, he would not have gone home but for the persistent efforts of Fr Boyer and Me Soulier. And here it is perhaps worth noting how often in French legal history miscarriages of justice have been averted or remedied by an advocate's close and continuing interest in a client. The relations between a criminal suspect or a convicted criminal and his counsel are one of the aspects of a case in which French judicial practice is in general more pleasing than ours, for with us the grotesquely overpaid barrister is rarely involved with his man's fate for more than a week or two at the outside and in the old days was not even expected to attend his execution.

In May 1963, there was a nasty, unsolved kidnapping case in Paris, in which an eleven-year-old boy, Thierry Desouches, was found dead. On the 23rd, two of its less intellectual members carried out, at Dampierre, one of the Richier château gang's most audacious raids, removing four chairs, five writing tables and a pair of vases, all priceless, while the bailiff watched television. In Morocco, a man had appeared in the life of Andrée, formerly Pauline, Dubuisson. He was an oil-mining engineer. A marriage was expected. Then it was off. At the second attempt in ten days, the proud murderess killed herself with barbiturates, while a gramophone record turned and turned until the neighbours broke in. That year, a famous murderess of the 'thirties, Violette Nozières, who had poisoned both her parents to the admiration of the *surréalistes*, was formally rehabilitated. Released in 1945, she had married and borne children. Her husband had just died. The restoration of her civic rights enabled her to take over a little inn near Rouen.

Within the same jurisdiction, at La Vieux Rue, the paternal grandmother, Louise Letondeur, had a stroke and, hemiplegic, occupied an ill-spared bed in the house of her son by her own father and his deaf wife, her niece, daughter of the same father, whose daughter Janine, anxious to be married as her sister Jacqueline had been four years before, had to stay at home and nurse the old lady, seven of whose grandsons were also at home and whose son, having recently fallen off a roof he was tiling, lay in bed all day reading detective stories. On October 28th, the more powerful André having refused, young, club-footed, bespectacled François was sent upstairs to strangle his paternal grandmother, which he did with a will, though it took him ten minutes. The bruises on her neck being concealed with a scarf, the doctor who inspected her next morning found some other cause of death and made out a certificate in due form.

Strangled the following week, in Arras, we are unlikely ever to know by whom, was a much younger woman, Monique Humbert. Within a fortnight, on November 15th, at Lille, without fatal result, another received eleven stab wounds at the hands of a thin man with a curious smile, Pierre Tavernier, the lover with whom she had just announced her intention of breaking. For this display of a violence for which he was locally well known, the *cour correctionnelle* withdrew Tavernier from circulation for a period of five years, the maximum at its disposal.

To have its later repercussions in France, a Hollywood episode of 1963 was the death, in the company of a former film star's wife, of Milos Milosevic. The verdict was suicide. The handsome young Yugoslav had been the companion and bodyguard of a currently successful French film star, Alain Delon, who paid for his body to be flown back to Yugoslavia The successor to Milosevic in Delon's service was another Yugoslav, Stefan Markovic. But of course the year's criminal event in the United States, by reason of its political importance, was undoubtedly the assassination, in classical style, of President Kennedy. This rocked everybody.

In the United Kingdom, the criminal event of the year was the Great Train Robbery on August 8th, remarkable for its careful planning and execution, the huge amount of money stolen and the small amount of it subsequently recovered, the protracted sentences awarded to certain of the participants, their prison escapes and later careers. From his maltreatment at their hands the engine-driver never recovered, and his death was certainly hastened by it, though not in so direct and demonstrable a manner as could usefully give rise to murder charges (which would have been 'capital'). Participants in the Great Train Robbery were known as Great Train Robbers and much admired.

LUCIEN LÉGER and his wife Solange lived in a hotel near the
École Militaire, behind the Invalides, on the Left Bank, though
not at all what we typically think of as the Left Bank. Across the
river and rather more than two miles to the north, in the Rue de
Naples, lived the Tarons with their eleven-year-old son Luc. They
were a prosperous and devoted couple, though Luc was sometimes
a trial, and M. Taron's business dealings had not always escaped
troublesome scrutiny. The Légers had been married five years,
but were childless, which was as well, for neither would have made
a good parent. Lucien worked as a male nurse at the Villejuif
asylum, to which he drove out daily in his 2CV. He was an
insignificant shrimp of a young man, who always wore dark
glasses and favoured heavy sweaters and plimsolls. He played the
clarinet in an amateur orchestra and had two guitars on the wall,
as well as a collection of Piaf and Aznavour records. Solange was
thin, jumpy, a heavy smoker and heavily made-up.

   Neither had a good background. Solange and her brother had
been brought up on public assistance. Her brother and Lucien
Léger had performed their military service together, and that was
how she and Lucien had met. His home had not been precisely
broken, but his enormously fat and ugly mother quite eclipsed
the skinny, near-imbecile man she had married (they are to be
seen posed grotesquely side by side at the entrance to the Law
Courts in Versailles). There were pretensions of taste. The young
couple read Camus and Giraudoux to each other. On the squared
paper of an exercise book, Lucien Léger wrote weak poems in
free verse and had sketched out the plot of a novel, *Journal d'un
Assassin*, of which the narrator kills perfect strangers for the
pleasure of reading about his misdeeds in the newspapers. The
two both ate far too many anti-depressant and tranquillising pills
no doubt brought home by him from Villejuif, and she seems to
have been intermittently on harder drugs, with breakdowns which
took her into hospital once or twice a year.

   A big school, the Collège Fénelon, stands in the Rue de Naples
and seems likely to have been the one Luc Taron attended. He
was not an exemplary scholar, and his parents toyed with the
idea of boarding him outside Paris. After his return from school
on Tuesday, May 26th, 1964, he went out straight after tea,
without doing his homework, which that evening consisted of

writing out the conjugation of the irregular verb *rire*, to laugh. While he was out, Mme Taron looked in her handbag and found that money was missing. Towards six o'clock, Luc came back, and his elegant, pretty mother gave him the rough side of her tongue. He had, it transpired, taken the money to buy her a present for Mothers' Day, but, whether this fact mollified her or not, he was out of the house again. It was not the first time he had run away, always returning a few hours later. On this occasion, he hung about the streets near his home, going no further than the Villiers tube station, where a young man in dark glasses asked him what was the matter and, being tearfully told about mother's unwarranted sharpness and the unfinished homework, offered the boy a drive in his car this lovely evening.

They drove south-west out of Paris, and at five o'clock in the morning Luc Taron's body was discovered in the woods at Verrières. He had been strangled with his face pressed either to the ground or to a softer surface. His parents had not yet reported his disappearance. This delay was regarded as a suspicious circumstance, and, after M. Taron had been to Palaiseau to identify the body, both were held for questioning for thirty-six hours. Their handwriting was compared with that on a note, written on squared paper from an exercise book and signed with three crosses, claiming responsibility for the murder, with convincing details, found on the morning of May 30th tucked under the windscreen-wiper of a car parked in the Rue de Marignan, off the Champs Élysées.

This was to be the first of more than fifty notes received at various addresses, including that of the *Daily Express* in London, in a little over a month. For the most part, they were signed 'the Strangler'. This was, said their writer, the crime of the century. At one point, he announced that he would strike again unless his name reappeared on the front page in the newspapers next day. Radio stations and ministries heard from him, as well as the police, not only in writing but also by telephone. In an automatic photograph booth, he photographed part of himself, revolver in hand, and sent the result to M. Taron. He described the sensation of blood pulsing in the carotid artery, said he knew it would have been easier with thumbs from the front and that the boy had taken ten minutes to die. On July 3rd, he wrote to the police to say that his car had been stolen by *l'Étrangleur* to take a corpse with battered head, that of a Montmartre gangster, out to Corbeil, and signed this letter with his own name (he had in fact abandoned his car outside working-class flats at Châtillon). Lucien Léger was arrested next day and taken to Versailles.

That was a Saturday. On Sunday, he wrote to his wife.

You must know everything now from the newpapers and radio. Not everything, for only I can know what really happened. I should like you to buy all the newspapers and read what they say, for no single one, picked by chance, can give you all the details.

I have picked one of the greatest barristers of our time, since it is said that my case is the only one in the world, and the most important this century, of its kind : Me Maurice Garçon has just left me. Outside, there is still a noisy crowd of journalists.

Yesterday, outside 1st Flying Squad headquarters, there was a yelling, threatening mob. The telly was there, transmitting live, and dozens of journalists followed us here : Radio Luxembourg, Europe, R.T.F.

The climax came here, at the Law Courts. The crowd succeeded in breaking through the ring of policemen and wanted to lynch me. It was through a barrage of shouted insults and punches (which missed) that I got inside. I had to leave by a back way, along corridors, to reach the prison. For what success amounts to, this is it. For the rest . . . that, too. Yesterday, I signed autographs by the score. I should think my memoirs will be worth a fortune!

Ten days later, he was feeling sorry for himself and wrote to his wife for sympathy. She did not reply or go to see him, in part, it seems, because she was in hospital again. Not till July 28th did she write, asking him to explain. Two rambling letters failed to satisfy her, and she started divorce proceedings.

The fact was that, even in his own limited field of endeavour, Lucien Léger's achievement had been small, even for those few years. He must himself have read of the Boston strangler whose career had reached its triumphant conclusion almost five months before his one poor effort. By then also, three of a succession of five bodies of strangled prostitutes had been found naked by the Thames, and the crusader was never to be discovered. In general, the communists manage to keep their murders to themselves, but hardly was Léger in prison before we began to hear of the 'Red Spider' in Poland. In France itself, the murderer of Thierry Desouches, a boy of Luc Taron's age, was still at large, as was the strangler of Monique Humbert. Within the jurisdiction of

Versailles, whoever shot Barbara Mehlfelt (a German student) at
Neuilly in October was to do so with impunity. In the north of
England, at the end of the Christmas holidays, took place the
murder of a girl-child, Lesley Downey, in circumstances of a
cruelty which, though inspired by an eighteenth-century French
writer, went far beyond the scope of our asylum attendant's poor
imagination.

SENTENCED TO death for the murder of three Britons, reprieved,
imprisoned, released, Gaston Dominici died, in his eighty-ninth
year, on April 4th, 1965. Ten days later, in the state of Kansas,
were hanged Richard Eugene Hickock and Perry Edward Smith,
anti-heroes of Truman Capote's non-fiction novel, *In Cold Blood,*
which in translation would be much read in France. In Normandy,
François's indiscreet talk about the strangling of the second
Letondeur grandmother came to the ears of a respectable uncle
and, through him, reached the police, so that the whole of that
large and incestuous brood was questioned and eight of its
members, with the husband of one, were held at Rouen on murder
charges. In the United Kingdom, a Labour government that year
suspended capital punishment and, in consequence, certain
provisions of the Homicide Act for an experimental period of five
years.

At Limoges on April 29th, a Dr Parat added his name to the
long roll of medical men who have killed intentionally. In the
prison of that town currently languished two men and two women
who, in December, had variously participated in the murder of a
garage-owner, Charles Vignaud, the two women being respectively
his wife and that of a gunman, Jacques Rossignol, hired by the
first wife's lover, whom the husband had been blackmailing.
Twenty miles outside Marseilles, in early May, Robert Blémant,
police superintendent turned gangster, was shot dead at the wheel
of his Mercedes. It remains uncertain which of the *caïds* or bosses
of the Corsican *milieu* had caused that old score to be thus
settled, but Blémant, although a Frenchman from Valenciennes,
had been at one time the right-hand man and later the rival of
the respected and (in Marseilles) seemingly all-powerful Antoine
Guérini.

At St Peter's prison in Versailles, Lucien Léger had grown dis-
satisfied with the newspapers' lack of recent attention to himself

and concluded that, if he was not to go down in a blaze of glory, it might be better not only to survive but to go free. Once acquitted, he could make fools of everyone with his memoirs. On June 11th, he therefore retracted all the admissions he had made and began to speak of a 'M. Henri' whom he had been shielding. Disgusted by this sudden change of front, the distinguished academician Maître Garçon refused to continue with Léger's defence and was replaced by Maître Naud, leader of the campaign to abolish capital punishment.

The last of our Moors murders (though of course that body would never reach the moors) was committed in the very smallest hours of October 7th, when, secure in the knowledge that he could no longer be hanged, Ian Brady threw caution to the winds and, ignoring the old lady upstairs, laid about him noisily with an axe, invited a visitor in to give a hand, dumped the body in his girl's bedroom for later attention and lay down exhausted but happy. Going home, the visitor also tried to sleep but, failing, got up and telephoned the police, who went round and arrested Brady and Myra Hindley. That month, a young German, Horst Goetze, went to Paris, strangled two prostitutes and returned home to Bonn the same evening, but, feeling that he had not yet sufficiently purified French morals, went to Paris again three days later and strangled another prostitute. On the 29th, the Moroccan Ben Barka disappeared in a manner which gravely compromised the prefectoral *police judiciaire* in the Quai des Orfèvres and was to lead to the loss of their comparative independence.

On December 4th, a Parisian prostitute in her sixties was strangled by a tall, gangling young man, Daniel Hugon, whose bulging forehead, pebble lenses and premature baldness were later found to be signs of a chromosome anomaly which had already made medico-legal history in Australia. The generation gap was visible that month also in the conurbation of Corbeil-Essonnes when, on the 12th, the girl leader of a juvenile gang knifed a near-octogenarian woman, a fortune-teller, first obediently knocked down in her own home by the girl's Arab boy-friend, then robbed at their leisure by the two.

IN 1966, the latest German sex killer appeared at Augsburg, and the Red Spider again struck twice in Poland. July's Speck murder of eight unprotesting nurses in Chicago rocked newspaper readers everywhere (and was to play its part in the XYY chromosome debate), while the chart on my wall shows also, for the United States, a homosexual murder at Ypsilanti. In the United Kingdom, no criminal event aroused so much interest as the Moors murder trial at Chester, though two murders committed in London were to arouse almost as much three years later.

On the evening of March 9th, a man (not, it is to be feared, of blameless life) called George Cornell sat drinking between two friends at the saloon bar of the Blind Beggar* in Whitechapel Road, East London. Two men entered, both armed with revolvers. One was Ronald Kray, a local big shot who also had night-club interests in the West End. The barmaid did not know his companion, whose name in fact was John Barrie. Kray went up to within five or six feet of Cornell. Cornell said, 'Look who's here!' Kray shot Cornell with fatal accuracy in the centre of the forehead. Barrie fired two shots at random with the evident purpose of causing other customers to keep their heads down, thus diminishing the possibility of recognition. Cornell's two friends took to their heels, and the barmaid fled down to the cellar. Kray and Barrie left the Blind Beggar and went to another pub, the Lion, in Tap Street, where the former's twin brother, Reginald Kray, awaited them. They drove off in a northerly direction to Walthamstow.

An unsolved crime in Paris that April was the murder of Jeanne Dubus, a schoolteacher, formerly an air hostess, found at her flat in the Avenue Péreire, on the 7th, stabbed twenty-one times with a bread knife by, it was thought with good reason, her brother, of whom no trace has since been discovered. The trial of Ian Brady and Esther Myra Hindley opened at Chester assizes on the 19th. They were jointly charged with three murders, of all of which they were to be found guilty. The trial was attended by such distinguished writers as Pamela Hansford Johnson and Emlyn Williams, both of whom would publish books on the case. It was also attended by the *doyen* of French crime reporters, Marcel Montarron.

---

* Historically, it is understood that Henry, son and heir of Simon de Montfort, was killed with his father at Evesham, in 1965, in battle against the forces of Henry III. A legend has it that he was tended by a noble lady, whom he married, and that he lived on as the blind beggar of Bethnal Green, whose daughter, pretty Bessee, was much courted and married a knight.

He was greatly struck by the immunity accorded to Smith as a Crown witness. In France, the very least Smith could have been charged with was non-assistance to a person in danger, not to this day a criminal offence in the United Kingdom. Montarron was also struck by the close cross-examination of witnesses, by the fact that the previous histories of the accused were not elicited in court and by the public hearing of scabrous details which in France would have been heard only *in camera* or, as the French put it, *à huis clos*. With forty years' experience of French criminal trials, M. Montarron was shocked by what he heard at this one, as well as by the smell of certain exhibits produced in court.

It was, indeed, all far worse than anything which came out at Versailles the following month, when M. Montarron further attended the trial of Lucien Léger. This was sufficiently disturbing, however. The former asylum attendant was afflicted with a petulant vanity remarkable even in France. For all one knows, he had convinced himself of the real existence of the 'M. Henri' whom, for a piece of *involuntary* homicide, he was supposed to be shielding. Sporting a bright red pocket-handkerchief, his eyes still concealed behind dark glasses, he danced up and down in the dock, insulting the father of the eleven-year-old boy he had strangled, delighted to be setting the public and all these lawyers (none more so than Maître Naud, his counsel) by the ears. Everyone loathed him. Nobody could feel the least pity for him. The jury, nevertheless, were out for two hours, returning with a verdict which meant life imprisonment, with probable direction towards the special prison of Château Thierry. Even then he was not finished. When the presiding judge had read out verdict and sentence, Léger cocked his head on one side and said : 'You have just committed a miscarriage of justice. Does M. Taron know Georges-Henri Molinaro?' Pressed, he gave an address for this 'M. Henri' in the Rue de Rennes. The proceedings were drawn out for two more days, while M. Molinaro was in fact found in the Rue de Rennes, a man who clearly had no idea what it was all about, who had never encountered either Léger or the Tarons, a name and address once noted by the former as he walked along the Rue de Rennes or picked by him from an advertisement or the telephone directory.

During the night of May 27th to 28th, a farmer in Sarthe, Gustave Legeay of Assé-le-Riboul, murdered his neighbour, a Mme Suru. Similar neighbourly action was taken in Champagne on June 7th by a woodcutter, André Paul, against Maurice Vachet, father of seven children, there being litigation between the two and a shotgun handy. A *crime passionnel* (wife killed, lover wounded) was committed on June 11th in the Paris suburb of Montreuil-sous-Bois, in mid-morning, at a bus-stop, as the wife got into her lover's red sports car, by Jean Susini of counter-espionage. In the late afternoon of July 8th, the body of Bernard Bel, aged fourteen, apprentice pastrycook and keen cyclist, was fished out of the Durance, near Briançon, the point reached the previous evening by competitors in the Tour de France, with their attendant mob of journalists, trainers, publicity agents, idle motorists, miscellaneous camp-followers and doubtless a fair sprinkling of pickpockets and small confidence men. There had been busy autograph-hunting by the local boys and a number of fights among outsiders.

In the previous chapter, in connection with the Deveaux case, I ventured the (quite unoriginal) opinion that, among the few cardinal rules in forensic medicine, the most cardinal of all was that wounds inflicted after death do not bleed. The second most cardinal I take to be that, once the victim has stopped breathing, water in which he may be immersed will not enter his lungs, so that the presence of water in the lungs indicates death by drowning, however many wounds or effects of poison may also show. The reverse is true. If there is no water in the lungs, then the cause of death was not drowning. This simple rule is of course well known to amateur criminologists and doubtless to many readers of detective stories. It will prove of capital importance in what, in a number of ways, has been the most interesting of all French murder cases of recent years, that of Armand Rohart, the mayor of Peuplingues. It would certainly be known to young Bernard Bel's father, a dispensing chemist at the winter sports sanatorium. The inquest showed no water in the lungs but signs of a heavy blow to the head. The police and the examining magistrate concluded that the boy had fallen off a wall, and the matter was non-suited. M. Bel was not satisfied. There was circumstantial evidence examining magistrate had not taken. At the age of fifty-eight, to which the police had paid no attention, statements which the M. Bel became his own detective and, two years later, would at least succeed in getting the case reopened.

Robert Heldenberg played first trumpet in the Republican Guards band in Paris and lived out at Noisy-le-Sec with his second

wife and their five children, making extra money by playing in
ad hoc orchestras and bands. He drank heavily and had twice
gone into hospital to be dried out. He also womanised and had
latterly been spending money on a love of his youth whose husband
had just died. The only one of his children for whom he showed
fondness was his red-haired eldest daughter, Isoline, who was later
to claim that his affection, which she did not reciprocate, went
beyond paternal limits. He beat his wife when he was drunk, and
at the beginning of 1966 she had sought and obtained a legal
separation which (and this seems very odd in England) authorised
cohabitation until the time of his retirement in September.

On the evening of the 26th of that month, a Monday, his fellow-
bandsmen, all those thirsty players upon wind instruments,
celebrated Sergeant Heldenberg's retirement with a *vin d'honneur*.
The worse for wear, he returned to his little detached house at
Noisy-le-Sec, where he was awaited, with some determination, by
his wife and two daughters, Isoline, already in her late twenties,
and Martine, then only fifteen. In concert, they murdered him,
first administering barbiturates and then strangling him with a
scarf. Afterwards, they pulled the furniture about or knocked it
over, scratched their own arms and went running to neighbours,
who knew that disputes were frequent in the Heldenberg house-
hold and that the trumpeter was sometimes violent enough in
liquor to excuse some degree of general rallying-round against
him. The case which the prosecution was to spend three years
preparing would, at any rate, allege that the murder of Robert
Heldenberg had been long and concertedly premeditated, with its
subsequent *mise en scène*, by his wife, *née* Raymonde Royer, and
two daughters, one of whom was therefore also guilty of parricide,
the other then of an age not yet able to bear full criminal
responsibility, all three bent on celebrating the trumpeter's retirement in their own way.

Half-Egyptian, a failure as a ponce and already in his late
thirties, Serge Barany, at about this time, went into partnership
with another man, Noël Marcucci, just out of prison at Tulle.
On October 11th, they began a series of *hold-ups* and *raids*
(operations for which the French language has never found words
of its own), principally in the departments of Var and Loiret, using
a succession of stolen cars and armed with three pistols of various
calibre. Three banks and a Martini warehouse were robbed with
skill and speed and not a shot fired. In Corsica, fourteen shots

were fired, in a hotel at Alistro, in the small hours of October 27th, at the end of a poker game. When the police came, they found the hotel proprietor dead, with two heavy calibre revolver bullets in him, a player whose leg had been broken by a stray shot and the owner of the revolver, François Memmi, unconscious with a fractured skull, the result of some brave intervener hitting him with a decanter. When he came out of hospital, they arrested Memmi. There were nine witnesses, including two women.

November was a quiet month, not so December. On the 12th, an associate of the Kray brothers, Frank Mitchell, known as 'the mad axe-man', was 'sprung' with remarkable ease from Dartmoor and installed with a blonde at a flat in Barking Road, East Ham. Barany and Marcucci, in a Citroën light van, had moved nearer Paris. On the 14th, at Villepreux, they were unlucky enough to kill a young bank messenger and made haste south again. On the evening of the 23rd, as Christmas approached, a Kray man called at the flat in Barking Road, gave the blonde a packet containing £100 and took Frank Mitchell away to a van parked round the corner, from which, shortly thereafter, the girl heard three or four bangs which she took to be shots. At that moment, the Red Spider was striking on a train near Cracow. The police at Mantes had not yet succeeded in identifying the young woman whose naked body had been found that morning in woods nearby, strangled with a dog's lead. She had in fact been a *call-girl* (the French have borrowed that expression, too), Gisèle Giannone, known as 'Corinne' in the Opéra district of Paris. The mystery of her death has never been solved. Barany and Marcucci were still out of luck. On the 29th, after a raid on the post office at Noailles, they had the misfortune to kill a sergeant of *gendarmerie* who pursued them on to a train at Cahors. There is some doubt as to which of them fired the fatal shot, though a third-class passenger distinctly heard a voice, presumably Barany's, say, '*Noël, fais pas le con!*' At any rate, that was the end of their partnership.

IT IS with sensations approaching those of personal guilt that I look back at the last dozen pages, as though I were somehow responsible for the miscellaneousness of crime in those four years, the mere diversity of their *faits divers*. The homicidal scene had been dignified by no great trial, despite little Lucien Léger's best attempts to create one, despite the intrinsic horror of the case of

Ian Brady and Myra Hindley (by the end of the year just one pair of the not quite innumerable murderous bores in prison). The assassination of President Kennedy was a shattering event, but its legal consequences were ludicrous. Among the French murderers, we shall yet see several awarded the brief dignity of a trial. The two murders laid at the door of the Kray brothers and their associates will come to trial in the United Kingdom with something like continental delay (but a third was yet unperformed). The fact is, however, that, although during what remains of our period there will be trials of the greatest interest, the miscellaneousness will persist and even increase.

The least, I feel, I can do is end this chapter with a trial in early 1967, the charges in the indictment relating to episodes in 1959 and 1963, the numerous accused having been in prison a year and a half. Taking things chronologically, I must even so first instance three January *faits divers*. On the 11th, in hospital at Arras, died Serge Defrance, aged five. As no difficulty was made about the death certificate, his mother, a fortnight later, was also to finish off his sister, Marianne, aged six, with a single extra sleeping-pill given her in water as she set off for school. Mme Defrance, who in the past had failed to rid herself of her husband and father-in-law by similar means, was to escape arrest until September. On January 16th, a simple-minded girl of fifteen was found raped and strangled on a building site near Villejuif. The mystery was never to be solved, but local young thugs were thought to have been enjoying a little collective fun. Three days later, an elegant young woman, a gynaecologist's wife, Françoise Besimensky, took a taxi in Paris and gave her address in Boulogne-Billancourt. The taxi was stolen, and the broken-nosed fellow in the driver's seat, Claude Buffet, at various times gardener, barman, wine waiter, chauffeur, drew out a pistol and demanded his passenger's handbag and jewellery. When she fought back, he first shot, then stripped and raped her. He was a great car-stealer and attacker of women, but it was for the attempted murder of a little girl that he was arrested a week before the Letondeur trial opened at Rouen.

This was on February 15th. There were nine people in the dock, Mme Letondeur, seven of her children and the husband of the younger of the two daughters. The youngest of the sons was discharged in the course of the first day's hearing, as having been under age at the time of the facts alleged. M. Letondeur was not charged. More literate than all but one of his children, it was his addiction to detective and spy novels which had kept him out of the dock, for, though present in the one house and the other on both occasions, he had taken no part in either murder but stayed with his nose in a book, his mind in a world of some writer's imagination, and paid no attention to what his family were up to.

The London press showed a fair amount of interest in this case, a block photograph in *The Times* showing the nine turnip heads of those in the dock on the first day. If I may here venture a little autobiography, this and the accompanying letterpress lie somewhat at the source of all my subsequent criminological interests, as well as of the novel, *The Shearers*, I was to draft out that year and publish two years later. What first struck me about the case was how utterly French it was, how totally unimaginable anywhere in the United Kingdom. This I then took as a challenge. I would so imagine it. The likeliest places to find such massive incest and tribal ways were in Ireland and North Wales, but I had to be able to do the dialect and so chose a remote part, a part I did not in fact know, of the North Riding, where also might still be found remnants of pre-Reformation Catholicism. My trial is longer, but otherwise all the dates in the story were the same. The names are closely paralleled ('Oldstreet,' Stonedale,' 'Shearer' for La Vieux Rue, Pierreval, Letondeur, and so on). The verdicts and the sentences barely differ.

In the Letondeur case, the sentences, I had perhaps better say here, were life for the mother and the lame son who strangled the second grandmother, twenty years for the younger daughter and ten for her husband (I sandpapered these down), suspended sentences for the elder daughter and two of her brothers, acquittal for the one with St Vitus's dance. It was not in fact much of a trial, considered legally or dramatically. Like the one the year before in Chester, it was conspicuous chiefly for the (less abominable) horrors revealed. Brady and Hindley had not been heard in evidence. The Letondeurs were inarticulate. The most memorable utterance was that of the old father to newspapermen, that it wasn't the first time old women had been given a push in those parts and that, but for his interfering brother, he could just have got François off to the colonies.

Trying the case before an imaginary English court of assize, I had to sort out some of the differences between proceedings at law in the two countries. I had to do this rather more thoroughly for the translation I undertook at about the same time of Balzac's *Splendeurs et Misères des Courtisanes,* of which the second half takes place almost wholly around the Palais de Justice and the Conciergerie on the Île de la Cité in Paris. And so I began the long course of reading which was to result also in three books on French crime and this one. But that will do about that. I now return to the murder scene in 1967, principally in France but first with a brief reminder of matters elsewhere.

THE MURDEROUS career of Poland's Red Spider (his name was Staniak) had ended, but the Augsburg sex killer struck once in 1967, and in Nuremberg Klaus Gosmann was brought to trial. In the United States, many death sentences were later to be passed, but the last for at least four years was carried out (by gas, in Colorado) on June 2nd. A crime whose roots lay in America was revealed by the finding of a body, that of Maria Domenech, off the west coast of Ireland. There was child-murder in England, quite unsolved in Berkshire, for the moment covered by the wife of a man called Morris in Staffordshire. In Scotland, at a young offenders' institution in Edinburgh, to which he had been sent at the age of sixteen for battering a woman to death, Peter Campbell stabbed, at eighteen, a fellow-prisoner to death and, having been sentenced to life imprisonment, was sent to a young offenders' institution at Dumfries. Of the two deadliest London gangs, the Richardsons were brought to trial that year, while in Jack ('the Hat') McVitie a suitable victim was found for the milder, homosexual Kray twin, Reginald.

In France that year, near Rouen, at the age of fifty-one, died Violette Nozières, poisoner of her parents a third of a century ago, a cult figure with the *surréalistes,* released in 1945, married and widowed, keeping a little inn. A murderess of the same period, Léa, the younger of the Papin sisters upon whom Genet's play *Les Bonnes* is based, was still working contentedly as a chambermaid in a luxury hotel. A much older woman, Rirette Maîtrejean, remote Egeria of the Bonnot gang, would see the year out, but not so Fernande Segret, Landru's last mistress, who was to drown herself in the chilly autumnal water of Flers Hall pond.

In Plaisir, near Versailles, lived the Décarnelles, Paul and Suzanne, she a rich heiress in her early thirties, he a man of forty, for whom she had bought a garage after his failures as a singer (she had once booked the Champs-Élysées theatre for him) and as a painter. Her interests were fast cars and show jumping, and as a competitor in this latter sphere she was herself almost of international class. She was tired of 'getting a mechanic's supper' and contemplated divorce, but was urged to swifter action when he refused to mend her Jaguar. He collected firearms, and from his collection, on March 3rd, 1967, she selected a 7.65 mm. automatic, with which she laid him low. She said it was in self-defence, but ballistics *expertise* showed otherwise. He had been bending down to get something out of a low cupboard in the kitchen. Nearer Paris, at Montreuil-sous-Bois, a Portuguese, aged thirty-four, equalised for the husbands. For the moment, his wife's body, with battered skull, lay in the garden, undiscovered.

In Paris, in the small hours of March 7th, a rich old gentleman brought two strong-arm boys with him to the luxurious apartment, in the Boulevard Suchet, of a German picture-dealer, Harry Wachs, who owed him several million francs loaned towards the purchase of a Rubens. The old gentleman's companions punched Wachs in the face, broke his spectacles, threatened his wife and children. He said he would get the papers, went into the next room, got a revolver instead, fastened the door, fired through it and mortally wounded one of the toughies, whom the other, with his rich employer's aid, took downstairs, drove north-east and dumped at the entrance to the Bichat hospital, by no means the nearest. Harry Wachs drove south to Orly and took the next plane for Milan. Later in the month, the unpopular mayor of a village within the jurisdiction of Beauvais was shot dead on his verandah in the evening, it was thought by a local stock-breeder using a rifle with telescopic sights, while in Grenoble a policeman was shot by (this was not to transpire for over two years) a very curious character indeed, a respectable Austrian photographer who, at night, went burgling accompanied by his son and who had killed his first French policeman eight years before.

The only note I have for April also concerns a policeman, superannuated but still under contract, the oldest of a drunken *ménage à trois* in outer Montparnasse, beaten and kicked to death, on Sunday the 2nd, by their common mistress's 'adopted son'. On May 3rd, at Mériel, it was the older man who shot his ex-mistress and her young lover when they broke into his house, as he had been waiting for them to do for four years past. On the 16th, in a scene reminiscent of Victor Hugo's *Claude Gueux,* a long-term prisoner killed a warder at Nîmes with a pair of scissors. On the

3 Robert Avril, wandering rapist.

4 Jacques Algarron and Denise Labbé arriving at court in Blois.

last day of the month, an old lady who lived alone near Nantes was battered senseless and robbed by her great-nephew, who, by the time of her discovery and death in hospital, had disappeared, leaving what was taken to be a suicide note. By then it was June, and June 1967 was something of a *mensis mirabilis* in French criminal history. Three murders (one of them twofold) committed that month were to reverberate, are still reverberating.

ARMAND ROHART had been mayor of Peuplingues for the past twenty-two years. At twenty-five, in 1945, he had been the youngest mayor in France. A few miles inland and south-west of Calais, Peuplingues is a village of between four and five hundred inhabitants. Armand Rohart farmed about three hundred acres. That is not a big farm in England, but in the Pas de Calais it was enough to make him the squire. His farmhouse was nobly called *La Bien Bâtie*. His wife came from not far away and was called Jacqueline. They had four children, young Armand and Marie-Françoise, in their late teens, and twins aged seven. Gentle, retiring and devout (*douce,* somewhat *effacée* and *pieuse,* regular in her attendance at church but not annoyingly *dévote,* not at all a church hen), Jacqueline Rohart, *née* Boidin, was universally liked. In general, M. Rohart was admired and respected. He was a capable administrator, attentive to the requirements of his commune at departmental and, if necessary, governmental level. He was a good farmer, though latterly, not with everyone's approval and not with immediately remunerative effect, he had turned land over from wheat and sugar-beet to apples and strawberries, as a result of which he owed (this was not generally known, though perhaps shrewdly suspected) almost half a million francs to what we might think of as a county district agricultural authority.

One of those who did not like Armand Rohart was the octogenarian parish priest, Father Fenet. This was no doubt in part due to a womanising which seems mainly to have taken the form of Rohart's exercising a *droit de seigneur* or *cuissage* on his farm girls. To one of these, Odile Wissocq, daughter of his gamekeeper, who was also *garde champêtre* or *garde forestier* to the small municipality, the squire's attachment was more than casual, though he neither acknowledged nor supported the illegitimate child she had borne him. The previous year, relations between the

D

two appear to have ceased, and Odile living in Calais, proposed to marry a young man she had met on holiday in Corsica.

A curious figure in the village was an elderly former soldier in the Foreign Legion, a man of Persian origin but known as 'the Turk'. His real name was Jacob Kerbahay or Karl Jacob. For the past twenty years, he had lived in a wooden bungalow on Rohart's land. He was short, swarthy, thick-set, thick-nosed, and he dyed his hair. He had won medals, and he lived on his Army pension, augmented by occasional work as a joiner. Some years before, he had served a prison sentence for violence against a woman then living with him. Though some worried about his interest in schoolchildren, the Turk was not an unpopular figure in Peuplingues. Both the squire and the village doctor frequented him. He possessed a miniature tape-recorder.

On May 23rd, 1967, Armand Rohart took out an insurance policy under which, in the event of his or his wife's death, the survivor would receive half a million francs, a million if it was death by accident. Understandably, the premium was high. On June 8th, the secretary of the regional agricultural board, whose name was Albert Calais, wrote to M. Rohart, pressing for repayment of the 400,000 francs loaned to him for improvements on his land. On the afternoon of the 9th, he and his wife drove to Escalles, the nearest village on the coast, presumably walking the half-mile of cliff path down to the beach and some way along the beach. It was a fine afternoon, though with some cloud and a little wind. The wind would hardly be felt at the foot of cliffs on a beach facing north-west, though perhaps there would be small breakers.

Between nine and ten o'clock that evening, a motor horn sounded insistently outside the house of the mayor of Escalles. The mayor of Escalles and his evening guest went out and in the twilight discovered the mayor of Peuplingues slumped across the front seats of his car, in bathing trunks but with a rug about him. The guest, who had done some first-aid, pulled back an eyelid and found the effect unconvincing. The two, however, left messages and drove Armand Rohart to the big central hospital in Lille, where also, pending encephalography, a simulated coma was suspected but the patient, no doubt nevertheless suffering from severe shock, kept in for the night under observation. As Mme Rohart was not at home, a search was instituted for her, and at four o'clock in the morning her body, in a two-piece bathing costume and draped with seaweed, was found near the water's edge on the beach at Escalles. There were facial injuries, including a broken nose.

Later that morning, Rohart was sufficiently recovered to tell his story and leave hospital. Hand in hand, he said, though neither could swim, he and Mme Rohart had walked into the water almost up to their chins. A wave had knocked her over, or she had stepped into a sudden depression, and he had lost her. He had gone under and seized her hair, but her flailing arms had knocked him away. At his last gasp, he had crawled up the beach on hands and knees, collapsed and, recovering consciousness briefly in the evening, found his car and contrived, automatically, to drive it to his friend's house, where again he had collapsed. This story, however, was inconsistent with the result of tests carried out on him in hospital at Lille or with the findings at his wife's autopsy. There were traces of barbituric acid in his blood. The scratches on his body did not suggest arms flailing at random but a conscious struggle. There was no water in Mme Rohart's lungs. There was dried blood on her face, so that those injuries had been inflicted before death. Neither that nor a lacquer spray applied the previous morning by a hairdresser in Calais had been washed away, so that she could not have remained immersed long enough for the tide to have returned her body to the beach. It would not, in any case, said fishermen, have washed her up at that point. Her body would have been borne by the current towards Calais.

A further odd circumstance was that, in her bloodstream, there was a fair concentration of alcohol, though everyone said she did not drink. At the time, young Armand was staying with relatives. When his mother's death was reported to him, his first reaction was to say, to a lieutenant of *gendarmerie*, that his father must have killed her (this was corroborated). Then followed what was to give the case its special *cachet*. On the 14th, while the sorrowing husband attended his wife's funeral, the Persian ex-legionary took his tape-recorder to the police and played back to them the recording of a conversation between himself and Armand Rohart. Later that afternoon, the mayor of Peuplingues was arrested and charged with the murder of his wife.

On the Turk's tape, the two voices were to be heard discussing ways to kill Mme Rohart without discovery. The Turk suggested divorce, but Rohart's voice said that that would upset the children, who would quickly recover from the death of their mother in what appeared to be an accident. The method he favoured was smearing a needle or drawing pin with the arrow-poison curare and placing it under the fabric of the driving seat of Jacqueline's car in such a position that she would be bound to sit on it while driving and would then crash the car. There had been further talk, said Kerbahay, of him going to Turkey, where the plant does not grow, to get curare. That the squire's conversation had been running along those lines he, the ex-legionary, had, he said, reported to several people, including the doctor, who had disbelieved him. In the end, he had made the recording to cover himself, fearing that Rohart might execute his 'perfect crime' in such a way as to pin it on him. Rohart's apparent motive for wanting to get rid of his wife had been to be free to marry Odile Wissocq.

JEAN-LAURENT OLIVIER, a young man of twenty-three, owned and farmed rather more than a hundred and fifty acres in the neighbourhood of Château Thierry, a hundred miles south-east of Calais, fifty east-north-east of Paris, in Champagne. An orphanage boy, he had come into possession of the land through contracting a shotgun marriage with the daughter of its previous owner, his employer. The date of Armand Rohart's arrest was a Wednesday, the 17th June, a Saturday. That day, neighbours of Olivier's, the Demarles, were moving, having been turfed off the land they leased by its owner. Too young to help with the move, their children, Lucien and Pierrette, just ten and rising eleven, were sent on an errand to a woman neighbour but otherwise left to their own devices. In mid-afternoon, some distance from what was still home, they were sitting under an apple-tree, eating the wild strawberries they had gathered in the woods. Nearby, with a tractor, Olivier was spreading manure on a field some three hundred yards from where he lived.

On Sunday morning, the children were found in the woods, the boy strangled, the girl raped and strangled simultaneously (presumably, a very little blood, with further indications known to pathologists but not to me). Olivier had assiduously joined in the search, had accommodated the Demarle parents during the night in a barn and, at first light, invited them into the house for coffee. He spoke of having seen a blue Renault 4CV stopped in the road. Other first statements contradicted his. There was a man who would have seen the blue Renault, but had not. Mme Olivier had heard the tractor stop and start up again, whereas her husband said he had worked without break. The rules of the French *garde à vue* seem not too dissimilar from our own. The police may hold a man for questioning for twenty-four hours, which a magistrate may extend to forty-eight. Within the extended period, the police got enough to bring charges.

It was at first a false confession. There had, said Olivier, been an accident. The boy had fallen in front of the tractor, one wheel of which had gone over his neck. In a panic, he had dragged the body into the woods, then caught Pierrette and strangled her as a *témoin gênant*, afterwards returning and raping her in order to disguise the crime as that of a *sadique*. This story would not do. Apart from the pathologists' point already mentioned, there was no blood on the tractor wheels. Already in custody and charged, Olivier changed his story. In order to have sexual relations with Pierrette, he had first strangled Lucien.

BETWEEN THE wars, the big shots of the Marseilles underworld had been Carbone and Spirito. The Guérini brothers, while acquiring night-clubs and influence, had not directly challenged their elders, who were protected by the political boss, Sabiani. During the Occupation, these three had collaborated, while the Guérinis had resisted. That had left them in clover at the Liberation, under Gaston Deferre. It may be remembered that in 1965 one Robert Blémant, policeman turned gangster, was shot dead at the wheel of his Mercedes and that rumour made the Guérinis responsible. On June 23rd, 1967, Antoine Guérini, the oldest and most powerful and popular of the brothers, accompanied by his son Félix and sitting at the wheel of his dark blue Mercedes-Benz, was filling up at a small garage on the outskirts of Marseilles, when a motor-cycle, bearing two masked men, pulled up alongside but kept its engine running. The man on the pillion held two revolvers, which he carefully emptied into Antoine Guérini. Then the pair drove off at speed. Rumour had it that they had been friends of Blémant's, but they were never traced.

This episode was therefore to have no direct juridical consequences. Nor, indeed, was there to be any directly ensuing *règlement de comptes*, which from a Corsican point of view was highly unsatisfactory. Remoter consequences were to be provoked by two foolish young men, one a Spaniard, one Armenian. At the news of Antoine Guérini's death, the flag was lowered to half-mast over the town hall at Calenzana, his birthplace. His body was taken there for burial, with a tremendous procession and flowers. While these solemnities were being observed, Claude Mandroyan and his Spanish friend broke into the mainland villa near Marseilles and stole the widow's jewels, which of course no receiver would touch. With his share of the loot, the Spaniard made tracks home. Mandroyan was advised that the best thing he could do was negotiate the return of the jewels with the late Antoine's brother, Barthélemy or Mémé Guérini, whose own interests had been centred on Aix but who would now effectively run the whole empire. Meetings were arranged. The jewels were restored.

This story, however, will take us into July, and I had better here first note three less reverberant incidents of June. A slave worker in Germany during the war, Romain Guinot had, at the Liberation, been granted a 100 per cent disability pension and a job as supervisor of a public garden in Orly, with a uniform and a revolver. Popular with the residents, he was a fiend at home. On June 15th, 1967, while he was cleaning a shotgun and uttering threats, his wife shot him three times with the municipal pistol. His last reaction seems to have shown a certain nobility.

'There,' said Mme Guinot, 'you won't hurt anybody again.'

'Don't call the police,' said her dying husband. 'Give me the gun. I'll say it was an accident.'

All situations which lead to murder are perhaps equally interesting. As a case, this one is notable for its treatment at law, quite unthinkable in the United Kingdom. It was to come up for hearing at the Central Criminal Court in Paris not much less than three years later, when Mme Guinot clearly had little to fear. After a fortnight in prison, she was to spend the whole intervening period at home with her children en liberté provisoire, not at all the same thing as on bail, for the British idea of bail, as temporary release against a monetary deposit, a caution, has only very recently come into use in France.

That piece of petty treason took place on a Sunday, the day after Armand Rohart was arrested. On the day of Antoine Guérini's death, police knocked on the door of a room on the fifth floor of the Helder Hotel in Paris, where they had reason to believe that a one-eyed man called Fourcat, an escaped convict, was hiding under the name of Dutto. A man's voice from inside asked them to wait a moment, but when they broke in nobody was there. The lock having been replaced, the room was occupied on the 25th by an American girl, Sandra Rowans, eighteen, whose parents had booked in the previous day and occupied a room two floors down. After eating out by herself at a Chinese restaurant, Sandra returned to the hotel and asked for her breakfast to be brought up to that room at eight o'clock in the morning.

The chambermaid found the door locked, apparently from inside. When it was opened with a master key, Sandra Rowans was found dead on the bed, strangled with her bra. A safety razor, uncleaned of soap and black whiskers, lay in the hand-basin, and a man's dirty shirt was found screwed up behind the bed. Only very briefly did it remain a locked-room mystery. Off the room was a cubby-hole giving access to the plumbing, and for somewhat over two days Fourcat had lurked there. This case was to be three and a half years before it came up for public hearing. The backlog of serious criminal cases in Paris was clearly becoming unmanageable.

July began with the body of a casual labourer fished out of the Seine at Corbeil-Essonnes. On Sunday the 16th, at a country fair not far away, in a row between two carloads of young louts, one, with an Arab name, in a stolen car, picked up a .22 rifle and shot another, who had a German name, through the head. The following Saturday, on the headland overlooking La Ciotat, the body, evidently tortured, its legs crushed, bullet-riddled, of Claude Mandroyan was found. Among those arrested were Mémé Guérini and his brother Pascal. At Soissons, in the small hours of Sunday morning, Jean-Laurent Olivier tried to hang himself in his cell but was cut down in time. On the 27th, at Corbeil-Essonnes, a joiner reported the theft of his wallet as he lay on the banks of the Seine sleeping off heavy midday drinking with a ragged pair of casual acquaintances.

These were Dédé and Chouchou, *clochards* who lived in a hut of branches in nearby woods. The body fished out of the Seine on the 1st of the month might also, it was thought, have been dumped there by them. They had of course 'real' names, respectively René Dubois and Léontine Brochard. Five years before, the man, a former legionary, had served eighteen months for assaulting a pea-picker, robbing him and pitching him in the Essonne, from which the shock of cold water had saved him. For Dédé's method was to get these seasonal workers drunk, lay them out with a rabbit punch (or, as we now prefer to say, karate chop) on the back of the neck, rob them and tip them in. Only the intercession of the gentle Chouchou had saved the joiner (who, after all, was asleep). During the past five years, eight bodies of casual labourers had been found in the Seine or Essonne in the neighbourhood, always in late June or in July. One by one, during the next few months, Dédé and Chouchou would remember them. Tatave, Jojo, the Breton, a North African. It would make a nice film.

The sex war in August produced at any rate five fatal female casualities, two wives, a mother-in-law, a middle-aged benefactress, a prostitute brought in off the streets by the André Pauletto, of Marseilles, of whom we have heard before, stabbing the woman in bed, taking an overdose of sleeping pills and lying down beside her, saying, when brought back to life, 'I loved her too much. I killed her.' This time, he was not to get off so lightly (with four years). The wives both lived in the suburbs of Paris. Mme Large and her husband both worked as chemists for the metropolitan water board. They were in their middle thirties. He did the housework and was very small. Mme Tourneur was fifteen years younger than her husband, who was in his late sixties. He drank. He shot his wife with a 7.65 revolver. Mme Large hit her husband with a bronze ornament, a reproduction of the famous Discabolus. He, packed for camping, took from his rucksack the mallet he carried for knocking in tent-pegs. Then he climbed out of the window and daringly descended, floor by floor, to the car park, where the police were already waiting for him. From details which, somewhat less than two years later, were to come out in court, it seems likely enough that Maurice Large might truly have claimed to have loved his wife too much and in the end to have hammered her senseless and finished her off by strangling for that reason.

Maurice Lazimi was a cynical little brute. He was twenty, his patroness forty-eight, a former cabaret dancer, Alice Bitoun. On prolonged sick leave from the Army, he offered to repaint her studio. This also was in Paris, at Popincourt. He stole cheques and successfully cashed one, but was told that Mme Bitoun's account did not cover the next one. When she discovered the theft and bawled him out, he was doing repairs in the kitchen and had a hammer. He cut up the body, packed the pieces into two suitcases and left them in the automatic left-luggage office at the Gare de

Lyon. He dropped the head in a dustbin, and it duly went to the municipal rubbish disposal plant. That month's mother-in-law lived in Lyons. So did Roger Volet, who blamed his wife's family for the fact that she had left him. On a visit to demand her address, he took a gun with him but left it in the car, fatally knifed mother-in-law and her brother, wounded father-in-law and fled.

I have nothing in France for September, though one note tells me that a French hero of the Anglo-Saxon young, Régis Debray, was brought to trial in Bolivia, another that the progressive mayor of New York that month cut the penalties for prostitution, with what effect we might have guessed. In October, a new châteaux gang carried out a spectacular theft of priceless old furniture. In prison, the butcher's boy, Jean-Marie Deveaux, cut his wrists deeply enough to sever a tendon. The Jesuit Fr Boyer was still working for a retrial, and the notion that a miscarriage of justice had occurred was gaining ground. There would soon be a bandwagon for journalists to jump on. Armand Rohart and Pascal Guérini had both booked René Floriot for their eventual defence, in the latter's case at a trial which would take place not at Aix but in Paris.

For the rest, both that month and the next and indeed somewhat the rest of the year seem to have been dominated by parricide and its obverse, the murder of children and juveniles. It was in the jurisdiction of Nancy that, in the early morning of October 10th, a young waster, André Vegnaduzzi, murdered both his parents with a flat-iron and several other instruments, then robbed them, wiped off his fingerprints and set out for Strasbourg, where he was arrested. His parents had opposed his marriage to a girl too good for him. It was in remote Var that, two days later, Jeanne Gandolfe, twelve, was found raped and strangled in a thicket near her parents' farm. Her father and his four brothers gave the *gendarmerie* no help but armed themselves and swore to find and deal with the murderer themselves. As was only to be discovered a year later, they were in fact bandits, who specialised in villas. They did not find little Jeanne's murderer. Nor was the murderer ever to be found of Charles Vassialadis, fifteen, who had run away from his home in Paris and was found smothered in woods near Versailles on the 18th. November's parricide shot his father while the latter slept drunkenly at midday in his room. This was at Courville, near Chartres. The father had been a grocer. The son had been prevented from pursuing his studies.

December's mother-in-law had seen her daughter deserted for a rich mistress in Montmorency. Late one evening, telephoning the son-in-law, Yves Le Goff, twenty-one, she got the mistress and asked her whether she had ever thought of paying her gigolo's debts. This last took a shotgun and his mistress's car, drove round to his mother-in-law's and, when she opened the door to him, shot her twice with fatal effect. With a mallet and for their money, a young farmer murdered an old couple among his neighbours in Touraine. Near Metz, a young woman helped her older lover to kill her husband and hide the corpse, for three months successfully. The month had been marked by the last but one guillotining to date, that of a child-murderer, Günther Volz, whose *recours en grâce* M. de Gaulle would not sign. It had been marked also by two murders of young children, memorable for quite different reasons.

IN CONFORMITY with French law, the surname of François X. has not been published, though no doubt it is widely known in Versailles. His parents were separated, and this boy of fifteen lived with his mother and a sister, Martine, three years older than himself, in the Avenue du Maréchal Douglas Haig, in a house backing on to woods, the Bois de Fausse Repose. Along the road lived the Malliarts, who had a boy of seven, Emmanuel, a fair-haired boy, a pupil at the St Jean de Béthune junior school, whereas François was a *lycéen* in the *troisième*. M. Malliart was a civil servant, at the Ministry of Defence. Though a cheerful boy, the apple of his eye suffered from asthma and was no doubt somewhat cosseted. François envied him.

On December 3rd, 1967, François occupied his Sunday afternoon by cutting words, letters and numerals out of boys' magazines and pasting them on a sheet of paper so as to compose a ransom demand for two million old francs, twenty thousand new. At noon next day, he met Emmanuel Malliart at the junior-school gate and played uproariously with the delighted younger boy, even, it seems, pushing him along in an old pram and calling out, 'Any old iron? . . . Rags, bottles, jam-jars. . . .' At any rate, he got the child into his own home, took him down to the cellar and opened his skull with what may have been the handle of the spade he was to use, later in the day, to dig a shallow grave in the woods behind the house. Through the Malliarts' letter-box he had meanwhile dropped his ransom note with, for proof that it was serious, one of the child's exercise books and two monogrammed handkerchiefs. That evening, he started telephoning, wanting the money to be deposited first in one place, then, doubled, in another. Women newspaper readers hung on the event. Mme Malliart broadcast an appeal. The Minister of Justice ordered the police to lay off for twenty-four hours while a Capuchin abbot and the leader of the Versailles bar association conducted negotiations. On Saturday, in the evening, his room and the cellar of his mother's house having been searched, François X. was arrested and remanded in custody in the juvenile wing at Fresnes.

At Châlons-sur-Marne, the day before François's arrest, a girl aged twelve, Marie-Claude Gervais had failed to return home from school, and that evening her satchel had been found ten miles downstream in the branch of the Marne channelled to feed a hydro-electric plant at Condé. On Sunday, this channel was drained and her body found. There were indications of attempted rape, and the skull had been cracked on both sides, it was uncertain how. Not until five weeks later, on January 18th, 1968, was a Polish bricklayer Joseph Kaczmarczyk, arrested. An earlier trail had led nowhere. Kaczmarczyk lived near and knew the Gervais family, and he had given Marie-Claude lifts before when taking his own son and her brother to school. He was in the habit of fishing in the arm of the Marne where the body had been found, and, as all Poles are supposed to be, he was moody. On the relevant evening, though commonly punctual, he had missed an appointment with a man who had a job for him.

The two dreadful child-murders had disputed space in the newspapers, and, as we shall see, a mood induced by the one had already affected evidence given with regard to the other. It had been a bad year for child-murder in the United Kingdom, too. Whereas in 1969 and 1970 there were to be less than half that number, in 1967 there were over thirty cases, less than half the victims (this is very unusual) being girls. Suspected relatives committed suicide in no fewer than eighteen cases, but even this is a smaller proportion of suicides among suspects than the nine for thirteen victims two years later. These facts, as I write, have just been revived by a newspaper in connection with the fourth little English girl to have accepted sweets from a stranger in 1971 with fatal effect.

Among new French murders in early 1968, two at least, one of two women in Nice, one of a saintly doctor, a cancer specialist, in Marseilles, both the work of young men, one a German, were unusual and interesting enough, but I shall, if I may, somewhat ignore them, as well as other criminal facts of the time, and here record only the reconstruction, in early February, of the movements, two months before, of François, fifteen, and his younger victim. The parked cars were crusted with snow. The sky was heavily overcast, and a vicious wind sneaked along the Avenue du Maréchal Douglas Haig. The party (police, lawyers, even journalists) had to nose round the young murderer's home (bedroom, cellar and so on), and, as M. Malliart would be with them, François's mother absented herself. His sister was there, Martine. Her eyes and M. Malliart's met, but the two did not speak. She and her brother did. He said, 'Don't cry, little sister!' He shivered a little, but himself did not cry. To the police he had said: 'I wanted to get myself sentenced to death, because I was miserable but not brave enough to kill myself.' In Châlons-sur-Marne, Mme Kaczmarczyk started divorce proceedings against her husband in prison at Rheims.

8 | THE TRIAL OF JOSEPH K.

PARIS ALWAYS had the best riots. Those of May 1968 marked the clear emergence of a new criminal class, that of the Western World's countless superfluous undergraduates. Our own welfare kids had done a fair amount of marching this way and that and shouting 'Fascist!' This word they had no doubt picked up from their Left-wing parents, for none of them had been born when fascism ended at least in Western Europe. One kind of seasonal marching had ended when the actress Vanessa Redgrave decided, doubtless on doctor's orders, to stop planting her fair bottom on the cold stones of Trafalgar Square. The French students had heard of Freud and Marx, whose names had bored Britons of my generation to a state verging on hysteria before the war but had somehow skipped Paris, where they had their own anarchist tradition. In Régis Debray, they had a little Che Guevara of their own, and for some reason they had paid more attention than our own young to the government-organised wrecking or cultural revolution in China the previous year.

For the most part, they stopped short of wilful homicide. They inflicted a great deal of grievous bodily harm, using iron bars and cobblestones against a police force limited to tear-gas and pathetically flexible rubber truncheons. Two thousand policemen were injured, several hundred permanently disabled. At least on the routes of marches, public lavatory attendants get a chance to start cleaning up as soon as the procession has passed, while in general Pop fans congregate in the open air, so that the dead grass can afterwards be sprayed. The Paris undergraduates blocked up the drains in theatres and university buildings until the stench became too much even for them. Then they moved out and left it all to the cleaners and decorators.

Even now atavistically respectful of the plumbing, German and Anglo-Saxon undergraduates also occupied fine premises, but in smaller numbers and for shorter periods. From the outset, the

thing had had its international side. Of the three most effective
Parisian juvenile rabble-rousers, one had been a half-Jewish
German educated at an English progressive, co-educational school,
Frensham Heights, so typical a product of the 'thirties. In the
private sector, the northern English part of the United Kingdom
set up that month something of a record for the youthfulness of
its murderesses.

On May 25th, a Mrs June Brown of Newcastle-upon-Tyne was
informed that the body of her son Martin, aged four, had been
found dead in a derelict house. The front door of the house was
locked, but a dear little girl called Mary Bell, aged ten, who
was standing outside, directed Mrs Brown and led the way
through a side door, downstairs to the back, by way of a hole
between two lavatories and again upstairs. They met an ambulance
man coming out with Martin in his arms. Three days later, Mary
came to Mrs Brown's house and asked if she could see Martin.

'No, pet, Martin's dead,' said Mrs Brown.

'I know he's dead,' said Mary. 'I want to see him in his
coffin.'

She was grinning, smiling. Mrs Brown was astonished that such
a young child should want to see a baby dead. Martin Brown's
aunt, Mrs Rita Finlay, had a son, John, aged three. Mary Bell and
a girl called Norma, aged thirteen, used to go round to Mrs
Finlay's house to play with John. They were always, Mrs Finlay
noticed, grinning and asking her such questions as whether she
missed Martin or cried for him and whether he would soon be
coming back from hospital. They laughed like anything.

A hundred miles farther north still, near Aberdeen, a rich
farmer, Maxwell Garvie, a nudist and Scots nationalist, was by
then falling to pieces under a pile of stones in a tunnel close by a
gem of Scottish baronial architecture. For some reason, his disappearance was not to give rise to comment until mid-August.
By that time, in Newcastle-upon-Tyne, Mary and Norma Bell had
evinced further curious behaviour. Another little boy in the same
neighbourhood, Scotswood, had a grown-up stepbrother, who was
courting a girl called Irene Fraser.

To Irene and a friend of hers Mary Bell showed some drawings
she had made and said :

'I know something about Norma that would get her put
away.'

Asked what she meant by this, Mary added :

'I'll not tell you, because you would tell the police.'

The two older girls assured her that they would not, and Mary Bell went on :

'Norma put her hands on Martin Brown's throat and pressed hard, and he just dropped.'

To illustrate what she meant, Mary put her hands on her own throat and did a little half-falling routine. Then she skipped away, dear little thing. The two twenty-year-old, sex-important creatures shrugged, giggled and thought no more about it until Irene's boy-friend's stepbrother, Brian Howe, three, was also found strangled.

That was on July 31st. As the body of Maxwell Garvie had not yet been discovered, we may perhaps here note a piece of international sadness connected, far south of the criminal event, with one of the few murders demonstrably stemming from the May riots in Paris. At the beginning of July, an English girl, Sylvia Collier, went to France to look for a young Frenchman, Yvon Fornari, known to her as Bruno de Kermadec, who, in London with false papers, giving his age as twenty-three whereas in fact it was only sixteen, had gone through a form of marriage with her in January and left her, pregnant, in March. She was twenty. With a friend, Caroline Grice, she made inquiries in Paris and went on to Aix-en-Provence, where she had stayed the previous year. Had she known it, 'Bruno' was in prison in Normandy, with seven others, of whom he, though the youngest, had been ring-leader, the body of the oldest of the band, a man of thirty known as 'Jimmy le Katangais', having been found, shot dead, the day before Sylvia and Caroline left these shores.

Her parents had learnt this, but she did not know it. On July 17th, she received a telegram from her parents, giving no details but telling her to go home at once. That afternoon, Sylvia Collier, who believed herself, though abandoned, to be Mme de Kermadec, went to the railway station and asked when the next train went. A rail car was due to leave for Grenoble in a few minutes. Sylvia left the station and walked along the track. The driver of the rail car will, he says, never forget.

It was 5.35. We had just left Aix station and were doing just under fifty miles an hour. I saw a young woman walking along the track. I pressed the hooter. She turned round. And quite without haste she lay down, placing her head on the left rail. . . .

I saw the smile on her face just as the train was about to run over her.

From the nickname of their victim, the whole band had become known as *les Katangais*. A decidedly pretty Tahitian girl student had joined them, but their first contact with university life had been when, with other young toughs, they moved into the Law School in the Rue d'Assas and, for a few weeks, enjoyed an alternation of policeman-bashing and educated cunt, before transferring themselves to Normandy and there, in the woods of Vernon, living a fantasy *maquis* life, stealing and roasting an occasional sheep. They had decided that 'Jimmy' was a big mouth and dangerous, and Fornari had deputed the second-oldest of them, who had served in the Foreign Legion, to shoot him in the back of his neck with a Luger they had. We ought not to know the name of Yvon Fornari, for, a widower at seventeen, he also was a minor and would have to be treated as such by the courts, but the name came out before his age was discovered.

Near Aberdeen, Maxwell Garvie still lay under a pile of stones in a tunnel. It was not politics but nudism and sexual high-jinks which had brought him to this position, for Brian Tevendale, who had shot him, was also a Scots nationalist, encouraged by Garvie to make love to Mrs Garvie while he occupied himself similarly with a Mrs Birse, a policeman's wife. The policeman had not always been left out. A girl had been found for him when his duties allowed him to join the usual mixed foursome, while a young man called Alan Peters had been engaged in some capacity for the night of the murder.

By the time Maxwell Garvie came, as we may say, to light in mid-August, French policemen were variously concerned with the murders of wives in Mériel and Martigues; of a hospital nurse near Cannes and of one Arab orderly by another in a Paris hospital; of a summer visitor to Corsica by a native whom the visitor had tried to stop beating his wife; of his former *fiancée* by a Breton farmer, a jeweller's daughter in Mâcon by a man yet unknown, a little girl near St Brieuc not, as some said, by her parents. A new law made cockfighting legal where it had an unbroken local tradition. In late August, most of the victims were women, but one woman finally shot a sadistic husband. In Brie, a driver for a cheeseworks, a keen trade unionist, shot one of his older workmates for working too hard, while on the road near Sélestat a hit-and-run priest ran over one of his parishioners, about whose neck hung a medal, given him by the priest, on which was inscribed: IN CASE OF ACCIDENT CALL A PRIEST. A maniac was setting booby-traps in strangers' gardens. He claimed a victim on the 26th. On the 29th, the satisfactory detonation of France's first H-bomb was announced.

September 1st was a Sunday. In the morning, the headmistress of a girl's school in Provence shot her mother and fled, taking a stock of barbiturates with her. In the afternoon, with a flick-knife, a young man in the region west of Paris stabbed his wife to the heart in the course of a quarrel about a saucy photograph he had taken of departing guests. That night in Montmartre, her last client stabbed and robbed a middle-aged prostitute. The next night in Nice, six revolver shots squared a ponce's account in a night-club, the Minnehaha. If the month kept up this brisk pace, the fact was obscured by preliminaries to a remarkable sequence of autumn trials. For the third time, Daniel Hugon, the gangling, bald, short-sighted man with the supplementary Y-chromosome, who had strangled an elderly prostitute three years before, attempted suicide in his cell at the Santé. Two riots, a fortnight apart, were organised in Brive prison with the idea of enabling Noël ('. . . *fais pas le con!*') Marcucci to escape, which he failed, however, on both occasions to do. The cases against them would be heard, respectively in Paris and at Tulle, in early October, as would those against Kaczmarczyk in Rheims and, amusingly, the non-homicidal, predominantly homosexual châteaux gang. One heard in September was that, at Laon, of Jean-Laurent Olivier, the young farmer who, the previous year, had stopped spreading muck on his field just long enough to strangle two children and rape one. His trial opened on the 26th. That day, a pretty woman in Paris shot her handsome husband, an Air France steward, altogether too systematically unfaithful. For some days past, nobody had seen Stefan Markovic, Yugoslav former bodyguard of France's most popular film star, Alain Delon.

THE OLIVIER trial was held *in camera,* though with journalists present on the understanding that they did not reveal scabrous details. In view of its gravity, it was a short trial. The verdict was brought in by one o'clock on the second day, with (need one say?) a death sentence. At first Olivier said he would not appeal, but was later persuaded to do so.

Before dawn on Tuesday, October 1st, the body of Stefan Markovic (not immediately identified) was found on a rubbish dump west of Paris, tied up in a sack inside a plastic mattress cover. As this was in the new department of Yvelines, it became a matter for the magistracy at Versailles. Later that morning, the trial of Barany and Marcucci opened in Tulle. They were a nasty pair, not least in the determination of each to save his head if he could at the other's expense.

Two firearms had been used on the fatal day. The bank messenger had been killed with a MAB 7.65, the policeman (an *adjudant-chef* of *gendarmerie*, in rank therefore equivalent to a W.O. 1 or regimental sergeant-major in the British army) with a service revolver, a P.38. In the railway compartment with the two gangsters when the police appeared was an air-force *adjudant* (W.O. 2 or company-sergeant-major rank) on leave. His evidence against Marcucci was decisive, for he was familiar with that type of weapon, heard Barany's words and saw from which corner the flash came. Dialogue of this kind is on record.

PRESIDENT OF THE COURT. It was you who fired, Marcucci?

MARCUCCI. No, Mr President.

PRESIDENT. So, Barany, it was you?

BARANY. No, Mr President. I fired a shot in the corridor, but not at the sergeant-major. I wanted to frighten him.

PRESIDENT. You admit having called out: 'Noël, don't be a cunt!' If you'd kept the only pistol, Marcucci couldn't have been a cunt! How could he have fired if you had the weapon?

BARANY. I said that without thinking.

PRESIDENT. What! But all this is quite incomprehensible.

FOR BARANY, ME NAUD: I wish Marcucci would at least yield on this point.

PRESIDENT. Oh, Maître, you don't often hear things admitted in court that didn't come out during the preliminary inquiry!

FOR MARCUCCI, ME LABROUSSE. What I should like the witness to tell us is how he could see the flash of a revolver in the corner of the compartment when his eyes were fixed on a man to his left, framed in the doorway.

This was demonstrated, with a court bench for the seat in the carriage and an usher collapsing as required.

On Tuesday night, Corsican gangsters were shooting it out near the Arc de Triomphe in Paris. On Thursday morning, in Rheims, the Kaczmarczyk trial opened. That day, verdicts of guilty were brought in and sentences of death passed on Barany and Marcucci. It was discovered, however, doubtless by Maître Naud, that the first bit of the dialogue above was too much on record. The official report of a court hearing (*procès-verbal*, minutes) is in France by no means a *verbatim* transcript. In particular, admissions or allegations, made in court, which contradict earlier statements may and should be set down, but only on the presiding judge's instructions or at the request of one of the parties, which means in effect prosecutor or defending council. Barany's admission, above, that he had fired a shot in the corridor, which was not in the *dossier,* was entered in his report of the proceedings by the clerk of the court on his own initiative, contrary to Article 379 of the Code of Criminal Procedure. The discovery and the acknowledgement of this fact meant that the findings of that court would inevitably be quashed *pour vice de forme* and a retrial ordered, with penal consequences which at that moment could not be foreseen.

That makes the trial interesting. Adventitious interest, had it been needed, was supplied in the Kaczmarczyk case by the fact that deadly Me Floriot represented the *partie civile* and that leading for the defence was fiery, younger and physically larger Me Isorni. This promised sport. For three years Jacques Isorni had been disbarred, and for twenty he had not been in ordinary criminal practice. First making his name as junior counsel for Marshal Pétain in 1945, he had more recently espoused the cause of the Algerian generals. He was, it need hardly be said, a fanatical anti-Gaullist and had got into serious trouble for allegations made against M. Giscard d'Estaing. As local opinion ran wholly against his client, he faced a difficult task and much initial hostility in Rheims.

The case against Kaczmarczyk seemed a strong one. That he knew Marie-Claude Gervais was evidence in his disfavour, since she had been pestered by a stranger before and would not have got into a stranger's car. Her spectacles had been found on a track off a road he admitted taking on the evening in question. The reason he gave for his outing that evening (to glance at a building site to which there was no immediate reason for him to pay attention) was unconvincing, and times he had given conflicted with those noted by a prospective employer. His own wife would swear that, on returning home, he had washed his shirt and sweater, which she had never previously known him do, and that next morning, although it was freezing, he had washed his car, without her help, which he usually enlisted. Evidence had been taken from a boy who said that he had seen Kaczmarczyk's car, with engine running, outside the cathedral at the relevant time. A girl (this would not have been allowed to be heard in an English court) that he had once shown a similarly depraved appetite in his approach to herself. The Gervais parents, though they knew and had been friendly with the defendant, had been won over by the police to a belief in his guilt.

But it had been five weeks before the Rheims police detectives had turned their attention to Kaczmarczyk, having previously sought in vain to trace a man on a yellow motor-bike. Marie-Claude's spectacles, presumably knocked off in a struggle, had, it seemed, lain all that time on a cart track much used by tractors, in winter weather, and were quite undamaged. The boy had not spoken of seeing a car like it and noting its registration number until a description of Kaczmarczyk's vehicle and number had appeared in a local newspaper, and his father was a policeman's drinking companion. As to the girl, there were very good reasons why her evidence in a case of this kind should not have been taken for submission even to a French court. The evidence of juveniles was indeed to play a large part in the trial, two others being called for the defence, together, at the last moment, with a man who had made statements to the police which they had chosen to disregard. The case against Kaczmarczyk could in fact have been fabricated wholly after it had been decided that, to meet public criticism (inflamed by the Malliart case, in which the Versailles police had shown more promptitude), a culprit had to be found and that the Polish bricklayer would do very well.

In his own account of the proceedings, Isorni admits that his manner at the trial was obstreperous. He complained at the outset that the report of the committal proceedings had been misdated by two days (this had to be admitted) and that two forensic scientists appointed to examine his client's sweater for traces of blood (who had found none) had not been calle One was out of the country, representing it at an international conference. Isorni demanded that the other be called and was given his way by the presiding judge, Councillor Servat. The indictment was read by the clerk of the court. M. Servat examined Kaczmarczyk, who spoke up well for himself. There were interruptions by Me Isorni during this *interrogatoire,* but the fun did not properly start until the evening of the first day's hearing, when police evidence was heard, notably in the person of Superintendent Brisset of the Rheims *police judiciaire* (or C.I.D.), who had been in charge of the investigation. Though indeed he reserved some animosity for the prosecuting *avocat-général,* red-gowned, be-ermined M. Pigny, this policeman and the local superintendent were Isorni's chief villains of the piece, nor did he spare the Rheims police in general, reminding the court that one of its members had been convicted of perjury in a case I have not touched on (an Arab case, in which also Me Floriot had represented the *partie civile*). A petrol-pump attendant from whom Kaczmarczyk said he had bought petrol on the evening in question had not, said Isorni, been seen by the police at all. Brisset denied this. The man, he said, did not remember. He could neither confirm nor deny the defendant's statement. But this fact had not been noted in a police report. At the time of his arrest, Kaczmarczyk had been told that his fingerprints had been found on Marie-Claude's school satchel and had replied that it was not impossible, since he'd more than once taken the child to school. But the fact was that no such fingerprints had been found.

It was also at this evening session that Isorni made his points (brandishing a copy of *L'Union de Reims* for January 25th) about the boy remembering a car number after it had been published (a week after the arrest) and the girl who, a week after that, had recognised from a photograph of Kaczmarczyk shown her by the Châlons police a man who had once molested her. More about Claudine C. was to come out later, but it is worth quoting Isorni's first comments for the sake of the patient interruption and quick come-back with which they and the day's proceedings ended.

FOR THE DEFENCE, MAÎTRE ISORNI. This girl had reported a man catching hold of the carrier of her bicycle on November 29th, 1967. But it isn't until February 2nd, 1968, that she 'recognises' my client. In the meantime, his photograph has appeared in the newspapers. But that isn't all. This urchin once accused her stepfather of tying her up and raping her in the woods hereabout! Now, there was found to be no case against this man : Claudine was discovered to be a sheer fabulist, an immoral liar. And it was on the basis of her story that

Superintendent Palisson wrote in his report: 'The suspect Kaczmarczyk *assaulted* a girl below the age of consent manifestly to assuage an abnormal sexual appetite, at any rate one not checked by the age of the victim, coveted and pursued on a winter evening.' That is the foundation on which the prosecution has ventured to build up its case!

PRESIDENT OF THE COURT, M. SERVAT. Maître, have you any further questions to put to Superintendent Brisset?

ISORNI. No, I won't put any more. If I did, he'd need his lawyer present.

A girl of fourteen was brought to the witnesses' bar and asked whether she confirmed a statement taken from her by the police, stating that Kaczmarczyk had enticed her and another girl into a house under construction. Tongue-tied, she was invited by M. Servat to come and stand by him, when she said that the police had put the words into her mouth and that they were wholly untrue. In the morning, a boy of nine came to the bar. He was the last to have seen Marie-Claude in front of Châlons cathedral on December 8th. He was a neighbour of Kaczmarczyk's.

MAÎTRE ISORNI, *pointing to Kaczmarczyk.* Do you know this gentleman?

THE WITNESS. Yes.

ISORNI. Do you know his car?

WITNESS. Yes.

ISORNI. If he'd been there, in front of the cathedral, in his car, would you have seen him?

WITNESS. Yes.

ISORNI. Did you see him?

WITNESS. No.

As witnesses for the prosecution, the boy who was supposed to have noted the registration number of Kaczmarczyk's car, his father and the policeman to whom the matter had been passed on were called. They had lost the various pieces of paper on which the number had been noted. The Gervais parents, the prospective employer, Kaczmarczyk's wife and his Polish parents appeared. The wife stuck to her story about washing the sweater, but otherwise supported the husband she had effectively nevertheless abandoned, ending her evidence with the firm statement that

Kaczmarczyk was incapable of having done what was alleged against him.

On the third day, Maître Floriot spoke for the *partie civile*, effectively but without the violence we have seen him display against Pauline Dubuisson and Denise Labbé. Before M. Pigny's *réquisitoire*, a last-minute witness, a middle-aged railway worker was allowed. He had seen another car, quite different from Kaczmarczyk's, driving at speed out of Châlons and in it a little girl wearing spectacles and holding a satchel. He had feared that it was a kidnapping, had reported it to the police and been sent packing. Isorni read out statements from two boys who had seen the same car. Their evidence also had been suppressed by Superintendent Brisset of the Rheims police. The *avocat-général*, M. Pigny, demanded Kaczmarczyk's head. Isorni rose to speak.

In the volume I list in my bibliography, he reprints the whole of this concluding speech for the defence (let us note here that, since he had called witnesses, he would not have had the last word in a British court). It was masterly. Its exordium was perhaps also a little theatrical. Me Isorni began by reading out passages from Me Floriot's *Les Erreurs Judiciaires* or, as it is called in English (through no fault of the translator), *When Justice Falters* (pages 18-21 and 23-4 of the translation). He then marched across the courtroom and flung the volume down before its author.

> ISORNI. Floriot, you should read it through at least once. You will find it contains some errors of fact. Those are not very grave. They are merely historical errors. . . . Gentlemen of the court, members of the jury, before you today Me Floriot spontaneously added a twelfth chapter to his book. This chapter might be entitled : 'How I Contribute to the Miscarriages of Justice I Denounce'. . . . I shall now demonstrate how, with Me Floriot's help, a miscarriage of justice may be fabricated . . .

This he most brilliantly did. The reader is, I hope, apprised of the elements of the case he was able to make out, and I shall not follow the speech through.

A point of some interest was what Isorni did not quote from Floriot's book. This lists a number of cases in which girls have made false sexual allegations against men, and more than one of these is reminiscent of that of Claudine C. The classic French case is that of the cavalry officer, La Roncière, and his commanding officer's daughter, Marie de Morell, in 1835. I have written about it elsewhere,* and there is a chapter on it in an excellent and widely read recent novel.† Floriot's volume devotes fifteen pages to the case and reverts to it twice. About Claudine C., what Me Isorni now told the court was that the *Procureur de la République* for Châlons-sur-Marne (a kind of local Director of Public Prosecutions, perhaps somewhat more like an American district attorney than any official known in England and Wales or Scotland), responsible for putting in her evidence, was the same who had earlier non-suited her complaint against her stepfather, describing her as a liar and fabulist, devoid of moral sense and in her own life of low repute.

Kaczmarczyk's Christian name being Joseph, Isorni did not fail to compare him with the archetypal Josef K. of Franz Kafka's novel, *The Trial.* This literary reference may not much have affected the jurors or even Councillor Servat and his two assessors, but the day was already won. After forty minutes' deliberation, they returned with an acquittal, to the great joy of the originally hostile public, who cried : 'Long live Joseph Kaczmarczyk!' and crowded around for his counsel's autograph. The triumph was to be incomplete, however. Divorced from his wife, it appears that Kaczmarczyk has returned to live with his parents and that, despite his acquittal, he is locally ostracised, retrospective reasoning having no doubt suggested that insufficient proof is not by any means proof of innocence and that, while planted evidence must be discounted, it may yet have pointed in the right direction. This is cruel reasoning, but it is neither illogical nor unsound and will always be heard when no case has been proved beyond all doubt against an alternative culprit. It is no doubt still heard about the butcher's boy, J-M. Deveaux. It may also be noted that Kaczmarczyk's claim to State compensation has been refused and that, so far without visible effect, Isorni has publicly (privately, no doubt, as well) appealed to Floriot to join him in a demand that the case shall be reopened. Not, that is to say, the case against Kaczmarczyk but the case presented by the murder of Marie-Claude Gervais, twelve. Members both of the police and of the magistracy connected with the case have meanwhile been promoted. An award of 125,000 francs was made in early 1972 by way of compensation to Deveaux.

---

* In *French Crime in the Romantic Age*, London, 1970.
† *The French Lieutenant's Woman*, by John Fowles.

ON OCTOBER 14th, 1968, in Paris, for strangling an elderly prostitute, Daniel Hugon, thirty-two, tall, myopic, moon-faced and prematurely bald, was sentenced to seven years' imprisonment, of which he had already spent three awaiting trial. The XYY chromosome anomaly might indeed, as Dr Lejeune's learned disquisition suggested, constitute a form of diminished responsibility, but hardly led straight to murder and, in any case, could not be cured except by death, which it showed little tendency to hasten. The subject is still one of medico-legal and of purely medical interest. The first British trial for murder of a known XYY case was to take place at Lewes two months after that of Hugon in Paris, a plea of diminished responsibility being accepted on the basis of medical reports which did not refer to the chromosome anomaly. More recently, an article in the *Journal of Criminal Law*, 'Criminology and Police Science' has suggested that its causative association with crime may be wholly mythical. That would be a pity. If crime were found to be due to vagaries of the Y chromosome, we should be left with only female criminality to account for.

9 | HOME THOUGHTS

MEANWHILE, THE forces of law and order in England and Wales with continental deliberation prepared their case against the Kray brothers, whose two expensive trials were to constitute the juridical festival of 1969. On July 3rd, 1968, a Mrs X., a barmaid, had attended an identity parade and picked out John Barrie as Ronald Kray's companion at the time of the shooting of George Cornell in the Blind Beggar. On October 15th, six men appeared at Bow Street magistrates' court on charges connected with the later stabbing of Jack ('the Hat') McVitie, whose body has never been found but is popularly believed to form part of the concrete of the Hammersmith fly-over.

On the 29th, a man in a drugged condition jumped from a hotel window in Leeds and landed on a car in the street below, somewhat breaking his fall but killing the driver. In November, at a two-car bungalow in Derbyshire, blonde housewife Mrs Gail Payne, twenty-six, mother of two small boys and formerly a singer in Manchester, took a hammer to bed and slew her husband, a successful thief and business consultant who beat her regularly twice a week. On November 15th, an engineer in Walsall, Staffordshire, was arrested and charged with the murder of Christine Darby, seven, the previous year. On the 19th, at the Old Bailey, majority verdicts having recently become admissible, a coal merchant, Stephen Jewell, received a life sentence for the shooting, in his car, on June 1st, of Tony Maffia, a very successful criminal indeed. On November 21st, under the somewhat different rules which obtain in Scottish courts, the case of the Aberdeen nudists, wife-swappers and provincial high livers opened before a jury of fifteen.

The verdicts were brought in on December 2nd. There were life sentences for Mrs Garvie and bearded young Brian Tevendale, the characteristic 'not proven' verdict and release for Alan Peters. The policeman's untried wife, Mrs Birse, Tevendale's

122

sister, complained that the neighbours would not speak to her and that Birse had lost his job, but she may have been somewhat consoled for these misfortunes by the extensive publication of her hitherto secret diaries in the *News of the World*. The first extracts appeared on December 9th. Next day, at Newcastle, the two little monsters, Mary Bell and Norma, faced a nervous jury, which heard the evidence of the mother of Martin Brown. On the 13th, at Burnham Beeches, took place one of a dreadful series of murderous attacks on women in Buckinghamshire, of which at any rate the last and worst would turn out to have been the work of a woman. On Christmas Eve, in Basildon, a young man, Brian Rolfe, was hit on the head at home with a bowling-alley skittle, his body being found late that evening in a car on a road in Essex, far from home. Suspicion fell upon his younger wife and her even younger lover, a car fitter.

The year ending with the murder of yet another little girl in Lancashire, Home Office clerks were able to start work on their 1968 criminal statistics. Those published a fortnight later, by Scotland Yard, for London alone, up to and including November, would not venture to single out homicide, for the old category of 'murders known to the police' no longer existed. The Home Office statistics which did eventually appear would be subject to tendentious interpretation but at least show what tiny fraction of even our modest total has been noted above or was ever much offered to the attention of newspaper readers. First provisional figures would show that in 1968 the number of killings investigated as murder by less than three quarters of the police forces of England and Wales was 282, whereas in 1967 the final and complete total was 225, itself the highest figure since the war. Since the last year of operation of the Homicide Act, the number of murders which, under that Act, would have been 'capital' had doubled, while the number of serious crimes involving the use of firearms had multiplied almost fourfold.

NEW YEAR's Day was a Wednesday. At least in south-east England, it was to be bright, dry and yet not at all cold for the time of year. London started notching up its 1969 statistics an hour before sunrise, when a man called Brian Hanmore went in pyjamas to the door of his flat on a sixth floor in Hoxton and was met with a blast in the chest from a sawn-off shotgun. This *règlement de compte* was said to be an episode in a new mini-cab war. Hanmore died at the Metropolitan hospital, Dalston, in his thirtieth year, rather more than an hour after sunrise, when of course, though dark, it was already January 1st on the eastern seaboard of the United States of America, though perhaps not yet in California, where, among bushes in a ravine not far from home, lay the body of the pretty daughter of Hans Habe, novelist and former crime reporter.

At about the cosmic moment, but not the local time, of its discovery, a man in New York State, a meat cutter by profession, burst into a family gathering in a small mountain village and repeatedly discharged a .22 rifle, killing his estranged wife, her sister, her sister's daughter and a boy and wounding eight other people. By then, it was Thursday in the United Kingdom, where for that day my documentation shows no wilful homicide although no doubt the usual twenty or so were killed on the roads.

On Friday morning, a delivery van drove away from the young offenders' institution at Dumfries, Scotland. Clinging to the underside was Peter Campbell, precocious double murderer. The dock of No. 1 court at the Old Bailey was occupied by a large, podgily good-looking young man, Dr Christopher Michael Swan, and his medical secretary, Stephen John Hartford. They were facing drugs charges mainly, but Dr Swan was further accused of soliciting Detective-Sergeant John Vaughan to murder Hartford and three other men. This incitement had taken place at Brixton prison, Swan having been led to believe that the detective-sergeant was a professional killer, procured for him by a departing fellow-prisoner. £10,000 was the sum offered. The interview had been tape-recorded. The tape was not played in court, but extracts from a transcript were read out.

As both Swan and Hartford had pleaded guilty on all charges, their trial should soon have been over, but the Recorder dragged it out, and there, in the dock of No. 1 court at the Old Bailey, wanted for the Kray brothers and their friends, Swan at least was still sitting on Tuesday the following week. That morning, at 3 a.m., at a highly genteel and expensive block of flats in Chislehurst, Kent, a young couple had heard banging and shouting from next door and seen the son of their neighbours in pyjamas cross the road to a telephone kiosk. Long before sunrise, his mother had died as a result of a blow behind the ear with a heavy instrument, his stepfather of stab wounds inflicted by her with a kitchen knife.

As Swan was still there on Thursday, the trial of the Kray twins and sundry others, but not their brother Charles, opened in No. 2 court. Moving to No. 1 the following week, this first Kray case was to last until March 5th. For this first instalment alone, apart from all other expenses, there would have to be met by the public, in the form of 'legal aid' both to the defendants and to the Crown, almost a quarter of a million pounds in barristers' fees. On January 14th, a Tuesday, belatedly captured in Torquay, a Great Train Robber appeared before a court in Aylesbury.

To anyone then in London, any such matter seemed to exist only in the shadow of the Kray trial. And yet by the 18th, this had quite disappeared from the national dailies and London evening papers. From across the Channel we heard that an arrest had been made in connection with the Markovic murder, that of a Corsican gangster called Marcantoni. Almost three years later, no further evident progress would have been made. Every now and then during that time, our newspapers could be counted on for an occasional photograph of the extremely photogenic Delons and their small boy or even of M. and Mme Pompidou, cheerfully harassed by Maître Isorni acting on behalf of Marcantoni. At the end of the month, the Krays were again in the papers for a while, Ronald Kray having named, as among his friends, Lords Boothby and Effingham and such show-business personalities as Judy Garland and Sophie Tucker, while Reginald was allowed to read to the court a poem he had written in prison to a little boy called Connie.

February was soon violent. On the night of Sunday, the 2nd, a schoolmaster in Beaconsfield, Bucks, heard screams across the road and found, barefoot, with a coat over her nightdress, outside the dairy where she worked and over which she had a flat, a girl called Sylvia Merritt, weltering in blood from stab wounds in back and throat. Signs in a garage at the back suggested that she had disturbed a fire-raiser. Not to reappear for three months, this matter abruptly disappeared from the news after two days, with the report that a woman had been seen running away. From this I deduce that by Tuesday evening the matter was already *sub judice*, and indeed it seems that the woman, Marlene Rolfe, had been arrested very shortly after the crime. It is perhaps worth noting that it would have been at just this point that French journalists would have got to work, unimpeded by contempt of court.

It is hardly possible to consider crime these past few years without some attention to the 'hijacking' of aeroplanes (new, for obvious reasons) and kidnapping both for the old and for new forms of ransom. Almost as characteristic of the period and not wholly dissimilar from either aerial piracy or ground-level kidnapping has been the open holding of a hostage against police siege. Some twelve hours of cosmic time after the savage murder of Sylvia Merritt, though by then it was Tuesday in Australia, police with tear-gas and shotguns rushed a house in Melbourne where a man held his former girl-friend hostage. He shot her, as he had said he would. For the past twenty-four hours at Cestas in the hinterland of Bordeaux, a man had settled down to what would turn out to be a fortnight's siege with his three children as hostages, promising to give them up only if the police would bring him his estranged wife so that he could kill her.

This demand seeming unreasonable, the *gendarmerie* sat round to wait. They did not propose to behave like the impetuous police of Melbourne, but rather like those in Shropshire, five months before, who, by a blend of persuasion, appeal and trickery, had resolved a similar situation without more bloodshed than is involved in wounding a fireman. The Cestas *forcené* (the word, meaning, broadly, a maniac, was coming exclusively to denote either this kind of person or, less frequently, one who ran amok in the street) had a rifle with telescopic sights. He killed a policeman who approached too close. This fact was kept from him. Nothing was said about it over the loud-hailer, and it was known that the batteries of his transistor had given out. The eldest child, a girl, got away by night. Great courage was shown by a priest, a doctor and the major of *gendarmerie*, who knew his man personally. Unfortunately, someone who got to the house under a white flag took not only milk and food but batteries for the transistor. The *forcené* was then able to hear broadcast appeals, but also to learn that he had already made himself liable to murder charges.

Meanwhile, at Stafford assizes, the case against Raymond Morris, rapist and child-murderer, opened on the 10th, counsel for the Crown stating his belief that the man's wife, who at first had told lies to shield him, would consent to appear in evidence against him. On the 11th, a Labour minister was demanding the removal from his Lancashire constituency of the eleven-year-old double murderess (or, rather, despite the tender years of her victims, manslaughteress), Mary Bell, who had been found a place at Newton-le-Willows approved school. On the 12th, Mrs Morris did appear and, defiant of one half of a schizophrenic public opinion, may be thought to have ensured that her husband would not return home for at least ten years (even supposing that his fellow-prisoners did not get him, 'as a cat will always get a canary'). On Sunday the 16th, in the darkness of a North London cinema, as mysteriously as in the smarter New York theatre setting of Ellery Queen's first novel, recently reprinted, and with some other of its attendant circumstances, a man was fatally stabbed.

That Sunday evening also, orders were sent from Bordeaux to the major of *gendarmerie* at Cestas. He announced them by loud-hailer.

> Fourquet, since you persist in neither giving up your children nor letting them go, tomorrow I shall be obliged to storm the house. I have a magistrate's warrant. I must carry it out.

At 8.05 next morning, listeners to France Inter heard the voice of a reporter at a microphone concealed from the house by trees.

> We here are sure that the outcome won't be long. The major has repeated his instructions over a loud-hailer directed at the little white house whose red shutters have remained closed these two weeks. . . . Wait a moment. Something certainly very serious is happening at this moment. Through my field glasses I can see armed men moving forward. We see a big red glow, several red glows, no doubt they are tear-gas grenades, those are warning shots you can hear. I know that the major's great preoccupation is to save the children. It is growing lighter, we can see better now. I can see policemen battering down the door. And there, yes, they're into the house. A vehicle is charging forward at full speed. It's an ambulance, it stops. They're bringing out somebody on a stretcher, I think it's Fourquet. A second ambulance has pulled up at the farm. Two more stretchers, that must be the children, Francis and Aline. The ambulances pass in front of us at full speed, in the direction of Bordeaux. I'll come back to you in a few moments. . . .

Ça y est, as the reporter said. The father had shot his two children and himself. Major Cardeilhac was in tears. France raged, and the sound reached London with the evening papers.

What he may have read in Washington there was no opportunity to ask him, but next day a black *forcené* barricaded
himself in a house there with two women and a boy. The police
did not sit that one out long, but did not even approach the
house until shots within had been reported and did not give
the assault until two of their own men had been wounded. It may
even have been that the two women had already been shot. The
assault started a fire. The man killed himself. The boy was got
out alive.

London had two deaths by shooting on Thursday, one of a
prosperous Maltese by another less prosperous, one of a jeweller
by the firearm-bearing member of a raiding gang of three otherwise equipped only with coshes. On Saturday, the Home Secretary,
Mr Callaghan, offered us a selection from the forthcoming
criminal statistics. It was designed to soothe and, let us hope, did.
That it was tendentious and disingenuous would soon be pointed
out, but still it was no doubt true that the streets of London were
safer to walk through than some, if not, as he claimed, those of any
other capital in the world.

It was not, after all, in London or in a street but in a hotel
bedroom at Worthing on the coast that, five days later, an
eccentric old creature of eighty-eight was battered to death. Along
the sea front, she had long been pointed out as 'the painted lady'
and, doubtless with the intention of keeping abreast with youth
and the modern world, had been accustomed to take her morning
coffee at a place mainly frequented by local specimens of the
former, who may not have liked her smiling old eye upon their
quaint rituals, but may also have thought her better-off than she
was.

It was in a street on the outskirts of Birmingham that, towards
noon on Sunday, an elderly man on his way to the local pub was
gunned down from a light-coloured car, not fatally. The first
instalment of the Kray trials ended on Wednesday, March 5th.
The reader may care to be reminded that this, the longer, had
been concerned with the deaths of George Cornell and Jack ('the
Hat') McVitie, not yet with that of Frank Mitchell 'the mad
axe-man', whose turn would come in mid-April, with a modified
cast of principals and accomplices in the dock. For their activities
on the two occasions, the twins were both awarded life sentences
with the recommendation that each should in fact serve not less
than thirty years. Their elder brother, Charles Kray, was given

5 Guy Desnoyers, former curé d'Uruffe, at the scene of the crime.

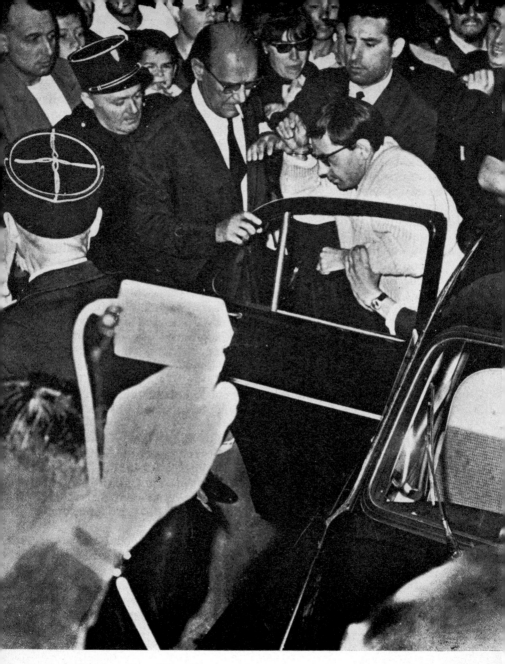

6 Lucien Léger, brought to Versailles.

ten years, and sentences ranging from two to twenty years were passed on seven other men.

For the murder of two children and the rape of one, Jean-Laurent Olivier was guillotined at first light on March 11th, a Tuesday. I saw no reference to this in English papers, which that week featured the hunt for a young man called Paul Beecham, who, it appeared, had shot, with a rifle, his parents and maternal grandparents in a riverside bungalow at Tewkesbury, Gloucestershire. To date, mid-March 1972, the guillotine has not been used again. At a second trial, Barany and Marcucci were indeed once more sentenced to death (as one or two others have been since), but they were to be saved by the presidential elections. It has been traditional for new Presidents of the Republic to begin with an act of clemency, but it soon began to appear that M. Pompidou was opposed to capital punishment, and, until the autumn of 1971, the general opinion in France seemed to be that Olivier's head would turn out to have been the last to fall.

In France, opposition to capital punishment has tended to thrive at a more popular level than in the United Kingdom, where an opinion poll published that March showed that an average majority of somewhat less than 70 per cent was in favour of the death penalty for one or another type of murder (the single question had not been put), a minority only for *crime passionnel*, presented as 'murder over a love affair'. For child-murder the majority was 83 per cent (in favour therefore of capital punishment for *something*). Majorities of up to eight out of ten were also in favour of corporal punishment not only for attacks on children, rape and robbery with violence but also for vandalism. They favoured specifically the birch, just as more were in favour of hanging than of any alternative mode of capital execution. Seventeen per cent thought hanging was still in force, while 8 per cent didn't know, in this respect women being better informed than men.

A decidedly smaller number of either sex would, I imagine, know specifically that capital punishment in the United Kingdom had been suspended for a period of five years due to end in sixteen months' time, when there might no longer be a Labour government to prevent the Homicide Act then automatically coming back into force, fewer still, outside the Labour Party executive, who knew that their present government planned to stop this happening. One who presumably knew or suspected this

E

was a Conservative M.P., Mr Duncan Sandys, who was collecting
signatures to a petition for the immediate restoration of hanging.
A curious sidelight on signature-collecting was cast later in the
month by a trial at Manchester assizes, when the last little girl to
be murdered in Lancashire was proved to have been battered to
death with a hammer by a workmate of the father of Lesley Ann
Downey, one of the victims of Brady and Hindley. At the time of
the Moors murder trials, this man, Harold Green, had gone round
collecting signatures to a petition of his own to the same effect as
Mr Sandys's.

THE NEW British murders, that late March, were those of three
old women in various parts of London, strangled in Stepney and
Tottenham, battered and in a trunk in a derelict house near where
I live, in North Kensington, and that of a red-haired schoolgirl
found raped, strangled and trussed in a mini-car on the M1
motorway, in connection with which a man called Kenneth Pike
was being sought. In April, an old woman who kept a sweet-shop
was strangled in Bethnal Green, where also a youth was killed with
a home-made spear. An old woman was battered to death in
Sutton Coldfield. Younger women were, respectively, strangled,
shot, stabbed, in Nottinghamshire, at Taunton, at Hitchin, and
pitched in the Medway, it was thought from a German coaster.
A number of little girls were assaulted in Hampshire, one battered
to death in the Rhondda, one reported missing in Norfolk. Far
from home, in Peru, an English professor of Law shot an English
barman who had attacked him for *crime passionnel* reasons.

In May, a girl of sixteen was battered to death, a child of
three strangled in its cot, both in Cornwall. A teenage boy was
found in a shallow grave in Hampshire. A young man was
murdered at his girl's home in Bournemouth, apparently by the
girl. A youth was shot dead by a young man in Southend. The
woman washed ashore in April had been known as 'the Tattooed
Lady' (also as 'Whisky Mary'). A tattooed man was found in
Epping Forest in May, stabbed eighty-nine times (it seems to have
been a *règlement de comptes* connected with the pornography
trade). In Staffordshire, 249 pellets were removed from the but-
tocks of a burglar known as 'Friday-Night Fred'. The householder,
fined £5, was nevertheless commended for his public spirit. At
the beginning of June, a baby kidnapped only the previous day

from a busy store was found buried on the Northumberland moors.

The investiture of our Prince Charles as Prince of Wales took place on July 1st, a Tuesday. It was rather expected that Welsh nationalists (who described that cheerful young man as 'this German oaf') would attempt some outrage. The day's first news was that two of them, as they made their preparations, had blown themselves up, dying instantly. Later, on television, policemen were seen chasing a man across a field. Rather less an occasion for mirth, a small rubber ball was thrown at the Queen's car by a long-haired youth, petulant among his enthusiastically royalist elders. Unpleasant in the extreme was an episode with a booby-trap, as a result of which the right foot of a policeman's son had to be amputated. Though connected with the investiture, that didn't happen until Saturday, the 5th. The previous day, a young woman was fatally stabbed in the street in broad daylight in Ruislip, a western outer suburb of London. The following Wednesday, near King's Lynn, a retired baker's man was done to death with a pickaxe. The murderer of March's old woman in Stepney, an escaped convict, had gone north to Glasgow. He had acquired three guns, and with these, when approached by the police, he first withstood siege, then ran amok, wounding thirteen people, but was shot down. That was on the 15th. On the 23rd, the young murderer of the yet older 'painted lady' of Worthing was brought to trial at Lewes. It was revealed in court, as it had not been in the papers at the time, that the word 'Whore' had been scrawled in lipstick over her ancient breast and thighs. Betweenwhiles, a girl research worker on a government ballistics project had been strangled, stripped and left in a Kentish ditch, where she remained for a week undiscovered, so that Interpol had been alerted and search made in France.

There, since we last glanced at the march of French crime, much the same kind of thing had been happening rather more frequently. Thus, for the period between the Olivier execution in March and the end of May, I have notes of some forty acts of wilful homicide committed on French soil. There was more infanticide and some parricide. Proportionately, fewer old women were killed, and one was a killer (infanticide by grandmother). In the conjugal setting, wives acquitted themselves valiantly, but in *crimes passionnels* they came off worst. A Yugoslav workman was killed by three French youths, one of the old women by a negro, a man of seventy by a prostitute and her Arab protector. Knives and firearms greatly outnumbered blunt instruments and bare hands, though, outside Strasbourg, a young woman did an Army officer to death with an axe. One of the wives was shot in a bank vault, a man in Poitiers in bed beside his wife, who heard nothing, a young woman in a Paris hospital by the man who had put her there.

A curious and gruesome episode was that in which a former legionary Pierre Coquard, who had several times been convicted of fire-raising and who currently earned his living by peddling blind-handicraft goods from door to door in Lyons, at the end of an evening's drinking repeatedly stabbed, with a crown-cork opener, his girl-friend and an older man who was with them, then decapitated the young woman, took her head to his hotel room, combed its hair, put make-up on its face and kept it for three nights on his bedside table, during the day taking it about with him on his rounds, in the bag in which he carried the articles he was offering for sale. That was in late April. In late May, on soil part French, part Spanish and part neither, normally crimeless Andorra had a murderess in its small prison. A Spaniard, she had shot her unfaithful French doctor husband.

THE TRIAL of Armand Rohart, mayor of Peuplingues, for the murder of his wife, opened on July 2nd at St Omer, where sits the court of assize for the Pas de Calais department. This department is not self-contained juridically. Its Parquet, which is to say its regional Directorship of Public Prosecutions, is at Boulogne-sur-Mer, which itself has no court of assize, but its court of appeal is at Douai, in the adjacent Nord. The presiding judge, M. Cogniart, was thus a *conseiller* of the Douai *Cour d'Appel*, but not its *premier président*, who should have appointed a replacement when one of the two original assessors fell ill, whereas Councillor Cogniart had done it himself. Maître Floriot, as Rohart's counsel, may, one supposes, have known of this irregularity already and resolved to play the card or not according to how the trial went. We cannot know. We do know that he had already tried, without success, to invalidate the committal proceedings on the ground that the examining magistrate in Boulogne had caused medical documents to be seized and that this contravened the right of professional secrecy.

Jacob Kerbahay, known as 'the Turk' (but in fact Iranian), had died a convincingly natural death in February, so that his voice would be heard only on tape. This fact might or might not help the defence, in that Floriot could argue without fear of contradiction that the recording must have been doctored but could not hope to lead Jacob into admitting that it had. Some hope might also be placed in the word '*hydrocution*' which had gained some medical currency. I have not yet come across the word in English. It was formed by analogy with 'electrocution' which was itself formed (not in France but in America and in the first place with penal implication, which it has lost elsewhere except with reference to American contexts) by analogy with 'execution'. *Hydrocution* was to be defined, by no means promptly, for readers of *France-Soir* as an abrupt cessation of the heart-beat

133

and of the operation of the nervous centres, causing death by asphyxia without the immersion of mouth or nostrils. It was described as the frequent cause of drowning (but death, then, would not be 'by drowning'), and it was said that recovery might result from artificial respiration or heart massage. Persons must have been known so to recover, for some of the onset symptoms described were subjective. These were a tingling in the legs, red patches on the arms, a clenching of the solar plexus and a sensation of intense heat. Hydrocution might, it appeared, result from fatigue, nervous shock, chill or indigestion (but was not the same thing as congestion). Well, of course, we have all heard of heart-attacks while bathing, as well as indigestion producing apparent heart-attacks, but there may be something medically respectable in all this.

Its bearing on the death of Mme Rohart, unaccustomed to sea-bathing, shortly after luncheon and with alcohol unusually in her bloodstream, on June 9th, 1967, seems fairly clear. If she had been hydrocuted before her head was submerged, she would not have taken water into her lungs. But the medical experts were emphatic. Mme Rohart had died neither of drowning nor of hydrocution. Death had indeed resulted from asphyxia, but this had been caused by blows received on the face, even though her nose had been broken after death (one possibility envisaged was that her face had been pushed into the sand, the breaking of her nose then perhaps being due to a last good bang to make sure). The motive might have been financial. It might have been the determination to marry Odile Wissocq (absent from the trial, in Corsica in a state of advanced pregnancy). It might have been a combination of both. Two motives are better than one.

The tape-recording indicated only the second motive. It was played to a hushed court on the afternoon of the second day's hearing. Behind the two voices, a clock ticked, and at one point two other clocks struck the hour. There had in fact been three clocks in the living-room of Jacob's wooden shack, as well as pin-ups, colonial trophies, an up-to-date wireless set and, of course, a portable tape-recorder. The deep, gravelly voice of the dead ex-legionary was heard first, the sharp, metallic tones of the man in the dock, two and a half years before, replying. There had, it may be recalled, been some question of Jacob going to Turkey for the arrow-poison, curare.

JACOB. You mean, well . . . something to do with getting rid of your wife?

ROHART. What you think. Have you any ideas?

JACOB. No. You know, the other day, I saw your daughter. It made me feel sick. . . . Tell me frankly, which do you love most, Odile or your wife?

ROHART. Odile, eh, no doubt about that. . . .

JACOB. You'll get married? When? After the accident?

ROHART. Odile, eh, no doubt about that. . . .

JACOB. A year?

ROHART. I should think so. Why?

JACOB. I was just asking. And the child?

ROHART. I shall acknowledge. . . .

JACOB. You'll admit . . .?

ROHART. When we're married, yes.

JACOB. Of course, yes. . . . You're still thinking of the same thing, the car accident?

ROHART. I reckon so, eh? What do you think?

JACOB. A car accident, you know, it's dangerous, isn't it? I mean, if there's somebody else about. . . .

ROHART. Not at five o'clock in the morning!

JACOB. No, I suppose not.

ROHART. Not so early in the morning, eh?

JACOB. You've got a big responsibility. There are four children. Especially now they're grown up. Still, it's your business, if that's what you want.

ROHART. I might still change my mind in the next few months. You never know.

JACOB. How do we fix it . . . for travelling expenses?

ROHART. Just as you like.
        (A clock strikes ten. Sensation in court.)

ROHART. You're certain to find it there, pretty well.

JACOB. We can try. If I go, it's what I shall look for. Suppose I don't find any?

ROHART. We'll have to think again when you come back. There are other things we could try, but that would have been the most practical. . . . Is that somebody at the door?

JACOB. No, no, there's nobody coming.
        (A second clock strikes.)

JACOB. I don't want to say this, but me, you know, I like your wife, she's very nice . . . even though I shan't have to do anything myself, you understand. . . .

ROHART. Oh, yes, whatever happens, you won't have to do anything yourself.

JACOB. I know that all right, of course, but still I should be a bit responsible.

ROHART. Obviously.

JACOB. How do you mean?

ROHART. And for me, it isn't much of a life any longer, either.

JACOB. Oh, I know that, yes, I can see. Me, if I was you, I'd go away somewhere else and get married there.

ROHART. No, impossible.

JACOB. Oh, why?

ROHART. It wouldn't fit. . . . There's always. . . . To begin with, Odile, she wouldn't want to, in the first place.

JACOB. Why?

ROHART. So long as my wife is there, Odile wouldn't want to be married, in the first place. In the second place, the children wouldn't like to go away, but if there was an accident. . . .

JACOB. What about the accident?

ROHART. With an accident, they'd be miserable for a week, a fortnight, the way people are when they've lost somebody, and then afterwards it's all right. It had to happen, it was an accident. Plenty of people have them. . . .

JACOB. True enough.

ROHART. They take place every day.

JACOB. Why don't you want a divorce?

ROHART. Impossible, the children would always hold it against me, if I get a divorce, they'll be unhappy. I couldn't have a divorce, no. Impossible.

There was more of all this, with talk of Interpol and the counter-espionage service. The Turk wouldn't go to the Middle East to look for curare. They must find something nearer home. The mayor's voice insisted that it must somehow work in with a car accident. Or an accident out shooting perhaps, with a shotgun. Either way, there'd be an autopsy, an inquest.

ROHART. You're always suspected, eh, even if you aren't

caught, you're always suspected. There are echoes. . . . That was the best formula, the needle and the curare. It ought to be managed somehow.

JACOB. Well, yes, that's it, there you are.

ROHART. Apart from anything else, it was the *best* formula. Early in the morning, you meet a car every half hour, between here and Boulogne. If that. As early as that.

JACOB. Yes.

ROHART. The trouble would be, if it wasn't instantaneous and she was able to stop.

JACOB. Yes.

ROHART. You did say it was instantaneous?

JACOB. Yes, yes.

ROHART. Without a moment of. . . .

JACOB. Without anything, without a thing. . . .

ROHART. At the first prick?

JACOB. First prick.

ROHART. That was it, you see, painless. Or else the car . . . if the car. . . . If the car. . . . What's that?. . . Is it a recording machine, that?

JACOB. Oh, there's no thingumajig on it.

ROHART. Look, what is it?

JACOB. No, no, it hasn't got a thingummy.

ROHART. You haven't turned it on to record?

JACOB. No, whatever for?

ROHART. You turned it on?

JACOB. No.

There was a click, which might have been on the tape or might have been the switching off of the machine in the courtroom. The presiding judge, M. Cogniard, asked the Mayor of Peuplingues to confirm that that was his voice. The man in the dock said that he had never uttered those words. The question arose, to what extent the recording might have been tampered with. Experts from French radio were heard. The regular ticking of the clock would have made complicated 'editing' difficult. On the other hand, said one expert, the ticking could have been added afterwards. Rohart jumped at this. Yes, he said, Jacob had stopped the clock while they talked. At this admission, Me Floriot put his head in his hands. At the end of the afternoon, he asked to have a copy of the tape. He would then, he said, bring it back next day with the sense entirely altered. His application was refused.

There had been a great deal of technical discussion on this point, and there was to be more. In the course of many years in broadcasting, some of it with French technicians, I had acquired a precise sense of what is and what is not possible in the way of editing magnetic tape, and I could have enjoyed joining in. The question can never be quite settled, however. If that particular tape had been tampered with, the job had been competently and skilfully done before it was copied. From what he was to say rather less than a year later, Floriot himself did not really believe that much had been done, but had merely wished to argue that it could have been.

Certainly, the evidence of Jacob's last tape was decisive. The case against Rohart had begun with it. There might have been none otherwise, despite the peculiarities of his behaviour that June afternoon and evening. Had there been a case against him without it, the tape may be thought to have done him good, since it stressed the *crime passionnel* side of the matter, whereas it might have been thought that he had killed his wife for the insurance money, which could have cost him his head. He was awarded life imprisonment. Then the irregularity of procedure was discovered and the verdict quashed. There would have to be a second trial. This would take place at Douai.

WHILE THE St Omer trial proceeded, a woman still young had strangled three of her six children at Thionville, an elderly man in Nice had stabbed his somewhat younger wife to death, and the undiscovered planter of booby-traps or *boîtes piégées* had claimed a fatal victim, a man of fifty-four. The day after the verdict, a German girl on holiday in Corsica was stabbed in her tent, it was thought by a compatriot, and a young woman in Amiens vanished (to be found eight days later, battered and strangled among the fortifications). The day after that, an exceptionally pretty prostitute, Madeleine Moklin, known as the Domino, who had broken away from *le milieu*, was found burnt to death in a car at the Val d'Enfer in Provence where Mistral sets the death of his heroine, Miréio. A theory was that this death had been ordered from prison by a ponce and gangster, Jean Breuil, who was to be re-arrested on drug charges the following year. Next day, near Lille, an old man was robbed and beaten to death by two brothers who had expected him to have more in his pockets. The day after that a young man shot his uncle dead in the Marseilles hotel room of his sister-in-law, a prostitute. In the department of Val d'Oise, an old woman and her middle-aged daughter were burnt to death in their house by a deliberate fire-raiser. There had been a similar case at Blaringhem two weeks before, but the arsonist then had been younger, his motive avowedly revenge on younger victims.

It was a remarkable summer, and the help of arsonists was not always needed. The sun burned through tarpaulins and set hay-stacks on fire, through the roofs of cars and rabbit hutches and roasted those within, left a factory blazing on the Seine east of Paris. The holiday season had started. Motorists assaulted girl hitch-hikers and each other, crashed into trees or plunged into canals, hit children or old ladies and ran. That weekend, the great hospital centre in Lyons ran out of blood for transfusion into the veins of the victims of road accidents. Departure by air was impeded by a strike of Air France switchboard-operators. Where elsewhere the local telephone system was blocked, other means of communication were adopted. In Lorient, for instance, a restaurant proprietor transmitted his requirements to the fish market by semaphore with flags.

People did not know what to do with their pets. Some were simply abandoned or tossed into rivers to take their chance. Nine Shetland ponies, rounded up among the traffic on a main road, were never claimed. Of two patients visited by a district nurse on the outskirts of Paris, one, unable to find it a place in a dogs' home or the queue at a veterinary surgeon's, had that morning hanged his white Pomeranian from a cherry tree, while the other, wishing to kill a tortoise and finding that it obstinately withdrew inside its shell, was sawing that in two. Babies also were abandoned, found in railway compartments or peacefully asleep on the stubble of reaped fields. As commonly happens in heat waves, bathing accidents multiplied. In one afternoon, nineteen youngsters from a holiday camp drowned in the Loire. The dreaded C.R.S. (Compagnies Républicaines de Sécurité), whom we commonly see as riot police hopefully whacking crash-helmeted students with their flexible truncheons, were put into bathing trunks and sent on beach rescue duty.

On July 5th, accompanied by her friend Sauveur Padovani,

who lived in Aix, the fair Harlette Boulbès, a woman of forty-
one, first visited the somewhat dilapidated Château de la Roche-
Rostolane at Puyricard, near Aix-en-Provence. It was owned by
the septuagenarian Vicomte Jacques de Régis de Gastinel. Mlle
Boulbès was on the look-out for a place she might turn into a
rest home for old people, and Padovani had recommended this
one. The game had been played before. At that very moment, a
nurse in Monmartre, a Mlle Dietschy, thirty-three, was within a
fortnight of being arrested for illegally restraining a Mme Loew,
seventy-nine, her aunt, and charged with 'extortion of signatures,
theft, receiving stolen goods and concealing letters'. The
proprietress of a home for old people in hither Normandy had
just embarked on a course of fraud, breach of trust and so on
which, by November, would see her in prison at Evreux. Of such
practices leading to murder British criminal history provides us
with a remarkable example in the case of Nurse Waddingham,
hanged in 1936.

It would not have been Mlle Boulbès's first venture in this field.
On property belonging to her mother, there had been a small
home for old people before, and several of these had died very
shortly after making over their money to the Boulbès family, on
whom suspicion had also lighted, that January, in connection
with a burst of sub-machine-gun fire and the lobbing of hand
grenades through a window of premises the occupants annoyingly
would not leave. A larger project was currently held up by a
failure to get bank loans, what the three operative Boulbès
(Harlette, her mother and a brother, Joseph, there being also
two respectable sisters) were able to offer in the way of security
being unimpressive to bank managers.

A formal arrangement for the sale of Rostolane to a company
had in fact existed for some months past, and money in respect
of this had been advanced only three days before Mlle Boulbès's
first visit. It was clear to her, however, that M. de Régis had taken
a fancy to her, and she formed the hope of persuading him to go
back on the arrangement. A witness, one of the estate's tenant
farmers, would later state that she had admitted to him that she
thought of marrying the unwashed, incontinent, alcoholic,
lascivious, stingy and largely immobile old man, who lived, mainly
in a chair, on the ground floor. Though somewhat heavy-jawed
and close-eyed, Harlette Boulbès had a good figure, good teeth,
nice hair, was nicely sun-tanned and wore a white frock buttoned

down the front. To the decayed, smelly old aristocrat, she had 'the beauty of the devil'. He gazed at her, an old servant noted, 'with eyes like those of the toad that died of love'. Certainly, she had a way with old men, acquired no doubt when in her first youth she had worked as a prostitute in Marseilles, under her mother's tutelage. She had three children by two men who, later, had successively kept her, but she remained unmarried.

In her way stood a long-established mistress-housekeeper, Lucia Isoard, who no doubt entertained financial expectations of her own. Mlle Isoard also had at one time made love professionally in Marseilles, but in her case it was long ago, for Mlle Isoard was sixty-four, though well-preserved and sexually still active, ministering to the *vicomte*'s little whims and also taking younger and more plebeian lovers. To poison her would be difficult, since it would require access to kitchen, bathroom or drink cupboard and cellar, all supervised by Lucia herself. As to drowning, neither the Rhône nor the Durance flowed nearby. A hit-and-run driver might, on the other hand, appear at any time on the stretch of road between the entrance to the drive and the post office, if only the housekeeper would appear on foot on that stretch of road at the right moment. Nobody would be surprised if Mlle Isoard were, in such circumstances, either killed or, badly injured, put into hospital for some weeks. Not that Mlle Boulbès would ever admit to entertaining such thoughts, while her friend Sauveur Padovani was highly respected and influential at Aix.

In Paris and elsewhere, criminal activities continued during the holiday period, which indeed facilitated housebreaking in large towns. There were horrors of the kind I grow tired of listing and the reader, doubtless, of counting. Roving gangs of youths beat up anyone they found alone at night, quite without age or class prejudice, for it was, for instance, a young lorry-driver whom, in St Denis, a small group with a girl blinded to forestall identi- fication. That same night, valuable pictures were stolen at Neuilly, and a body too many was found in the cemetery in Montparnasse. That was Friday, July 25th. The lower courts were still clearing up arrears. On the 17th, defending two young thieves from Swansea, a woman barrister, just back from California, suggested to the jury that, instead of burdening the French taxpayer, they should be sent back to be hanged in their own country. On Sunday, at a hotel in Deauville, the manager's wife killed him with a kitchen knife, while yet another policeman was shot in Lille.

The accident to Lucia Isoard took place on Monday afternoon. At noon, the postmaster had taken a message from a caller in Marseilles to say that he would ring Mlle Isoard again at four o'clock. Before she appeared out of the drive, the engine of a white Citroën, which had been standing on the bend for the past hour, started and was tensely held in top gear. Within seconds of her appearance, it had mounted the footpath and killed her. There was a witness on the other side of the road, a Mme Chaix. The car at once swerved across and made for her, but, with great presence of mind and some agility, she jumped into the ditch. No doubt trembling and dusty, she hurried home. Her father-in-law had noticed the car waiting. Together, they at once went to the police. A Captain Drobecq of the Aix *gendarmerie* was put in charge of the investigation. By Wednesday, journalists from Paris and the Marseilles-based crime reporters of national newspapers were at Puyricard, booked in at hotels in Aix, a short four miles away.

Two prompt discoveries were that Mlle Isoard's room had been rifled the evening before her sudden violent death (in the search, it was thought, for the name of some person she knew in Marseilles, from whom the telephone message could be said to come) and that Mlle Boulbès and Sauveur Padovani had both been at the château when the crime occurred but not at that moment in conversation with the *vicomte,* so that they could have signalled to the driver of the white Citroën when Mlle Isoard was seen to go down the drive. It further transpired that Mlle Boulbès and Sauveur Padovani had been in Marseilles at the time the telephone message was sent. The car, with a smashed headlamp, was found abandoned. It had been stolen on the afternoon in question. A young man whose description tallied with that given of the driver by Mme Chaix and others had twice been to the estate farm, to buy potatoes, in the company of Padovani. He was identified as Gaston Costeraste, a small-time crook, a *demi-sel,* known in the Marseilles underworld as Jo l'Aixois. He had vanished. He was still at large when, on August 9th, Padovani was charged and remanded in custody, Harlette Boulbès being for the moment released after making a statement.

On the same date, in Midfield near Birmingham, Alabama, a *forcené* armed with five rifles and a shotgun, threatened with eviction, killed his parents, a minister of religion, a woman neighbour and himself, and later, farther west (by then, it was

next day in France), the incredible Manson girls performed their
famous massacre in Hollywood. In the month's remaining horrors
in France, Poles and Arabs played a disproportionate part, both
as murderers and victims (Arab of Arab, Pole of Pole), while the
Austrian photographer, thief and multiple killer, Adolf Bauer,
was shot down by police in Grenoble. There was, it is true,
nothing foreign about the peasant farmer in northern France
who confessed to savagely killing two little girls with a bill-hook
for trespassing (friends of his own daughter, they were picking
flowers in one of his meadows on a Sunday afternoon). The case
was compared with that of old Dominici, to whose victims friends
of the late Sir Jack Drummond had, earlier that month, placed a
memorial stone at the scene of their death. By then, somewhat
nearer that scene, 'Jo l'Aixois' (Gaston Costeraste) had been found
and, after questioning, to everyone's astonishment, released.
Harlette Boulbès was still at liberty. Vicomte Jacques de Régis de
Gastinel had gone into hospital at Aix, was receiving treatment
in the neurological ward.

11 | THE LITTLE DEBATE

THE NAME of Waite has its place among the classics of American and, indeed, more broadly of Anglo-Saxon criminal history. The famous Waite was an ill-qualified young doctor who, in 1916, tried various other means but in the end poisoned his parents-in-law with arsenic. He had always somewhat tended to theft, and his motive for murder seems to have been purely financial. He was of a literary turn of mind, read Ibsen, Maeterlinck, Poe and Keats. At autopsy, after electrocution in Sing Sing, he was found to be suffering from a slight meningitis of the left side of his brain and an abnormally large heart. To this latter, in a metaphorical sense, he had always laid claim. Those who like their murderers explaining have made what they could of the meningeal infection. It may indeed have accounted for his curious alternation between heartless calculation and erratic foolishness, but hardly for his early criminal disposition or for the murder project, which he entertained before marriage, choosing a wife who had parents suitable for murdering.

I have no reason to suppose that Lord Leigh's chauffeur, William Waite, who in 1969 was found to have poisoned his wife for love (not of her, but of a younger, prettier woman), was of a literary turn or even that he had ever heard of his namesake. He used, it seems, arsenic, at first in small doses over a period of eight months and then, on September 7th, massively in a glass of Lucozade.

The case had something of a classic, a conventional, quality, which always suggests reading, especially since as poison is not as a rule a man's instrument of murder, except among members of the medical profession (and then, as a rule, something better than arsenic). I suppose one could always write and ask Mr Waite. It is strange how reluctant we are to take advantage of the fact that murderers are now simply pensioned off. They must find time hang heavy between the psychiatrist's occasional visits and might gain a rehabilitating sense of moral worth from doing a little something to earn their keep.*

That crime took place in leisured Warwickshire. A more contemporary type of culpable homicide was committed, three days later, in Luton, when three men, described by a witness as 'of swarthy, Italian type', gunned down a postmaster, made off in one vehicle, abandoned it and switched to another, but without stealing anything. What happened next day just after breakfast in central London, though without fatal consequences, was even more up-to-date. Four men in stocking masks, with sawn-off shotguns, efficiently lifted £15,000 in wages being delivered to W. H. Smith's off Holborn, merely 'blasting a security guard in both feet'. The following week, on a Tuesday evening in Putney, an old woman was beheaded, apparently by her daughter, without evident motive. The reader may remember the case of Pierre Coquard, who, after killing his *fiancée* and the older man to whom he feared he was losing her, kept her head by him at night to remind him of vanished love. The Putney case lacks that pathos. The previous month, there had been a decapitation case in Belgium in which a wife kept her husband's head in a plant-pot, the marked difference between her and Keats's or Boccaccio's Isabella being that not two rich and snobbish brothers but she herself had separated it from the trunk which she had dumped on her doorstep, so mutilated as to suggest a Mohammedan ritual murder, with the result that local Arabs were first suspected.

So, it may be remembered, they had been in the Deveaux case before the apprentice butcher was arrested. In that case, the suspicion seems to have been better founded, since more than one neighbour claimed to have seen an Arab suspiciously lurking and one to have noticed what might have been a bloodstain on his chest. When the case came up for retrial, in Dijon, after six years, that September, a pathologist for the defence argued learnedly that the wounds inflicted on the master butcher's little girl pointed to Moslem methods of butchery. This retrial opened

---

* Since the T.U.C. denies long-term prisoners all possibility of productive labour, I have sometimes thought that murderers at least, in whom most people take some interest, might be kept in conditions resembling those of the drearier animals at the London Zoo. There, when not required for interview, they might indeed be allowed the privacy of their straw, but, once they emerged into the light of their yards, become subject to public scrutiny and such conversation as they chose to engage in. Notices would discourage visitors from either feeding or pelting them.

towards the end of the month, on the 24th. Next day, also in
Putney, as the culminating episode in a phase of 'queer-bashing'
by juvenile gangs, the unmistakably homosexual but otherwise
respectable Michael DeGruchy, a solicitor's clerk, was beaten up
and left dying outside cemetery gates. A row between black
labourers in Dalston seems to have produced the month's last
victim of a fatal knife wound in the London area.

The month in France had begun with the suicide of Gabrielle
Russier, a schoolteacher prosecuted by the otherwise liberal and
permissive family of the pupil with whom she had an affair. This
was a sad business, about which even M. Pompidou felt impelled
to express himself, but it lies outside my field. The planter (if
there was only one) of exploding *boîtes piégées* claimed another
fatal victim. The long-sought 'man with the iron bar' (a long-
haired youth who had spread terror and caused one death in
woods near a big new building estate), was arrested. Guest of
honour at a luncheon given on the 12th by the Anglo-American
Press Association in Paris, the prefect of police, M. Grimaud,
admitted, on his manor, a murder-rate of one a day (with more
than sixty daily car thefts and three house-robberies every hour).
Next day, a young American from Delaware, a deaf-mute, his
face viciously slashed before he was strangled with his own belt,
helped to make up that month's total of victims. That same day,
in the neighbourhood of St Denis, an Arab cut his daughter-in-
law's throat, performed a kind of rough hara-kiri on himself and
then jumped out of the window.

If the reader remembers the Republican Guard trumpeter
strangled at home on the evening of his retirement three years
before, he may care to learn that Mme Heldenberg and her
daughter received, on September 23rd, 1969, five-year sentences
of which they had already served more than half awaiting trial.
The Deveaux retrial began on the 25th. That ended in acquittal,
to almost everybody's relief. The reddest face was that of a policeman, though some expert witnesses cannot have been happy. The
judge who had first tried the case in Lyons was dead. The
triumph was chiefly that of a Jesuit prison visitor. The plump,
dim-witted butcher's boy had become a highly articulate, thin,
edgy, bespectacled young man with false teeth. He has since
married.

I MUST somehow have missed the English newspapers for October 1969, since I have notes of only two murders in the United Kingdom that month, one near the beginning and one three weeks later. This took place at Witham, Essex, on the 22nd. A man hammered his wife to death and then hanged himself. He was a Frenchman with a fine Resistance record, an O.B.E., and night-club interests in the West End of London. The murder on the 2nd was, on the other hand, to the best of my knowledge, wholly English and northern. A girl of fifteen was found done to death, by what means and whether or no with signs of sexual assault I have never discovered, on the golf course at Southport, Lancashire.

What I also have are a court report from my local paper, the *Kensington News*, dated October 3rd, and a selection of readers' letters from the London *Evening Standard* in mid-month, torn out, as I remember, in Deal, where, as throughout south-east England, the paper enjoys a limited sale wherever Lord Beeching left railway stations in use. The *Kensington News* extract reads as follows.

DEATH SENTENCE MAN TELLS COURT OF BLACKMAIL

Frederick Emmett-Dunne, who was sentenced to death while serving in the Army in July, 1955, at a general court martial in Germany for murder and whose sentence was later commuted to one of life imprisonment and who was released in July, 1966, claimed at Marylebone Court that he had been blackmailed by two men into obtaining goods by deception.

Emmett-Dunne, aged forty-seven, described as a garage manager, of Fulham Road, Chelsea, said that as he was leaving Barclays Bank, after depositing the firm's money, the two men, whom he had last seen between 1962 and 1964 while in prison, were waiting for him at a car park where he normally left the company's car.

They referred to him by name and said they wanted something doing. He replied that he had no intention of getting into trouble. They said they would 'pop the bubble' and he would lose his job because his firm would not have a convict working for them. He committed the offence in a moment of weakness.

Emmett-Dunne pleaded guilty to obtaining by deception clothing and shoes worth together just over £60, from three shops. He also admitted and asked the magistrate, Mr John Phipps, to take into consideration, two similar offences of obtaining goods dishonestly and an offence of stealing a Barclaycard.

The accused told the magistrate that he had worked diligently since his discharge from prison. His employers were now fully aware of the situation and had sufficient confidence in him to promote him to general manager on October 1st. Since his employment with them he had deposited sums of money in the region of three-quarters of a million pounds sterling.

Mr Phipps fined Emmett-Dunne a total of £75 and said if anyone approached him again in the manner he had described there was only one course to take and that was to go to the police straight away.

The Emmett-Dunne murder case is not one of those I have so far listed, and the reader may care for some account of it here, though my purpose with it may be thought purely auto-biographical.

The victim had been a fellow-sergeant, what in the Army was in my time called a 'short-arsed' fellow, no more than five feet two, a Sergeant Watters, found in the small hours on December 1st, 1953, hanging by the neck from banisters in barracks in Duisburg, a bucket kicked over beside him. A verdict of suicide was brought in at the inquest. Six months later, Sergeant Emmett-Dunne married the dead man's German-born widow, Mia, whom he had (accidentally, he claimed) met again in Leeds. It was, apparently, gossip and speculation in the unit which led his C.O. to report the matter to Scotland Yard. The body of former Sgt Reginald Watters was exhumed and examined by the Home Office pathologist, Dr Camps, who concluded that death had been caused not by hanging but by a blow delivered, before suspension, possibly by the edge of a hand. An Irish regular, Emmett-Dunne had been in a commando unit during the war, and the blow was described as a commando blow, though of course it was taught in 'unarmed combat' to other troops, to the present writer, for instance, as a harmless gunner. It was, I suppose, a piece of elementary *karate*, which required no artificially hardened edge to the hand, since its target was the soft front of the neck and the Adam's apple. I had never thought of it as a killer, only as a stopper, like a knee in the balls. I had, indeed, sometimes imagined, when tempers were rising in a public house, that it might have to be my way of stopping a stronger man if he attacked me, its great advantage being that, if attack seemed likely but not certain, the hand could be raised in a gesture which might seem merely protective or at worst to threaten a backhanded slap across the face. For that sort of purpose, as it seemed to me, very little force indeed would be needed. The man would simply choke and cough for a while and go and sit down, while his friends slapped his back and the temperature subsided.

Luckily, the occasion never arose in my particular case. The situation in Duisburg cannot have been imaginably the same, if only because Emmett-Dunne was at least comparatively the big man, Watters the small one. I don't in fact know how big Emmett-Dunne was and is, though his face, in a photograph before me, is that of one solidly built and perhaps tall, not a bad-looking face at all, the jaw massive but the features regular, with no hint of obvious criminality, à la Lombroso, about them, not, one might guess, a particularly good-tempered or amiable man, but not of any mad fixity or quirky malice either. Appearing at Bow Street, he claimed that, as a citizen of Eire, he could not be tried before an English court for a crime allegedly committed in Germany. He was taken to Düsseldorf and there charged before a military court, though with eminent prosecuting and defending counsel, respectively Griffith Jones and Curtis-Bennett.

His case was that he had killed Sergeant Watters in self-defence, the latter having threatened him with a revolver, Mia Watters and he being suspected of a guilty association with each other. He had indeed, with the help of a half-brother in the same unit, thereafter attempted to simulate a death by suicide. The prosecution had built up a detailed circumstantial account of Emmett-Dunne's movements on the evening of November 30th, 1953, and showed an altered entry on the guardroom time-sheet for that evening. There was evidence that Watters had been killed outside barracks and subsequently brought in, but this did not destroy Emmett-Dunne's case in essence. The real issue was premeditation, and the evidence for this was hearsay, that of a Sergeant Browne, who stated that his co-sergeant, a week before the fatality, had averred that Mia Watters's behaviour seemed likely to lead her husband to adopt desperate measures, that in fact he might well hang himself. To those who want to know *what really happened*, all this is fascinating, but the important thing is that the court was convinced that there had been premeditation, and that a verdict of murder not of manslaughter was adopted. Lucky perhaps in being a citizen of Eire, Sergeant

Emmett-Dunne also (if benefit it is) benefited from the fact that capital punishment, even for *Möchelmord*, had been abolished in West Germany.

And so, sentenced to life imprisonment, he had come out in 1966 and gone into the garage business, presumably under a false name, and, after a bit of trouble, had landed on his feet, with a lot of good sense and even generosity of mind shown all round, a sort of happy ending if we avoided questions about Mia and supposed that no unhealthy curiosity was being exercised in Fulham Road, a road, I may say, which I know quite well and in which, about that time, I had intermittent occasion to visit a hospital. I did not feel strongly impelled to look up the garages in it. Under whatever name he now flourished, I wished Mr Emmett-Dunne well. The fact was, I thought he had been hanged some fourteen or fifteen years before.

I had just finished a book, *French Crime in the Romantic Age,* and started working out a chronology for, anywhere and everywhere, crime between the two world wars, thinking that I would do that period next. But I also wanted an idea for a novel. The idea which presented itself required a closely bounded chronology for the United Kingdom between the end of the Second World War and the Homicide Act of 1957. I had got this out and taken it with me to Deal, first chosen as a suitable base for hithering and thithering across the Channel by hovercraft from Pegwell Bay, careless of the currency restrictions then in force. The weather was splendid, and it was nice to be out of London, where the dustmen were on strike.

The idea might, I thought, do better for a play, because then perhaps I could count on the physical appearance of the actors, skilfully made-up, and the accents adopted by them to create a growing sense of who they were really meant to be before at least some of the numerous verbal pennies dropped unmistakably and emphatically at the curtain, say, to the first act. The second act would provide ingeniously managed retrospective development, the third a horrid climax. Not, I thought, until late in the second act would I bring on the character most immediately recognisable visually, dome-headed Christie, aged seventy-seven, at a point at which laughter would provide a desirable relief from accumulated tension. For by then it would have become almost clear that all the characters were murderers hanged, in real life, between 1946 and 1955. The scene was to be a hotel. The manager would be

Heath, the manageress Rose Ellis, the elderly, crop-haired reception clerk with the north-country accent Margaret Allen; the arrival at curtain-up Daniel Raven; an elderly permanent resident, foreign and artistic, a Mr Hepper; Haigh running the local taxi service, Bentley one of his most reliable drivers; two Evanses and a Harries, Welsh, among the handymen, as well as a Whiteway. The two who arrived meaning to make things awkward, threatening to 'pop the bubble', would be Burns and Devlin, who had always worked rather as a pair and were plain slobs. The convention was that, already in 1946, the Attlee government had put an end to capital punishment, partly revived by the Tories in 1957.

At first I thought to situate the hotel in mid-Wales, but then decided on the south-east coast, where the Kentish coalfield accounts for many north-country and some Welsh accents. I rather thought that, in the last act, Heath should murder Ruth Ellis with every refinement, if that is the word, of sadistic cruelty. Certainly, at the beginning of that third act, Ruth Ellis's face would be seen outside at the window, as, fourteen years before, it had been at that of a public house in Hampstead. I had a fair number of such details worked out and even wrote one or two opening pages (arrival of Raven, publicity tycoon), but then thought I'd try a novel after all. This would be narrated by Leonard Mills, an experienced crime reporter and failed poet, obsessed from the age of nineteen with the idea of the perfect crime and taught by experience that the best way to get, and get away with, your scoop is indeed to be there before the crime is committed but not to commit it yourself, rather to play on the circumstances and provoke somebody else to commit it. I thought I might let him provoke several crimes, every other character somehow repeating his or her behaviour of between fourteen and twenty-three years before.

It is, I hope the reader may agree, an idea not without possibilities. On the point of abandoning it, I mentioned it in a letter to Nigel Morland of *The Criminologist* and got back what I quoted earlier in connection with Heath and Haigh. My correspondent had also once 'wangled an interview' with Mills, who 'mentioned a crime novel which "helped" him', and had been well acquainted with Norman Rae, the *News of the World* crime editor who played so unusual a part in this case. His letter was, I thought, a pretty fair return for a copy of the Emmett-Dunne cutting from my local paper.

There was in fact, it may be recalled, an attempt made under the Attlee government to put an end to capital punishment. Thrown out in due course by the Lords, the Criminal Justice Bill, passed by the Commons, caused a temporary suspension of capital sentences, from which, in 1948, several convicted murderers benefited, notably James Camb and Donald Thomas. In the absence of *corpus delicti*, a Polish ex-soldier, Onufrejczyc, was 'commuted' not long before the execution of Ruth Ellis, between which and the passing of the Homicide Bill in 1957 there was a wave of reprieves, among those who benefited being Ellul, Morris Clarke, Burdett and Freda Rumbold. My problem being rather to keep my cast down to manageable proportions, I was glad enough not to be burdened with these. I felt also that I could reasonably dispense with more than a passing mention of Mrs Christofi, presumed returned to Cyprus, where her experience and publicity appeal would be useful to the fiendish Makarios, and with Peter Griffiths, presumed killed by his fellow-prisoners, by reason of the strong prejudice of all other villains against child murderers. Omitting a large number of lesser brethren, my *dramatis personae*, in the order in which in real life they had been executed, would thus have been Heath, Rowland, Haydn Evan Evans, Russell, Haigh, Margaret Allen, Raven, Timothy Evans, Burns and Devlin, Giffard, Bentley, Christie, Harries, Henry, Mrs Merrifield, Whiteway, Hepper and Ruth Ellis. In a play, I had not found a proper use for Mills, though in a novel he would have been of the first importance.

Had they not been executed, the order in which they came out would have been much the same, beginning with Heath in, say, the year of the Homicide Act (which would have made him watch his step for the next eight years) and ending with Ruth Ellis, who, for good conduct and a history appealing to the sympathy of other women, would hardly have been released later than 1964. In 1961, Mills would still have been short of thirty. When they were restored to society, the ages of the others would have ranged from under thirty to over seventy. At the time of my story, in the mild autumn of 1969, they would have seemed the stars of that first generation of the reprieved.

I gave up the idea, because I decided that people would take my novel (or play) as an argument on behalf of the retention of capital punishment or, as was to turn out, for its restoration. I was not, indeed, a convinced abolitionist, but neither was I fervent retentionist. My private objection was not to the point of view seemingly urged but to the likelihood that a general point of view would seem to be urged. I will not write propaganda under the guise of fiction. If I can help it, I will not even seem to be doing that. My purely hypothetical situation must have suggested future analogies of a kind unwelcome to any but those who implicitly believe that the abolition of capital punishment is a step on the way to abolishing murder, a belief I believe, though unexpressed, to be common and think silly. There will never be, I feel quite sure, a society in which murders are committed on appreciably less than the present British scale.

Although the Government proposed to deny it parliamentary debate, by mid-October the matter had been raised in the editorially abolitionist *Evening Standard*. I did not see the case for abolition initially made, on Monday the 13th, by, of all the available kinds of people, a pushing juvenile, president of the National Union of Students, or next day's contribution by the brilliantly wayward Philip Hope-Wallace, who, it seems, 'presented the dilemma of those who seek an objective, liberal view'. Objective *and* (as currently understood) 'liberal'? It seemed to me a contradiction in terms, but perhaps that was the 'dilemma' (taken, I felt sure, by Philip in his stride). On Friday, readers 'had their say'. They included a Labour member with an Irish name sitting for a Yorkshire constituency, the *dépaysé* Yorkshire novelist John Braine and the mother of a young married woman slaughtered by a young soldier in 1963, before the eyes of her four-year-old daughter. The grandmother was, it need hardly be said, in favour of capital punishment and fearful of the soldier's imminent release. Mr Braine refuted the opening writer's American statistics, and the member for Hull North was brief.

House of Commons, S.W.1

Sir,
        I have just two words to say to those who wish to restore capital punishment – Timothy Evans.
                                        Your faithfully,
                                        KEVIN MCNAMARA

This struck me as a classic of the same order as that of another Labour member, Mr Leo Abse, brother of the poet, whose comment on the convictions of Brady and Hindley had been,

'We are all guilty'. Not, of course, that one failed to take Mr McNamara's implicit point, that, with capital punishment in force, a miscarriage of justice might become irrevocable.

Of all that happened in France that month (which included husband-murder, infanticide and three examples of parricide in one day), two matters will most concern us, one quite new. This was the kidnapping, on October 24th, of Sophie Duguet, known as Little Red Riding Hood, daughter of a rich farmer, in Soissons. Within four days, the ransom (in sterling, some £75,000) had been paid and the child restored, unharmed. The kidnapper was a man called Michel Fauqueux, and the police seemed to know this. He was to enjoy (if that is the word) a good run for his money. At Aix-en-Provence, Harlette Boulbès and Gaston Costeraste ('Jo l'Aixois') were both in custody. Their delayed incarceration had been due in part to political considerations, arising from the fact that Jo had worked for the only recently cleaned-up S.A.C. (Service d'Action Civile), the strong-arm branch of the gaullist party, on the eminently necessary job of protecting bill-stickers at the time of the presidential elections. Padovani, on the other hand, who had enjoyed less immunity, had been S.A.C. representative in Aix.

FROM ALL I ever learned, it looks, improbably, as though there had been only one November murder in the United Kingdom, that of an inoffensive youth by three young thugs in Birmingham. I see that on the same day, the 9th, a Sunday, a French *au pair* girl committed suicide in London in circumstances which compromised an unnamed baronet. An interesting advance in criminalistics was announced from Glasgow, where, by the use of fine lead powder and a process known as electronography, clear fingerprints had been shown on a dead body. Towards the end of the month, with the aid of photographs and tape-recordings, *The Times* controversially substantiated charges against senior C.I.D. men at Scotland Yard.

There was more discussion in the papers about capital punishment, the Government having by then made its intentions painfully obvious. On the 6th, the *Daily Mail* played with statistics, concentrating on what had indeed given rise to general alarm, the increased use of firearms in organised robbery. On the 15th, the *New Statesman* and *The Spectator* both carried substantial articles, the former's by C. H. Rolph, the latter's by Auberon Waugh, gifted son of a great comic novelist. Mr Rolph's piece was of course wholeheartedly abolitionist, but written with admirable restraint, not at all the kind of thing suggested by its title, surely not his own, 'The Hangmen Fight Back'. Mr Waugh's views on the central issue were as unemphatic as even the present writer could wish, but it seems to have been he who first made the point that, in its handling of the question, Parliament would inevitably show its contempt for the electorate. He also argued that the Labour Party's purpose was not so much to settle things its own way while it could as to prevent the matter becoming, in the summer (when the Act of 1965 was due to come up for reconsideration) or early autumn, an electoral issue, for then it would certainly lose them votes. A similar contempt, said Mr Waugh, was evident in the Government's clear determination to 'go into' the Common Market against the will of the majority. Mr Waugh could hardly be expected to foresee just how attentive to the common will the same people would become when they were the Opposition. Towards the end of the month, attention wandered for a moment to the fact that the birch was still used in the Isle of Man.

The month's most evocative crime in Paris was the shooting of a barman and a waiter and the rape at pistol point of the proprietor's daughter, on the 5th, at five o'clock in the morning, at a night-club, the Gavroche, in Montmartre. The name of the club is, of course, that given by Victor Hugo to the dreadful but infinitely pathetic and touching urchin in *Les Misérables*. It was also evocative, however, of a whole past age of gangsterdom and *le milieu*. For the proprietor of the club was Jo Attia, former lieutenant of Pierre Loutrel ('Pierrot le Fou') who, in the immediately post-war years, had been Public Enemy No. 1, an odd association since, while Loutrel had worked for the Gestapo, Attia had resisted and spent three years in a concentration camp. Attia, whose real name was Brahim, had shown a remarkable aptitude for avoiding serious conviction, so that he was known as *le roi du non-lieu*, which we might attempt to translate by calling him Jo ('No Case Against Him') Attia, but he was a sick man, still feeling the after-effects of recent hospitalisation with a cancer of the throat. The active management of the Gavroche was conducted by a woman with the delightful name of Carmen Cocu, herself once a powerful gangster, who had succeeded the prostitute mother of his daughter, Nicole, in Jo's affections. As it seemed not unlikely that the Gavroche killings and rape constituted a *règlement de comptes* which might herald a large outbreak of gang warfare, he no doubt feared for his own life and is reported as, that afternoon, calling a council of war in a small bar at Belleville. Nicole Attia, for her own protection, slept that night on a camp bed at the Quai des Orfèvres, with policemen on guard. As it was to turn out, however, despite the fearful insult to Attia inherent in the rape of his daughter, the killer's sole grudge had been against the barmaid (who had a husband serving ten years in prison near Toulouse). He, the killer, was in fact a young nut called Christian Jubin, who, since his discharge, cured, from an asylum in June, was believed to have taken part in thirteen hold-ups in Paris and would presently be found pursuing his activities in the neighbourhood of Versailles, careless of the vengeance of *le milieu,* of which police notices warned him, suggesting that, for his own safety, it would be best for him to give himself up.

The old life of poncedom and protection racketeering went on, when no new consignment of drugs was to hand. On the night of November 13th, five men were arrested while threatening to wreck a bar in the Rue du Chevalier de la Barre. On the night of the 24th, a prisoner recently released went with three other men into a bar in the Passage Wattieaux. The other men told the manageress to go out for a walk and, during her absence, 'executed' the unfortunate fourth, who must have wished briefly that he was back inside. A less hurried ceremony was held in Provence on the 13th, when a helicopter took part in a second reconstruction of the crime at Puyricard. I have note of twelve other murders in France that month, none of much originality, whether as to motive, means employed, quality of the persons involved or the relations between them.

LYONS, TOO, had its *milieu,* with regular bloody adjustments of the score among ponces and their women, but the place was remarkably free of Corsicans, Arabs and Yugoslavs. The previous year, their determined attempt to disguise as an accident the murder of a ponce in a brothel called *Fétich's Club* had led to the discovery of extreme corruption in the anti-gang squad of the Lyons police. By December 1969, no doubt in consequence of these revelations, one of the two principal Lyons big shots had been in prison for almost a year, and on the 3rd the other was taken to the mortuary after a bank raid in which a cashier, a policeman and another bandit were also shot dead. That cashier was not the month's first to be shot dead. It had happened the previous day to one in a savings bank at Vaulx-en-Velin, within the jurisdiction of Lyons.

On the 5th, a mother strangled her intelligent dwarf child near Metz, and at Ferrières-en-Brie a Yugoslav, with a .22 rifle, in front of his six children, shot their mother, two women neighbours and the son of one of these. Under observation for appendicitis, he had discharged himself from hospital the previous evening, walked eight miles home in his pyjamas, slept peacefully all night but, that morning, got out of bed on the wrong side. In Lens on the 8th, a man due to go into hospital resisted the ambulance men and shot a policeman they called to reason with him (this also with a .22 rifle). Mothers' attempts on the 15th to murder their children were successful by strangulation on the Somme, abortive by stabbing on the Oise.

It is perhaps a little odd that the more notable or at least more noted French crimes that first half of December all took place in the provinces. Paris began to catch up on the 18th, when an elderly woman was fatally stabbed in the Rue de la Croix-Nivert by a mental patient allowed out. The following evening, a positive massacre took place in a chemist's shop in the Boulevard Richard Lenoir, from which the young armed robber got away with a five-franc piece, which he dropped in the street. A few hours later, a gunsmith was badly wounded by a man with a sawn-off shotgun who got away with nothing. In what was taken to be a gang règlement de comptes, Arab brothers were killed in their Montmartre bar on what to Christians was the day after Christmas, known to us with increasing meaninglessness as Boxing Day. That day at Pau in the Pyrenees unfolded a dreadful scene whose cinematic possibilities must be evident to the least imaginative of us. Revolver in hand, a blind ex-paratrooper groped about a house new to him, then heard his wife washing clothes in the scullery, crept up behind her, forced her to her knees and shot her in the back of the head.

Among French criminals whose names we have noted, the author of the Gavroche bar killings was arrested two days later in Versailles, where, the day before, for what seems no good reason, Lucien Léger, *l'Étrangleur* of 1964, had been heard again, telling again his story about a Molinaro whom he had been shielding (his drug-addicted wife had in the meantime served a prison sentence for attempted extortion from M. Taron, the bereaved father of *le petit Luc*). From time to time, a numbered ransom note in circulation gave some hint as to the whereabouts of Michel Fauqueux, the kidnapper and prompt returner of Sophie Duguet. His common-law wife, Thérèse Lemadre, in and out of custody, was at Christmas released on bail, a new procedure in France. At the beginning of the month, Marcantoni, still facing charges in connection with the murder of Stefan Markovic, had also been turned loose provisionally.

That had been on December 3rd. In the United Kingdom that day (specifically, at Edmonton, London), an elderly butcher was clubbed to death with an iron bar by his assistant, who then stole somewhat less than fifty pounds in order to buy a motor-cycle and become a Hell's Angel (he already had the crash helmet, boots and studded leather jacket). In the United States, warrants were out in connection with the Sharon Tate murders, and on Monday the 8th Charles Manson and five other people were indicted. The English county of Hertfordshire had by then found darkness again, but at about the same local time on the same date, a young married man, John Kenneth Danby, if not yet committed for trial at the assizes next March, had been remanded in custody at Welwyn Garden City, charged with a fearful sex murder on Friday evening, when much beer-drinking had diminished his sexual capacity and the girl had laughed. In Durham, Ian Brady was on hunger strike in protest against a refusal to let him see Myra Hindley, whom he described as his common-law wife.

On the 10th, in Milan, with no more than minutes in hand, police arrived at the crematorium and prevented the incineration of a man of seventy-eight who had not, after all, died a natural death. In the same Italian city, on the 12th, bombs exploded in a bank, killing fourteen and injuring more than a hundred. In Spanish air-space that day, Ethiopian security guards shot two Arab hijackers dead. Champagne was offered to the passengers who remained alive. To his parents in the small town of Kaltenbrunn, Bavaria, a fat young man wrote from prison in Coburg:

Please forgive me for the heartache I have caused you. I am in good health. Nobody has hurt me, and I am happy.

Into that matter also, sexual incapacity had entered.

During the summer, two local girls had been found stripped, bound and stabbed to death. A third, whose name was Sieglinde, had disappeared. She had last been seen accepting a ride in his car from heavily built Manfred Wittmann, but the police had not bothered him much. At twenty-six, he was chairman of the local society for the protection of animals, president of the sports club and acting chief of the fire brigade. Everyone in Kaltenbrunn liked the young man with the odd, fixed smile, who blushed furiously when girls spoke to him and whom his friends knew as gentle and harmless. Then a girl called Irmgard had been found, also stripped, bound and stabbed but still alive. She said her assailant had been a plump, dark-haired young man, with a pale face and educated voice.

'He stopped the car', she said, 'in a deserted spot and forced me to get out.

'He told me, "Do what I tell you, and you won't get hurt".

'But he tore my clothes from my body. He used my nylon bra to tie my hands behind my back. He tried to assault me but failed.

'Then he stabbed me in the breasts with a knife again and again. That's the last I remember.

'And all the time he was smiling oddly.'

But those will be the English reporter's short paragraphs, not Irmgard's.

When she felt better, the Bavarian police had arranged an identification parade of plump, dark-haired young men with pale faces and educated voices.

Irmgard pointed at Manfred.

'That's the man who attacked me,' she shouted.

Even then he smiled. He is not smiling in this *News of the World* photograph. Apart from the clothes and the hair, he looks like a baby sitting on its pot. Helga is smiling nicely, and Nora looks quite cheerful, while Sieglinde, between them, is positively laughing. Aged sixteen, she is a chubby little blonde with widely spaced eyes and chewed hair. There is no photograph of Irmgard.

Said Police Chief Karl Sprecht: 'I questioned Manfred for eight hours before he broke down and cried out, "Yes, I am the Phantom!"'

Well, then Manfred takes Karl and other fuzz to a secluded

spot ten miles from Kaltenbrunn, where, in a shallow grave under the fir trees, they find the body of Sieglinde. She is naked, as if we didn't know, and her hands are still tied behind her back.

Standing at the graveside, Manfred says :

'I selected Sieglinde because she was pretty and shapely. I didn't want to harm her. I wanted to make love to her. When I failed, I lost control. I am not a complete man.'

Karl was worried about imprints of the girl's bare feet on the grass.

'Yes,' says Manfred, 'I forced her to dance for me. After killing her, I went back to my sports club.'

'He used the murder weapon to cut bread and sausage for his friends,' Herr Sprecht went on.

'Manfred then told us how he had taken Helga and Nora to the woods and killed them.

'First he made them dance or play hide-and-seek. Then he bound their hands and stabbed them to death.

'He was already planning another attack and had begun stalking the girl.

'When we took him to prison at Coburg, where he awaits trial, two hundred middle-aged women crowded around the police car shouting : "Hang the Smiling Killer !" Manfred listened with that odd, contorted smile on his face.'

Nobody hurt him. Nobody was going to. The fat Phantom was happy. While he wrote smilingly to Mr and Mrs Wittmann in Kaltenbrunn, asking their forgiveness for the heartache he had caused them, we may imagine three distinguished journalists in London putting the finishing touches to articles for the quality Sundays of December 14th, their last opportunities to express themselves influentially on the subject of capital punishment.

The *Sunday Times*, having (like the daily *Times* and the *Evening Standard*) turned Leftwards under Lord Thomson's ownership, was against it of course. Even so, editorially, it criticised the Government's haste in pushing its measure through. Had they waited until, say, February, the arguments for abolition could have been deployed and 'the delusions of the hangers' exposed. In a signed article, Mr Eric Jacobs put the statistics into what was certainly a perspective and concluded that the provisional abolition of 1965 had proved nothing about the practical consequences of hanging.

7 Jean-Laurent Olivier, executed March 12th, 1968.

signs of preparation for dinner. A bill-hook or *machete* lay on the carpet in the lounge, broken glass beside an empty handbag. The front door had been forced, the telephone in the hall wrenched away from the wall. Muriel's jewels had gone, and so had she.

12 | KIDNAPPING AND ITS CONSEQUENCES

NEW YEAR'S Day was dull and cold, even in Provence. In a private room at Cavaillon hospital, a man barely five feet tall had lain for the past fortnight in a coma from which he was not expected to recover, by reason of a fracture of the petrosal or otic bone, the result of him skidding into a tree in a borrowed Alfa-Romeo. The man's name was Mondoloni. His hair was dark. Had they been open, we might have seen that his eyes were almost colourless, a washed-out blue if anything. Taken in conjunction with that small, bitter mouth, they had been frightening eyes, those of a dedicated killer, for whom the revolver was in more senses than one an equaliser (but to be small is a positive advantage if you are the target, as also for getting away in a crowd). Elsewhere in the hospital, expected presently to be up and about, was his effective stepmother, who had been with him in the car when it crashed. The adjacent room was occupied by his young cousin, Félix, there to keep an eye on him on behalf of the family, who had many enemies and whose two senior male members were in prison in Paris, awaiting a trial due to open there early next week. For Antoine-René Mondoloni was the natural and adopted son of Mémé (Barthélemy, to his parents doubtless Bartolommeo) Guérini and a nephew of the late Antoine (Antonio?) Guérini, who had died bullet-riddled outside a garage on the outskirts of Marseilles two and a half years previously.

Then a schoolboy, currently a law student, Félix Guérini had been present on that occasion, too. The hooded men who came now, threatened but did not harm him. He thought there were five of them. The night sister was too frightened to count. They made six small, round holes in little Mondoloni with what the police surgeon thought must have been a stiletto. Having made a statement, Félix took refuge with his mother, Alice Guérini, at her villa outside Marseilles.

163

Mondoloni's funeral took place at Cavaillon on Tuesday, January 6th, 1970. The short coffin was lowered into the grave. A fair-haired woman with a head-scarf, the widow, and a handsome old creature, Mondoloni's mother, bent forward to pitch lumps of frozen earth ringingly on to the lid. Cameras clicked. One whirred. There were even flashes, as the light was poor. A man in dark glasses and a raglan overcoat held the arm of Mondoloni's mother. He was her second husband. Her first, who had worked for the Guérinis, had a hotel in the town. Though Mémé subsequently adopted him, Mondoloni had continued to bear the family name of the first husband, since remarried to the woman still in hospital. The second husband's face was crumpled with tears, though he could hardly be thought a chief mourner. This was no sort of gangster's funeral, if one remembered the crowd and the flowers at that of Antoine Guérini in Calenzana, during her absence at which the unfortunate Mandroyan had been foolish enough to steal Alice Guérini's jewels.

In Paris, the clerk to the court read out the long indictment or act of accusation. The old, fluted oak panelling remained, but the courtroom had been splendidly redecorated. The beading of the ceiling and cornices shone with new gilt. The lustres were very lustrous. There were nine people in the dock, rather oddly arranged. At the front, from left to right, were, first, a young man called Marcel Fillot, then a policeman, then Mémé Guérini, policeman, Pascal Guérini. Tiered behind Filliot were men called Poli (wearing dark glasses) and Rossi. Behind the first policeman were two other policemen. There were microphones directly in front of Filliot and the two Guérinis. Below the dock extended parallel benches for the defence lawyers, with tables between them. Of the two best-known of the Parisian lawyers, Floriot sat at the extreme left, Isorni at the extreme right. The white-maned, handsomely Jewish advocate behind Floriot was Émile Pollak, star of the Marseilles bar, one of no fewer than six counsel for Mémé Guérini. Floriot was one of two for Pascal Guérini, Isorni one of three for Poli, the gunman. Pale and bespectacled, M. Dubost occupied the ministerial box. Between his mutes, the assessors, M. Fournioux presided. The jury consisted of eight men and one woman.

The Guérini brothers had grown old in prison. Mémé suffered from respiratory troubles, and what was said to be some kind of polypus in nose or throat made him almost unintelligible, however much or little the microphone was turned up. Filliot was a good-looking young fellow, with eyes of a dreadful candour. He was not charged as a principal. Had he not gone back on his first statements, he might have been a prosecution witness. The chief prosecution witness was pretty, peroxided Janine Prillard, who had been Mandroyan's girl-friend. She had not been present on Monday when the roll of witnesses was called. She had been kept in Belgium, under police protection. She appeared on Wednesday, with great effect, though in fact her evidence amounted to little more than that Mandroyan had been afraid of the Guérinis and didn't want to go to see them and that, when she heard of his death, she had immediately *known* that it was they who had killed him. Naturally, she would think so, and just as naturally he had been nervous when they sent word to say they wanted to see him about the jewels.

Mémé's wife, Lili, wore a panther-skin coat. Her hair was henna-tinted. The fair-haired woman who sat with her was English. Her name was Jacqueline Edwards. She lived with her mother in Cannes and had known the Guérinis for six years. Mémé Guérini had always hated gang warfare, she said to journalists at the adjournment. He would not have agreed to the killing of young Mandroyan. The journalists thought otherwise. The insult to the family had to be avenged somehow. Latterly, too many people had taken liberties with the Guérinis. The score for the great Antoine had not yet been settled. It was possible, on the other hand, that those who had killed him had also killed not only Mondoloni but also Mandroyan, either to lay the Guérinis under suspicion or because Mandroyan knew too much. That Wednesday, the Court of Cassation quashed the St Omer verdict on Armand Rohart, the mayor of Peuplingues. He would have to be tried again at Douai.

On Saturday evening, Solange Léger, wife of the Strangler still protesting his innocence at Château Thierry special prison (and grumbling about the rate of pay for his work), was found dead at the foot of her bed in an easterly part of Paris, the accidental termination of a long, slow suicide. In Durham prison, Ronald Kray half-heartedly cut his wrists in protest against separation from his brother. At midnight on Sunday, a door of the night express from Strasbourg to Paris was opened and a girl pushed out on to the track by, it was thought, a young man wearing a tartan scarf and violet socks. In the morning, at a magistrates' court in Berkshire, a Welsh pilot was charged with variations on the hijack theme, plots to blow up an El Al aircraft at Heathrow and to freeze four prominent British Jews for transport in boxes to Amman. On Thursday, a Yugoslav fatally stabbed his wife in the street in the Paris suburb of Pantin, and a listed note from the Duguet ransom was reported by a bank near Grenoble. On Friday, a Welsh Labour M.P. appeared at Bow Street on spy charges. On the Yorkshire moors, the young Crown witness at the trial of Brady and Hindley led police in a search for two graves still untraced.

Later that day, the Guérini verdicts were brought in. Mémé got twenty years, Pascal fifteen, as did Poli and Rossi. Filliot was acquitted and discharged. For the rest of the month, I shall note only two new murders, one of them triple. In my immediate London neighbourhood, a young American from California had been foolish or unlucky enough to take a room in Clarendon Road. There in the street he was found stabbed dead on Wednesday, January 21st. Two of the Notting Hill Gate hippies were promptly arrested and charged. Two others had left London. At a hotel in Amiens that Saturday, the proprietor, his wife and their daughter were found with shattered skulls. This was thought to be the work of Pierre Tavernier, a local man with thin features and a curious smile, whose brutal disposition we briefly noted earlier. For early February, we may note a *forcené* at Besançon and a hijack failure at Santiago, Chile. The Besançon *forcené* was an Arab. The hostages were his French wife and their two children. What he wanted was his mother-in-law, who had been unkind to his wife in childhood. A co-religionist persuaded him that it could hardly be the will of Allah that he should therefore kill his wife and children. The Chilean domestic aircraft was refuelling for the inevitable Cuba when police came aboard disguised as mechanics and shot the two student hijackers, also winging an air hostess.

ALTHOUGH PROTRACTED search had failed to turn up a body, the Hosein brothers, Arthur and Nizamodeen, of Rooks Farm, Stocking Pelham, Hertfordshire, were arrested on February 10th, 1970, and charged with that between December 29th and February 7th within the jurisdiction of the Central Criminal Court they did murder Mrs Muriel Freda McKay; and that on divers dates between

December 30th and February 6th within the same jurisdiction they made with menaces an unwarranted demand upon Mr Alick McKay that the said Mr Alick McKay should pay to them one million pounds for the safe return of his wife, Mrs Muriel Freda McKay, contrary to Section 21 of the Theft Act, 1968. Aged respectively thirty-three and twenty-one, the brothers were, as we might say, West Indian East Indians of Moslem background. Arthur Hosein had first come to the United Kingdom from Trinidad at the age of seventeen, had performed his military service in the Pioneer Corps, had set up as a tailor in Hackney, East London, and had there married an established hairdresser, ten years older than himself. They had two children. They had bought Rooks Farm two years before, and Nizamodeen and a younger sister had lived there only since November. Arthur Hosein had friends both locally and in London. Friends from London had stayed at the farm only ten days before (they proposed to offer the children a home while he remained in custody). The district was very lightly populated, but one local friend lived no more than a hundred yards away. The livestock on the farm consisted of pigs, ducks and two bullocks. It was in pig-raising that Arthur meant to branch out. He had two cars. He continued with his tailoring, taking orders for trousers especially. The police believed that Mrs McKay had been kidnapped in mistake for the wife of the chairman of the *News of the World*, the celebrated Mr Rupert Murdoch, at that time out of the country.

Despite the comparative isolation of Rooks Farm, it had not, to my mind, been a promising kidnap situation, principally because the Hoseins were coloured foreigners and conspicuous. I do not think that they could have got away with it anywhere in the United Kingdom or, indeed, the British archipelago or perhaps even Europe at all. To 'get away with it' means, of course, that you must, on the one hand, collect the ransom and, on the other, not find yourself faced with murder charges. Indeed, unless murder was part of your original plan, to murder at all is a sign that you have failed. The murder will have been improvised out of fear of discovery of the lesser offences, commonly in sheer panic. That it so often results in murder is the principal argument against kidnapping with a ransom demand, from everyone's point of view. The Hoseins had not received the ransom money. It is thought likely, on the other hand, that, as with the boy Malliart in Versailles and his captor, the juvenile François X., murder had been done before the ransom demands were properly made. The situation in Soissons was quite different. There, it may be recalled, in October, the ransom (a million francs, about £76,000, in 500 franc notes whose numbers had been listed and would later be published) had been paid promptly, the child (Sophie Duguet, known briefly to journalists as Little Red Riding Hood, because of what she was wearing when taken from her nursemaid on the open road in broad daylight), promptly restored in good shape. From the outset, the police had suspected Michel Fauqueux, a former garage-owner, who in August had escaped from prison at Cambrai, patiently removing stones from one wall of the cell to which traffic in stolen cars had brought him, a traffic out of whose proceeds he had just bought the garage, which it seems likely he intended to run straight. Aged twenty-eight, he was small, thin as a match, dark-haired and sallow but with blue eyes, inherited from his widowed mother, a Polish immigrant. He wore a moustache and, while on the run, had also grown a chin-strap of beard.

The Duguets farmed between four and five thousand acres in the departments of Aisne and Loiret and also had large industrial interests (sugar refining, wholesale bakery, potato crisps). Between spells as a factory worker, Fauqueux had done occasional days' labour on their land. His mistress's father had worked for them all his life. The mistress was Thérèse Lemadre, a dumpy peasant girl, fair, of low IQ (though uneducated, Fauqueux was rather intelligent) but steadfast character. They were unmarried only because, having once allowed the banns to be published, Lemadre had withdrawn his consent at the last moment, Thérèse being under age. She had borne Fauqueux three children. It was in her cottage in the direction of Lille that little Sophie Duguet had spent three pleasant days before her father delivered the ransom. Charged as an accomplice in December, Thérèse Lemadre had been released, on not bail exactly but *liberté provisoire*, because of the children and perhaps also because Fauqueux was expected to visit her, as indeed he had done more than once. The bulk of the ransom money was, moreover, hidden under her bath. A policeman, a member of the Lille *gendarmerie*, called on her daily.

There could hardly have been a nicer kidnapping or one that might have been more successful if Fauqueux and his girl had known what to do with the money once they, so promptly and no doubt unexpectedly, got it. He, certainly, could have got away. During the past four months, he had been in Belgium and in Spain briefly, doing something about false papers and a vague plan for them all to go to Mexico. A great many difficulties remained, but they were not, I should have thought, insuperable, even when it is granted that Fauqueux could not, or did not propose to, live without his common-law wife and their children. There is room for endless speculation here. On Saturday night, however, February 21st, the police caught Michel Fauqueux climbing the wall of Thérèse Lemadre's garden. Though armed with a pistol, he made no attempt to resist arrest. He was taken to Lille, though, after a maximum of forty-eight hours' *garde à vue,* he would have to be taken, on Monday, to Soissons to see his examining magistrate, a woman.

THE ARABS of Arab countries had taken with delight both to sky-jacking and to blowing up aeroplanes in mid-air when the passengers least expected it.* The principal achievement of two Jordanians was the destruction of a Swiss aeroplane with thirty-eight people aboard. The bomb they had put on an Austrian aeroplane indeed exploded shortly after its take-off from Frankfurt, but little damage was done and nobody killed. In Latin America, the fashion was political kidnapping. That year's wave started in Guatemala, where, first, the communist bandits or *guerrilleros*† rapidly exchanged that country's Foreign Minister for one of their band in prison but then, in early March, killed a young man from the United States embassy for whom they were expecting a larger exchange. Of two French *forcenés*, one, on March 8th, a Sunday, shot a policeman dead, wounded three other people and turned the weapon on himself, while another, next day, was talked out of blowing himself up in a large block of flats.

On the 24th, an American diplomatist was kidnapped in

* The originator of this practice appears to have been a young man in Denver, Colorado, John G. Graham, who had taken out a large insurance policy on his mother's life, in 1955. He was tried only for the murder of his mother, the deaths of forty-three other people having been clearly unpremeditated. Graham's infernal machine had been home-made with fourteen pounds of dynamite and an alarm clock. Someone had provided the two Arabs with an altimeter, so that the aeroplane automatically exploded when it reached a certain height.
† Not, for goodness' sake, *guerrillas.* A *guerrilla* is a little war. Those who wage little wars are *guerrilleros.*

Santo Domingo, on April 6th a German one found murdered in Guatemala. During the course of that month, kidnap threats were uttered against the son of our Princess Margaret and the daughter of Sir Gerald Nabarro. In Paris, Arabs kidnapped the daughter of rich Arabs and, demanding a comparatively modest ransom, got away with it in twenty-four hours. At Soissons, the kidnapping of Sophie Duguet was reconstructed in the rain, and Michel Fauqueux was to be seen carrying a life-sized doll, while the young woman examining magistrate tied a scarf over her head and shivered. The second trial of Armand Rohart, Mayor of Peuplingues, opened at Douai on the 20th and closed on the 24th. The tape of his conversation with the dead Turk was played over again. Rohart adopted a more ingratiating attitude in court, but the verdict was the same as at St Omer. He had undoubtedly murdered his wife on the beach at Escalles three years previously. For the second time, he received a life sentence. In the United States, another Kennedy was in trouble.

On Wednesday, May 27th, Michel Fauqueux and Thérèse Lemadre were married. She, pregnant, had been in custody at Laon since his arrest, their three children in public care, visited indeed by a married sister of Thérèse's. The civil ceremony was conducted, at Soissons town hall, by a mayor's deputy in tricolour sash, a simplified religious ceremony, the merest blessing, by a priest in the prison governor's office. As the new Mme Fauqueux was driven away back to Laon, schoolchildren shouted, 'Long live the bride!' On Monday, June 8th, at the close of a session with the examining magistrate, during which his handcuffs had been removed, Fauqueux nipped through a side door and out of the prison, stole a motor-scooter and was at liberty for twenty minutes. The following Monday, towards midnight, an intruder at the house of the Duguets, clearly no practised hand, though his carbine was fitted with a silencer, broke into their bedroom, clouted Philippe Duguet several times on the head with the butt and then fled, leaving the weapon. A week later, the land tycoon was to be found sleeping at his father's house, afraid for his life.

For the fact was that, in this matter, popular sympathy lay wholly with the kidnappers. On their rare public appearances, people had booed Duguet and shouted sympathetically for Fauqueux and his girl. This was, as none of our murders had properly been, an episode in the class war. When la petite Sophie had first been abducted, the journalists had begun building up their usual picture of her as 'Little Red Riding Hood' and of her mother's anxiety. Mme Duguet had also been pregnant, and a fool of a doctor had told her that, because of all the emotion, her child might be born deformed. But Sophie had spent only three nights in sufficient contentment away from home, while Thérèse Lemadre, by a kind of State kidnapping, had already spent months without her children (and they without her or their father). Duguet had got his money back, all but a few thousand francs spent by Fauqueux while he was on the run. There was nothing he stood to gain by punitive legal action against a pair who, whatever their fault, seemed personally amiable, as, of course, Philippe Duguet did not.

He could not, certainly, single-handed have quite turned off the heat. Nor, perhaps, could anyone. Since the facts were not in doubt, the case against Fauqueux could hardly be thrown out either by the examining magistrate herself or by the Court of Appeal at Amiens. The Fauqueux would have to stand trial at assizes on charges for which severe penalties were laid down in the Penal Code. When the matter came up for hearing in September, much would depend on the jury. To lead for Fauqueux's defence, no less an advocate than Maître Pollak had let it be known that he would come so far out of his way from Marseilles. At this news, not Philippe Duguet but his father constituted himself *partie civile* and announced his intention of retaining counsel of equal weight. That could have been thought to show vindictiveness on old Duguet's part.

The date of the attack on Philippe Duguet in his own home was June 15th. On that date and at much the same hour in world time, the unedifying spectacle of the trial of Manson and his girls started its long run in Los Angeles. On the 22nd and 29th (these three dates were all Mondays), respectively at Versailles and Evreux, the trials of François X. and of *les Katangais* half-opened, being held *in camera*. As, at the time of the murder of his seven-year-old schoolfellow, François had been a minor of under sixteen, he was tried in the children's court without jury. At the time of the murder of 'Jimmy le Katangais' in the woods of Vernon, one of the nine in the dock at Évreux had been a minor between the ages of sixteen and eighteen. He could have been tried separately, but, as he was considered to have been the ringleader, it had seemed natural to take all nine together, and so the whole of the main proceedings had to be held *à huis clos.* He, it may be recalled, was the one who, with false papers giving his age as twenty-three, had married, impregnated and left an English girl, Sylvia Collier, who had subsequently lain down in front of a train on the railway track outside the station at Aix-en-Provence. He and the member of the gang who, on his orders, had actually fired a bullet into the back of 'Jimmy's' neck were given six-year sentences. The others were acquitted, though two remained in custody, having yet to appear at La Roche-sur-Yon on charges of armed robbery. Even at the close of the Versailles proceedings, the name of François X. could not be made public, though his fifteen-year sentence would take him well beyond the age of majority.

The Puyricard trial opened at Aix on July 8th, a Wednesday, the day after the Katangais verdict. Harlette Boulbès, Sauveur Padovani and Gaston Costeraste ('Jo l'Aixois') were accused not of wilful murder but of assault and battery (*coups et blessures*) resulting in death. The sentences passed (at 1.00 a.m. on Sunday morning) were twelve years on Boulbès, eight each on Padovani and Costeraste. This story was yet to have its wry and sufficiently amusing pay-off four months later. For the moment, we may note that, by some process of civil law, the *châtelain* of La Roche-Rostolane, Vicomte Jacques de Régis de Gastinel, hospitalised in Aix, appears to have been found incapable of administering his estate and a brother to have been empowered to sell the house and its treasures off, though not to his own immediate benefit. Jacques de Régis was furious and swore revenge.

Throughout the first half of the year, new murders of the usual kinds, unlisted here, had accumulated on the eastern side of the Atlantic at what had ceased to seem an unusual rate. The trend was clearly to be maintained in the second half of the year, and in late July and August there was plenty in Britain and France to engage the encyclopaedic criminologist's interest. In so far, however, as the significant trend was in kidnapping and other hostage-holding, ending or not in murder and with political rather than merely financial ransom demanded, even European eyes were, that summer already, directed across the Atlantic and not wholly to Latin America. It was, indeed, in Uruguay that, on August 10th, a United States official was found with hands chained and two holes in the head (the release of no fewer than a hundred and fifty political prisoners had been demanded and refused). It was, on the other hand, in The Hague, that, on the

4th, a Brazilian diplomat was found with his throat cut. It was into a Californian courtroom that a black gunman bounded, armed by pale-brown Angela Davis, intellectual Egeria of the oddly beglamorised Jackson brothers, handed out weapons to two other blacks, took the elderly judge, two women jurors and the district attorney hostage and ended up dead in the street outside, with his two friends and the judge. That month also, President Nixon committed his own contempt of court with a comment on the Manson case, still uproariously proceeding.

The trial of the Hosein brothers opened at the Old Bailey on September 14th, by ordinary standards a long trial. It was still going on when, on the 28th, at Laon, that of the recently married Fauqueux opened and, indeed, when it closed a few days later, on the 1st of October. As the facts were not in question, a substantial part of the Fauqueux trial was devoted to the 'expert' testimony of psychiatrists, whose pompous ineptitudes made everybody laugh, including the two accused. The public warmly applauded Me Pollak. Then came the turn of the jury, who found extenuating circumstances for Thérèse Fauqueux, née Lemadre (or, as the French rather have it Thérèse Lemadre, épouse Fauqueux, for a Frenchwoman's maiden name remains with her all her life), but none for Michel Fauqueux. A French judge has little latitude in passing sentence, once the verdict is in, and, by a lenient interpretation of what is laid down in the Penal Code, this meant a mere three years for Thérèse but fifteen for her husband. Though he might indeed not serve the full term, there was clearly something excessive about this.* The court had manifestly accepted Fauqueux's assurance that, had the ransom

* The severity of the sentence had nothing directly to do with the age of the 'victim'. The kidnapping of adults for ransom has not been common in France, but there have been two cases within the past ten years. As I write, there have been no judicial consequences to that, in March 1971, of an (if she will forgive me, for it is surely relevant) rather plain adolescent girl from the car park of a block of luxury flats in Paris. A ransom of half a million francs was paid. Seven years previously, the wife of the aircraft manufacturer, Marcel Dassault, had been picked up by a group of men outside her home. A ransom of four million francs was demanded. It was not paid, but Mme Dassault returned home, all smiles, three days later. The man considered to be the leader of the group got twenty years. As I write (October 19th, 1971), a young Englishwoman, who had kept a baby for more than five weeks, has just been given three years. Her parents, admitted accessories after the fact, were not even charged. There was, it is true, no question of a ransom, and the young woman has been excused on the ground that she had just had a miscarriage.

not been immediately forthcoming, he would simply have decided that the attempt was a failure and still returned the child unharmed within a matter of days. The severity of the penalties for kidnapping took account, as possibly it should not, of the hardship commonly endured by the victim and the possibility of the thing ending in murder.

Early the following week, Arthur and Nizamodeen Hosein were to be awarded, respectively, twenty-five and fifteen years for kidnapping Mrs McKay, in addition to life sentences for murdering her, fourteen years each for blackmail and ten for sending threatening letters. As, however, all these sentences were to run concurrently, it seemed likely that Nizamodeen at least would be out as soon as Fauqueux, who also has additional sentences acquired two months later at Cambrai (these, certainly, were very lenient, a total of fifteen months, with fines, for fraud, forgery, escape and thirty-seven out of fifty-eight admitted car thefts). Yet you would have to be very fond indeed of all coloured immigrants to see the Hosein brothers as anything but a pair of unspeakably evil little beasts, while in Michel Fauqueux even the element of anti-social resentment was good-humoured and un-emphatic, his determination to shield his wife so unswerving that, if in court she admitted doing this or that at his request, he would at once jump up and say that he had not asked but ordered her to do it.

The trial of the Hoseins ended on October 5th. That day, we had the news that, in Canada, a British trade commissioner, James Cross, had been kidnapped in Montreal by Quebec secessionists. Five days later, Pierre Laporte, Labour minister for the province, was similarly abducted. For the release of Cross, that of twenty-one 'political prisoners' was demanded, the first additional demand for a financial ransom of half a million dollars having been dropped. The Canadian government had offered no more than a safe-conduct for the kidnappers. In the different fates of the two men, numerous factors were no doubt at work. The most important I take to be that Laporte was locally known. The police were 'tipped off'. They began to close in. It is inherent in the kidnap situation that at that point the kidnappers will panic and behave desperately, generally murdering the hostage. The likely fate of Cross inevitably gave rise to anxiety, but the fact that he was not a local man might have justified a favourable prognosis.

The date on which we ḷrned about the Laporte murder was October 19th. It was difficṿ to avoid some feeling of shame when a political kidnapping wɪ a fatal outcome, the first in a civilised country since thᵢ Second World War, took place on territory from which the ᴜnited Kingdom was not yet quite detached. True, the perns most directly involved were of French 'culture' and mighᵢeven be Frenchmen, for, although the F.L.Q., Front de Libératᴴn Québecoise or du Québec, was a communist organisation, i⸱was said that many members of the former O.A.S., the 'fascisᵗ Organisation de l'Armée Secrète, had fled west and joined then In fact, the affair was to have repercussions back in France. ᵗhe most notable or at least most noted of these was, it is true, a *ᵢglement de comptes* between Canadians. Two of the gang followᵈ a third to a northerly suburb of Paris and, after breakfast on March 29th, 1971, put three .22 bullets into his head. The Moᵗreal papers anticipated further incidents of the same kind, wheᵗer in France or in Algeria or in Cuba.

THERE MAY be unexᵖected fatal consequences. Of three children kidnapped in Paris ᵢ 1970 (two from the same school by the same Tunisian taxi-ᵈriver), one was no more than fifteen months old, and a party tᵒ the kidnapping was a maid engaged by the child's mother onlyᵗhe previous day, November 16th. It was she who, the following January, for the most part in a suitcase on a beach in Normanᵗy, was found dead, so beheaded and dismembered that heᵗ identity, though quickly suspected, took some time to establish. The last I heard, it was supposed, though it had not yet beᵉn proved, that this was the work of her two male accomplics, arrested (in Normandy), before the gruesome discovery. The child was all right.

A case for which it is difficult to find the right epithet without seeming heartlᵢss, took place in Germany in April 1971. For the restoration of Renate Putz, sixteen, abducted in Munich on the 5th, her kidnappers demanded one third of a million marks within three days. Her parents, on holiday in Switzerland, found the ransom note when they returned home on the 15th. By then, their daughter's body had been lying for a week past in a gravel pit outside the town.

13 | AUTUMN TRIALS

OF SIX French trials for murder in th autumn of 1970, four were for crimes committed more than thr; years before, and for the man convicted of the earliest of the: his murderous activity, it would turn out the following year, as not yet by any means over. Of the countless *faits divers* of tose two years, it would be foolish to attempt to say which coul be safely forgotten and which might yet provide great trials. C the few new murders I shall still record here, the juridical outcme may be unknown to me when the book leaves my hands. O the late 1970 and the early 1971 trials I record, the reader wil find that the criminal occasion of each was in most cases noted a it occurred.

What seemed likely to be the most notworthy episode in the case of Claude Buffet had occurred on Janary 18th, 1967, when, driving a stolen taxi along the Rue de l'Asomption, Auteuil, he was hailed by elegant young Mme Besinensky and given an address in the suburb of Boulogne-Billanourt. Arrested three weeks later on another charge, he had, he told the examining magistrate, set out that evening with the idea of killing somebody, 'to see how it felt' (*'pour voir l'effet que cela fait'*), and the rich doctor's wife, a former model, after spending the evening pleasantly visiting sisters till then less fortunate than herself, had been very unlucky indeed. When, after the murder, his taxi stopped for lack of petrol, it is credible Buffet had stripped the shot and robbed woman and done other things to her body in order to disguise his crime as that of a *sadique*. Though broken-nosed, he was a good-looking fellow, successful with women up to a point and enormously vain. When, on October 8th, 1970, he appeared before the Central Criminal Court in Paris, the charges against him were concerned not only with the murder of Françoise Besimensky but with forty-four bag-snatchings and numerous car thefts. Beside him in the dock sat or stood a regular mistress, Marie Ansoine, who had accompanied him on many of his

176

expeditions, always by car, but had spent the past eight months *en liberté provisoire*.

In their answers to the presiding judge, M. Fournioux, and under what passes for cross-examination in French courts, the pair made no attempt to shield each other. It was, we might say, rather a Barany and Marcucci than a Fauqueux and Lemadre double act, a head (but only one) being theoretically in play. An hour after the murder, said Marie, Claude was sleeping like a log. In the course of the judicial inquiry, he had tried to pin the murder on her, but in court insisted that the pistol had gone off accidentally. There was also a legitimate Mme Buffet, who had a son by him and gave evidence on his behalf, though at one time he had introduced his mistress into the house and (first version) made his wife sleep on the floor (in a second version, he had slept on the floor). One of the *partie civile* lawyers called for the death penalty, saying that only in decadent countries had this been abolished. The official prosecutor, M. Dubost, would be content with life imprisonment. The famous and experienced Maître Naud had undertaken Buffet's defence, but, at the beginning of the trial, been repudiated by the latter, who was then left with only two youngsters to defend him. One of these said, with charming modesty, that his client had wished to be found guilty and had therefore entrusted the case to himself in order to make sure of being ineffectively defended. In his *réquisitoire*, M. Dubost had quite forgotten the woman in the dock. Upon being asked by M. Fournioux what he proposed for her, M. Dubost said that, as she'd been out of prison for so long, he didn't see much point in sending her back.

Before the jury retired on October 15th, Buffet was asked in due form whether he had anything further to say in his own defence. He thus addressed the astonished jury:

> Be generous! Grant me sentence of death! The prosecution doesn't want me to be guillotined. It wishes me to expiate my crime between the four walls of a prison, to the end of my days. But that is not what I want! I have killed, I must pay the price!

There were some who doubted his sincerity, but it is one of the arguments against capital punishment as a deterrent that there are some who would prefer it to prison (in French criminal history, most notably Lacenaire, a man positively in love with the guillotine, in 1835). What was to ensue, alas, can only be taken as an argument for capital punishment. But that was to be the following year. For the moment, Claude Buffet would be off to Clairvaux prison with a life sentence. Marie Ansoine was given three years, most of which she had already served.

In Amiens that day opened the trial of Pierre Tavernier, forty-two, for the murder, with a hatchet, of M. and Mme Sovaux, hotel keepers, and their daughter Micheline, who had broken off her engagement to the man on learning that he had spent five years in prison for inflicting grievous bodily harm (with a knife) on a former girl-friend. This case had come up for hearing with something like British speed, since the triple murder had been accomplished only that year, on the 24th of January, in the entrance hall of the hotel, La Crémaillère. Tavernier had not confessed, and his counsel, a woman, Maître Anne-Marie Page, was to plead not guilty on his behalf, while he put on an act of wilting sarcasm and got, indeed, some laughs but also growls of anger. His thin, aquiline face and the curiously ambiguous expressions on it, expressions tried-on but essentially inward, uncommunicative, withdrawn, sensitive in their way, a smile which was no smile but yet not quite a sneer either, stay with one, make one look for the same thing in other people. On the third day of the trial, there was one of those characteristically French visits of the whole court to the scene of the crime. That was on Saturday morning. In the evening, the jury allowed extenuating circumstances, but the sentence was life.

In Paris, next Monday but one, the 26th, the crime considered was again more than three years old. It was that noted in Chapter Seven, a young man's murder of his benefactress, whose head he cut off and tossed in the dustbin, so that it went unnoticed into the municipal waste disposal plant. The following day, Tuesday the 27th, interest shifted from the Law Courts to the home of a manufacturer of telecommunications equipment, Pierre Aimedieu, who lived in the Vaugirard district, almost three miles west-south-west, in the Rue Léon-Morane, No. 15, on the first floor. Thither, at eight o'clock that morning, the caretaker directed a respectable-looking but insignificant caller, wearing heavy-rimmed spectacles with bifocal lenses and carrying a briefcase. He asked, she said, whether they had a peephole in the door and, on being told that they did, murmured that in that case either they would or would not let him in, journalists differed, and perhaps she was in doubt. It was a matter of some interest, since the Aimedieus were, it seemed, extremely chary of letting anyone into the flat, but at that time the daily help was expected. Within the next two minutes or so, without arousing interest in the house, inside the Aimedieu apartment, a 7.65 mm. pistol had been emptied of its eight bullets. M. Aimedieu had received a scalp wound. Mme Aimedieu had been hit twice in the jaw and twice elsewhere. Laurence, their daughter, a girl of twenty-three, was dying from a single shot which (some journalists) had gone straight to the heart or (others) had severed her carotid artery. And the caller, minus hat and spectacles, had left the house, later to be traced by a police dog to the Commerce underground station, where the dog lost the scent, as well it might.

Neither from the hat nor from the spectacles, nor from an identikit portrait based on the observations of M. and Mme Aimedieu and the caretaker, could the murderer be identified. There was no apparent motive. M. Aimedieu was a model employer and a good neighbour. Though prosperous, he lived very modestly and worked long hours. Mme Aimedieu also worked, as a dentist. The daughter had been studying dentistry and was about to announce her engagement. Her brother was doing his military service. The family went each weekend to a house they had in the country, where M. Aimedieu spent his time tending the vegetables they brought back for the week, buying none outside. It was a first-class enigma, permitting boundless speculation. It need not have been, had M. Aimedieu recognised his assailant, as he might well have done, for they had met before, and there had been an argument, and M. Aimedieu had reported the matter. Yet the thing was to remain an unsolved mystery for eight months.

It would be solved in the end by a ballistics *expertise*. For it was a bullet from the same weapon which, the following June, hit a motorist in the leg when he was parking to the displeasure of a former police superintendent, Georges Villaret, a country neighbour of the Aimedieus, with whom there had been a bit of a motorists' quarrel ten years before. Before and after his war years with the police he had served with the Army in Indo-China and Algeria. A defeated and demented patriot, his politics had generally been of the extreme Right. Latterly, however, he had taken to the study of Marxism and come to see M. Aimedieu as the archetypal capitalist. At the age of sixty-one, he was on the point of foundering into incurable madness. His face bore no resemblance to that in the identikit picture.

AMONG THE many who had read of the drama at Puyricard was the widow of a Belgian colonel, a Mme Irma Rees, aged sixty-one, who, twenty years before, at a regimental dinner in Marseilles, had met Vicomte Jacques de Régis de Gastinel. In May, she had travelled to Aix-en-Provence and gone to see him at the geriatrics' refuge there. She had got him out and taken him to Fréjus, where on November 5th the two were married. Three weeks later, as the consequence of an operation, he died, leaving her his sole heir. Not unexpectedly, his brother contested the will. The last I heard, there matters stood. An attempt was still being made to annul the convictions of Harlette Boulbès, Sauveur Padovani and Gaston Costeraste ('Jo l'Aixois'), but in February 1971 these were upheld by the Court of Cassation.

The aged aristocrat, much cleaner than he had once been, was in the fifth day of his married bliss when, before the court of assize in Paris, appeared André Fourcat, *dit* Dutto, thirty-one, blind in one eye, accused of having, on the night of June 25th, 1967, murdered by strangulation Sandra Rowans, an American girl of eighteen, in Room 19 on the fifth floor of the Helder Hotel. He was defended by Maître Pollak. The Rowanses were not at the trial. The next hopeless case, on Friday the 13th, was that of another petty crook, Serge Lemerger, who, at the age of twenty-three, had found himself committing a murder by firing at a policeman in the police station in Montmartre to which he had been taken with his brother as a result of their attempts to sell a stolen camera, on November 19th, 1968. Lemerger was defended by Maître Naud. The presiding judge was still sharp-featured, bespectacled M. Fournioux, with his fine head of hair. The official prosecutor, red-gowned with silly ermine and jutting underlip, was still bald, heavy-jowled M. Dubost. On the 23rd, the same magisterial pair faced Me Floriot, defending the German picture-dealer, Harry Wachs, who had not unwarrantably, on March 7th, 1967, through a closed door shot one of two young thugs brought along by a creditor to intimidate him.

Me Floriot's principal December assignment was in Brittany, where his persuasiveness did not save the author of a *meurtre passionnel* from a sentence of fifteen years. In Paris, in January 1971, he got Liliane Dupuy, who more than two years before had shot her faithless husband, the Air France steward, off with five years' suspended. Further reflections of the conjugal war that month were the trials, at Orleans, of Madeleine Chauvet for shooting her husband and, in Paris, of Colonel Chanoine for strangling his wife and her dog, a boxer, Bobby, tying them together with a 20 kilo (just over three stone) weight and dumping them in the Oise. Many new murders of the time were also of a domestic nature. Floriot's next client to appear before assizes in Paris was again a wife, Odette Picard, who, with a .22 rifle, had shot her husband in bed (he was snoring), then gone to fetch their son, a doctor, who slept on the top floor.

There were *forcenés*, too, managed by the police without more than the original loss of life. In Toulouse, there was a use of hostages in a bank robbery, and the police positively bowed the raiders on their way, pressing money upon them. There were two examples of men who *did it again*, thereby, alas, undermining the case against capital punishment which the deputy speaker was even then preparing to lay before the National Assembly. On February 13th, in Marseilles, a Mme Savin, his septuagenarian landlady, was strangled and robbed by a wartime child-murderer who, imprisoned for life in 1945, had been released sixteen years later for good conduct. On March 7th, in the neighbourhood of Nîmes, a man who had just completed a twenty-year sentence for murdering his mistress was arrested for the murder of a neighbour, his contemporary. At that time also, a famous child-murderer of the 'thirties, Gabriel Socley, was again at large, having escaped from the asylum at Sarreguemines to which he had been sent in 1960 when, after his release from Château Thierry, he had been caught molesting a little girl in Dijon. He was full of murder threats, but luckily carried none out.

The old *milieu* of ponces and their women was not dead. In a recent book on prostitution, Marcel Sacotte, a highly placed legal dignitary, had calculated that in Paris alone ten thousand men lived on the immoral earnings of women and that their daily rake-off was about five million francs. Three of the ten thousand were in court at the end of February 1971. The previous year, at St Cloud, they had spent five hours breaking a young woman's jaw, closing her eyes and otherwise ill-treating her, in a vain attempt at persuasion for which they received, respectively, sen-

tences of eight and five years and eighteen months, with twenty
thousand francs' damages to pay. To judge by their names, these
three were mainland Frenchmen. We need hardly ask where
Jean-Jean Bernardi came from, and in fact he was a first cousin
of the Marcantoni already so long bound over on charges connected with the murder of Stefan Markovic, Alain Delon's
former bodyguard. Whatever his remoter provenance, Gilles
Klotchkoff was, though of substantial family, a hippy by Parisian
standards, long-haired but good-looking and evidently virile.
Among the bars he hung around, one belonged to Bernardi, and,
to his cost, one of Jean-Jean's women, Josiane Boirin, known as
France, fell in love with him.

It would make quite a novel. Also in love with Gilles was a
beautiful young countess, recently widowed, Claire Lefèvre de
Longeville. The two had met through Gilles's brother, Jean-
Claude Klotchkoff, a prominent businessman. For some months,
the two women had shared Gilles's attentions. More recently, as
France would not (dared not, she said, as we may well understand
from the case above), give up prostitution, Gilles had broken with
her and gone to live with the countess at a house she had bought
in Provence. France and her friend Kim, another of his women,
had then in fact left Bernardi and gone into hiding, an intolerable
affront to the ponce and one for which the laws of le milieu
demanded that he should obtain either remuneration or revenge.
He had once been round to France's studio, armed and accompanied, when she and Gilles were together, and the latter had
escaped through a window. Latterly, both France and Kim had
telephoned him at his brother's to warn him that Bernardi was
after him. The course of events in early May appears to have been
as follows.

On Saturday the 1st, Klotchkoff arrived in Paris to pick up a
car and other of the countess's belongings. On Monday evening,
Bernardi was seen in the company of Marcantoni. On Tuesday
evening, at about 7.30, he was in his bar, which bore an English
name, In the Wind. That morning, Klotchkoff had been found,
with six 7.65 bullets in him, in woodlands east of Paris, where
he had certainly been left for dead, but had been taken to
hospital at Coulommiers and was able to speak, as Bernardi must
have quickly discovered, for, after a brief reappearance in his bar
on Wednesday morning, he vanished, as for the moment, though
unincriminated, did poor, harassed Marcantoni. The tale told by

Klotchkoff was that, on Monday evening, Bernardi and a man called Tony had come to his brother's flat, demanding to be told where France was. He did not know. He did not even know that she and Kim had left Bernardi. That made his position worse, whether Bernardi believed him or not. Had Jean-Jean been able to find the two women, he might have made them pay. As he could not, somebody had to be killed to save his face. And so Gilles Klotchkoff had been taken for a ride. As we have seen, the *milieu* is no respecter of hospital beds, and he was still in danger. Also given police protection were the countess, who had come up from Provence to be at his bedside, and his brother. As to the two girls, they were in dire peril and not to be found.

In this plight, I fear, we must leave them all. I note only two further matters within the jurisdiction of French courts. The reader may remember that, in August 1969, in northern France, two little girls were murdered while picking flowers on a Sunday afternoon, a crime to which the owner of the pasture soon confessed and for which he had motive, means and opportunity, the motive being a pathological hatred of trespassers on his land, a hatred which he had recently demonstrated, though without fatal effect or indeed grievous bodily harm, on two Belgian girl cyclists. I knew that he had later retracted his confession, but that is a very common episode in any French judicial inquiry. Not until June 1971, when the case against him was formally non-suited, did it transpire that a year before he had been released provisionally. No alternative murderer had been found.

A little more must be said about Claude Buffet, convicted murderer of Françoise Besimensky, the gynaecologist's wife. By September 21st, 1971, he had served eleven months of his life sentence at Clairvaux, a splendid prison which has, as its name may suggest to us, grown up on the site of the Cistercian monastery, St Bernard's own. Each prisoner had his own cell, with hot and cold water, radio, white sheets and tasteful decoration. That morning, Buffet and another long-term prisoner, Roger Bontems, reported sick with tummy upsets and were taken to the hospital block, one concealing a sharpened spoon-handle, the other a similarly treated piece of bedspring. The nurse and warder on duty were both temporary replacements for others on leave. There were six patients confined to bed and a trusty on hospital duty. Buffet and Bontems barricaded themselves in and, by telephone, demanded, as the price for releasing their hostages, two cars fitted with radio, three revolvers, a machine-gun and a supply of cartridges (which would be tested to make sure they were not blanks). The prison governor communicated with the Minister of Justice, René Pleven, who said that the firearms must not be issued. Buffet and Bontemps refused to leave without them. The parleying went on all day and into the night. The governor repeatedly asked that the warder held as hostage should be brought to the telephone. When this was not done, he concluded that the young man was already dead. In Paris, M. Pleven stayed by his telephone. In the small hours, he authorised a forcible end to the siege, and this was agreed to by the warder's wife and the nurse's husband. The other prisoners were yelling in their cells. The nurse lay in a terminal coma, stabbed in the neck and belly. The warder had been dead some time, his throat cut. He had earlier been badly knocked about, and barbiturates had been forced down his throat.

THE PREVIOUS week's *Kensington News* had announced that for Sunday, November 8th, 1970, an organisation called See Britain was organising a murder tour of the former royal borough, inevitably somewhat concentrated on my own part of it, since two out of the three principal sites, the Pembridge Court Hotel (Heath) and the renamed 10 Rillington Place (Christie and Evans) lay north of the Bayswater Road/Notting Hill Gate/Holland Park Avenue axis, while even the Onslow Court Hotel (Haigh) was not far south of it. I telephoned the paper's offices. They did not think that any special facilities had been granted. A small mob would simply walk (or, as it turned out, in large part drive) round from one place to another and gape at the buildings from outside. I decided I would save my five shillings. The tour seems in fact to have taken place three weeks later. I missed a display of indignation in Ruston Close, once Rillington Place. Many of the houses, including No. 10, had been pulled down, and No. 2, which was derelict, had been renumbered for the occasion. The lady next door had put up placards, protesting, it seemed, not so much against the tour as against living conditions in Ruston Close. 'It's murder!' she said.

Two days before, in, of all places, Manila, a zealot from, improbably, Bolivia tried to murder the travelling Pope with a wavy-bladed Malayan kris, but the dignified little Italian survived to make inflammatory statements about Ireland, a country which he has not yet visited and whose unique Catholicism he could never hope to understand. A fortnight later, there were trials of Basque nationalists in Spain, and of these he no doubt received a satisfactory explanation. It was Advent, and on Christmas Eve, at Pirbright in Surrey, near an Army camp, a girl of fifteen, Janet Stevens, set off with presents to her grandmother, for which reason (it is true, she carried them in a red bag) our journalists called her Red Riding Hood, a title which, unlike her life, she was to keep somewhat longer than her younger and smaller French counterpart had kept hers. As so often, the drunken and licentious soldiery were unjustly suspected.

Unofficial statistics in the New Year showed that in 1970 violent crime had, like wages and prices, maintained a steady upward trend, in the United Kingdom as in France, while in the United States it was thought already to have reached the saturation point to which we tended, a notion more comforting to our American cousins (who, indeed, needed comfort), than to ourselves. Like that for voting and for marriage without parental consent, the age for robbing and killing had dropped. Even without increase, it would be some years before (when the time since abolition of the death penalty equalled the average duration of a 'life' sentence) the number of convicted murderers in our prisons found its own level and the number of those annually released became constant.* By reason of a suspension decreed four years previously, American prisons had accumulated more than six hundred under sentence of death. From the other side of the Atlantic, this looked like an insoluble problem. A later ruling of the Supreme Court had decreed that executions might start again, according to the practice of individual states, but it never seemed possible to envisage what, to the rest of the world, could only be regarded as a federal massacre. The United States might, one felt, be forced to reprieve all those murderers, whether or no it were then felt possible to start again from scratch.

In the United Kingdom, statistics for the first half of 1971 showed a continuing trend, with yet more violent crime and younger people perpetrating it. Anecdotally, old women seemed increasingly to be the chief victims of the generation gap. The

---

*Three, recently released, who had been convicted of further murders or resolutely attempted murder that year were Donald Forbes, Norman Parker and Stephen Szabo.

kingdom had grown less united, however. As was only to be expected, Civil Rights agitation had given rise to almost constant rioting in Belfast and Londonderry. The I.R.A. murders got under way on March 10th, when three young Scots, off duty and out of uniform, were lured from a public house, ambushed and taken for a ride. As I write, this kind of thing is still very much with us, and there seems little doubt that the government of the Republic and the hierarchy have both connived at it, the latter somewhat less openly than the former. The world is painfully ready to believe those who say they have acted from political motives and to regard these as somehow more respectable than other motives for murder. Irish fellow-feeling for others similarly motivated seems unlikely, however, to have extended to the Mahommedans who, on Sunday, April 4th, massacred two hundred Indian Catholics and their Italian priest in a church near Jessore.

There were I.R.A. murders on July 12th, on which date three young French campers were shot dead in our Midlands by an English youth who then had the decency to write out a confession and, as the French would put it, *se donner la mort* or *se faire justice*, as impulsive murderers are much inclined to do, perhaps more frequently in France than here. It was a nasty month, with knives also much out. August had wife-murder, young men killing each other in Poplar and an old man of eighty-two in Southwark, little girls murdered in Birmingham and Watford. On the last day of the month occurred, across the Atlantic, the death of Nathan Leopold, a famous co-murderer of the 'twenties. Apart from the French Dr Bougrat of the same period, he had been the only reprieved murderer I can think of whose later life was truly edifying. Few others have attained even a modest rehabilitation. It would clearly have been a pity to execute him. His accomplice, Richard Loeb, had been executed long ago by fellow prisoners.

One began to wonder whether old-fashioned murders took place any more or whether it simply was that policemen, doctors, insurance companies and neighbours had lost interest in anything more obscure than yesterday's scenes of violence. Though not yet under attack on quite the American scale, our police were kept busy defending themselves. Two of their number had been fatally shot in Reading in June and Blackpool in August, and the month of October was, or at least its newspapers were, largely occupied with the trial and sentence in one case, the hunt for and capture in the other, of those who had killed them. There was, as there always is on such occasions, a public outcry for the restoration of the death penalty for murderers of policemen. Not so much in connection with these murders as with a capture of armed raiders in Bethnal Green, the question also arose whether our police should be regularly armed, since it appeared that hardly a day passed without weapons having to be issued to men on specific duties.

As INTERESTING as anything on the British murder scene in the closing months of 1971 was the renewed attention given to earlier cases within the period covered by this book. Interest in the Evans and Christie cases had been revived by a film based on Ludovic Kennedy's ten-year-old volume. A volume on the Hanratty case of 1961-2 was published, another on Craig and Bentley; both these aimed at showing that irrevocable miscarriages of justice had occurred. It seems an infallible recipe for success, and both volumes have had some, the second leading directly to or at least stimulating new police inquiries. I never thought Bentley should have been hanged, and the degree of his guilt (or Craig's), is unaffected by the possibility that P.C. Miles was in fact killed by a stray bullet and not by one fired at him by Craig with undeniably murderous intention. The Hanratty case was one to which I had not paid much attention at the time. When, in consequence of the book, the matter was discussed at unusual length on the wireless, I noted that the soberer and more judicious of those taking part, including Mr Blom-Cooper, remained convinced of Hanratty's guilt, while, with one exception, those on the other side came over the air simply as bad and incredible witnesses, either shifty in manner or speaking with a vehemence of which the true origin was concealed.

At the same time, without benefit of literature, a new investigation was being made into a less remote murder, the shooting, in May 1967, of John James Buggy, known as 'Scotch Jack' and found off Seaford Head, as his body detached itself from the concrete slab to which it had been roped. This was gangland stuff on a great scale for London. Buggy had evidently been a strong-arm man in the protection racket around Mayfair gambling clubs, in one of which it was believed he had been shot, while there was talk of dark-complexioned men from Tangier, of the interest of the American Mafia and of unrecovered loot from the Great Train Robbery. Among new British crimes, one noted the continuing youthfulness of some of those facing murder charges, a boy of twelve at the Old Bailey, a girl of fourteen at Warwick. Perhaps as a result of progress in their integration, one might have noted also some departure from the common rule that immigrants kill within their own ethnic group. The December victims of two young coloured women, one a nurse, were both white, one of them an elderly retired man, the other a child. Both these crimes were committed in the London area, south of the Thames.

Home Office national statistics take time to appear, but at the end of the year Scotland Yard figures for London alone promptly showed that 'murders known to the police' (some would still be sandpapered down to manslaughter), were up by more than a third on the previous year. As even so the figure was less than a hundred, our literate, stay-at-home murderers must have felt a sense of discouragement on reading that, during the same period, those of New York had raised their productivity by four hundred to a total of over sixteen. On the other hand, many British husbands and wives may have taken heart on learning that, the previous year, almost two thousand Americans had successfully disposed of their spouses.

INEVITABLY, THE printed sources for this book and especially its later chapters have been newspapers rather than bound volumes. The choice has been wide and largely accidental, but I have kept my eye on British crime rather in the pages of the *Daily Mail* or *Evening Standard* than in those of *The Times* and the middle-class Sundays, while for France *Le Monde* and *France-Soir* share the chief honours, but with close if intermittent attention paid to *Le Journal du Dimanche, Le Figaro Littéraire, Le Nouvel Observateur, Sélection du Reader's Digest, Lectures Pour Tous, Le Journal de la France,* even (for the Rohart case) the radio and recording enthusiast's *Son* and other pleasurable or instructive publications, variously high-minded. At one time, I had a subscription to *Détective.* The London editions of *True Detective* and *Master Detective* deal largely with American matters, but sometimes get round to French cases, as does the *International Herald Tribune. The Criminologist* is weak on its French side, but indispensable to anyone who attempts to keep up with developments in forensic science or with changes in police and courtroom practice, large questions of delinquency and so on.

Not all the books in English I list are equally serious or even amusing, but none is without something of interest relevant at least to cases I may have noted only very briefly or lumped together in some generalisation. Again inevitably, all these cases belong to the earlier part of our period.

Besnard, Marie, *The Trial of Marie Besnard,* translated by Denise Folliot, with a preface by Sybille Bedford, London, 1963.

Browne, Douglas G., and Tullett, E. V., *Bernard Spilsbury: His Life and Cases,* London, 1955. (Antiquis)

Capote, Truman, *In Cold Blood,* London, 1966. (Hickock and Smith)

Deeley, Peter, *The Manhunters,* London, 1970. (Maria Domenech, Peugot kidnapping)

Fabian, Robert, *Fabian of the Yard,* London, 1950. (Antiquis)

Firmin, Stanley, *Murderers in Our Midst,* London, 1955. (Margaret Allen, Antiquis, Camb, Christie, Dr Clements, Cummins, Dobkin, Evans, Haigh, Heath, Raven, Straffen, Malinowski and Grondkowski, unsolved child-murders)

Floriot, René, *When Justice Falters*, translated, with an introduction, by R. H., London, 1972. (Besnard, Dominici, Jaccoud, Labbé-Algarron, Léger)

Foot, Paul, *Who Killed Hanratty?*, London, 1971.

Forsyth, Frederick, *The Day of the Jackal*, London, 1971. (Attempt on the life of President de Gaulle)

Fowles, John, *The French Lieutenant's Woman*, London, 1969. (La Roncière)

Franklin, Charles, *World-Famous Acquittals*, London, 1970. (Besnard)

Giono, Jean, *The Dominici Affair*, translated by Peter de Mendelssohn, London, 1956.

Goodman, Derick, *Crime of Passion*, London, 1958. (Yvonne Chevallier, Demon, Pauline Dubuisson, Gelfand, Hilaire, Labbé-Algarron)

Greenwall, Harry J., *They were Murdered in France*, London, 1957. (Dominici, Janet Marshall, Jacqueline Richardson)

Huggett, Renée, and Paul Berry, *Daughters of Cain*, London, 1956. (Margaret Allen, Mrs Christofi, Ruth Ellis, Mrs Merrifield)

Humphreys, Travers, *A Book of Trials*, London, 1953. (Camb, Haigh)

Johnson, Pamela Hansford, *On Iniquity*, London, 1967. (Brady and Hindley)

Kennedy, Ludovic, *10 Rillington Place*, London, 1961.

Knowles, Leonard, *Court of Drama*, London, 1966. (Haigh, Hepper)

Knox, Bill, *Court of Murder*, London, 1968. (Manuel)

Leitch, David, *The Discriminating Thief*, London, 1968. (Xavier Richier and the château gang)

Morland, Nigel, *Hangman's Clutch*, London, 1954. (Haigh)

———, *Pattern of Murder*, London, 1966. (Camb, Manuel)

Morris, Terence, and Louis Blom-Cooper, *A Calendar of Murder*, London, 1964.

Phelan, Jim, *Nine Murderers and Me*, London, 1967. (Heath)

Roberts, C. E. Bechhofer, *Famous American Trials*, London, 1947. (Leopold and Loeb)

———, editor, *The Trial of Ley and Smith*, London, 1947.

Rowland, John, *Unfit to Plead?* London, 1965. (Ley and Smith, Straffen)

Symons, Julian, *A Reasonable Doubt*, London, 1960. (Camb, Merrett-Chesney)

Tennyson Jesse, F., editor, *Trials of Timothy John Evans and John Reginald Halliday Christie*, Edinburgh, 1957.

Thorwald, Jürgen, *The Century of the Detective*, translated by Richard and Clara Winston, London, 1966. (Besnard, Hume, Merrett-Chesney)

Traini, Robert, *Murder for Sex*, London, 1960. (Byrne, Christie, Dowdall, Heath, Whiteway)

Tullett, Tom, *Inside Interpol*, London, 1963.

Veale, F. J. P., *Crimes Discreetly Veiled*, London, 1958. (Nuremberg trials)

Watts, Marthe, *The Men in My Life*, London, 1960. (Messina brothers)

Webb, Duncan, *Crime Is My Business*, London, 1953. (Antiquis, Haigh, Heath, Malinowski and Grondkowski, Messina brothers, Raven)

Whitehead, Don, *Journey into Crime*, London, 1960. (Haigh)

Wilson, Colin, *A Casebook of Murder*, London, 1969. (Rohart)

—— and Patricia Pitman, *Encyclopaedia of Murder*, London, 1961. (Yvonne Chevallier, Dominici, Pauline Dubuisson, Jaccoud, Labbé-Algarron, also most of the British and American cases noted to 1960)

Yallop, David A., *To Encourage the Others*, London, 1971. (Craig and Bentley)

Batigne, Jacques, *Un Juge passe aux Aveux*, Paris, 1971. (Begum's jewels, *Combinatie*, Dominici, Guérini brothers)

Chenevier, Charles, *De la Combe-aux-Fées à Lurs*, Paris, 1962. (Memoirs of a superintendent of the Sûreté Nationale, noted for his bloodless arrest of Émile Buisson and more remotely concerned with the Dominici case)

Clavel, Bernard, editor, *L'Affaire Deveaux*, Paris, 1969.

Duché, Jean, *Pourquoi Jaccoud a-t-il Tué?*, Paris, 1960.

Isorni, Jacques, *A Reims le Procès de Joseph K. . . .* , Paris, 1969. (Kaczmarczyk)

Jouhandeau, Marcel, *Trois Crimes Rituels*, Paris, 1962. (Labbé-Algarron, Évenou, Curé d'Uruffe)

Laborde, Jean, *Amour, que de Crimes.* . . . Paris, 1954. (Yvonne Chevallier, Demon, Pauline Dubuisson, Gelfand)

Larue, André, *Les Flics,* Paris 1969. (A dazzling volume chiefly devoted to personalities of the Quai des Orfèvres and the Sûreté, but with useful information also on Attia, Bastien-Thiry, the Begum Aga Khan's jewels, the abduction of Ben Barka, the *Combinatie* raid and its consequences, the Dominici case and Watrin)

Manceaux, Michèle, editor, *Les Policiers Parlent,* Paris, 1969. (A volume of taped interviews with policemen, arising largely out of the May 1968 riots. The policemen come out of it very well, though accepting Mlle Manceaux's smug assumption that it is really very odd to be a policeman, while of course perfectly natural and even noble to be a journalist)

Montaldo, Jean, *Les Corrompus,* Paris, 1971. (The Fétich's Club murder and the complicity of the Lyons police)

Montarron, Marcel, *Les Grands Procès d'Assises,* Paris, 1967. (Curé d'Uruffe, Dubuisson, Labbé-Algarron, Léger)

——, *Histoire des Crimes Sexuels,* Paris, 1970. (Goetze, Olivier, Brady and Hindley)

——, *Histoire du Milieu,* Paris, 1969. (Begum's jewels, *Combinatie,* Guérini brothers)

——, *Tout ce Joli Monde,* Paris, 1965. (Léger)

——, editor, *L'Affaire Denise Labbé-Algarron,* Paris, 1956.

Mouton, Jean, *Littérature et Sang-Froid,* Paris, 1967. (Hickock and Perry, Truman Capote compared with Stendhal)

Sacotte, Marcel, *La Prostitution,* Paris, 1965.

——, *La Prostitution, Que Peut-On Faire?,* Paris, 1971.

Sebeille, Edmond, *L'Affaire Dominici,* Paris, 1970.

Sicot, Marcel, *Servitude et Grandeur Policières,* Paris, 1959. (Dominici, Trébert)

Thévenin, Raymond, *Criminels, Fous et Truands,* Paris, 1970. (Barany and Marcucci, Guérini brothers, Hugon, Kaczmarczyk, Olivier, Pauletto, Rohart)

——, *Meurtriers sans Aveux,* Paris, 1971. (Deveaux, Mémé Guérini, Puyricard, Rohart)

Vincentanne, Stéphane, *La Bande à Pierrot le Fou,* Paris, 1970. (Propounding anarchist views, this is yet lively and informative not only on the post-war period's first Public Enemy No. 1, but also on such survivors as Attia and Boucheseiche and on the scandalous disappearance of Ben Barka)